BUILDING
A REVOLUTION

To my parents,
who brought me up during
those turbulent years in China

BUILDING
A REVOLUTION
Chinese Architecture
Since 1980

Charlie Q. L. Xue

香港大學出版社
HONG KONG UNIVERSITY PRESS

Hong Kong University Press
14/F Hing Wai Centre
7 Tin Wan Praya Road
Aberdeen
Hong Kong

© Hong Kong University Press 2006

ISBN 962 209 744 8

All rights reserved. No portion of this publication may be reproduced or transmitted in any form or by any means, electronic or mechanical, including photocopy, recording, or any information storage or retrieval system, without permission in writing from the publisher.

Secure On-line Ordering
http://www.hkupress.org

British Library Cataloguing-in-Publication Data
A catalogue record for this book is available
from the British Library.

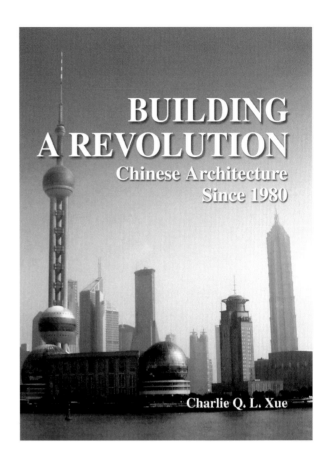

Printed and bound by United League Graphic & Printing Co. Ltd., in Hong Kong, China

CONTENTS

ACKNOWLEDGMENTS

The idea of writing a book in English on Chinese architecture germinated in the late 1980s when I was trained at the University of Hong Kong, supervised and influenced by a group of planning and construction scholars with a global outlook and a remarkable insight into Asia. Professor Sivaguru Ganesan sharpened my eyes in viewing the place I had been raised and later worked as an architect in for years. My nomadic academic life in Britain and the United States coincided with the booming of China. The distance across the oceans allowed me to watch and contemplate China's building revolution, while I benefited from communication with leading scholars including Chris Abel and the late Dr Stewart Johnston.

The prelude to this book is a text/handbook written for Hong Kong: *Building Practice in China*, published in 1999. It was a timely reference for busy building professionals and a text for Hong Kong and American students who learn Chinese or international practice in their courses.

Encouraged by the success of *Building Practice in China*, I began work on another volume about modern Chinese architects. Initial comments by Professor Kenneth Frampton of Columbia University and Dean Raymond Yeh of University of Hawaii provided me with much guidance and challenge. Professor Jennifer Taylor of Queensland University of Technology (QUT), with her deep understanding of the Asia Pacific, posed timely questions and made valuable suggestions. My frequent discussions and debates with Professor Miao Pu of the University of Hawaii in the past twenty years often reminded me of the importance of critical thinking. Miao will find that some of his brilliant ideas and insights are recorded in this book. An early reader of my draft, Leigh Shutter, often expressed his views about this project while we were jointly running the QUT program in Hong Kong. The same is true of my colleague Kevin Manuel, during our many visits to the Chinese mainland and in discussions of our continuously updated curriculum on Chinese architecture. I am indebted to all these renowned scholars for lending me an international perspective.

The active Chinese architects are the heroes of this volume. Their outstanding works form the major story, and their generous contributions of drawings and pictures shine throughout the book. Particular thanks go to Professors Mo Bozhi, Qi Kang, Dai Fudong, Peng Yigang, He Jingtang, Bu Zhengwei, Cheng Taining, Zhang Jinqiu, Xing Tonghe, Guan Zhaoye, Lu Jiwei, and Xiang Bingren. They supplied materials for this book and inspiration for me in my formative years. For architects in my own generation — Chang Yung Ho, Miao Pu, Zhang Lei, Liu Jiakun, Wang Shu, Teng Kunyen, Ma Qingyun, Dong Yugan, Zhao Bing, Meng Jianmin, Wang Lifang, Fei Xiaohua, Gong Weimin, Yin Jia, Li Linxue, and Zhang Jiajin — we once faced the same puzzles and explored them in similar ways, and I hope we can work side by side in future.

The project was supported by several research assistants from mainland China: Zhang Xiaochun, Chen Xi and Wang Hongjun, doctoral students from Tongji and Southeast Universities. Their contributions are credited at the beginning of the relevant chapters. Other doctoral students, Chen Xiaoyang and Shi Wei, collaborated with me in studying the trade of architectural design and the system of tendering in China. Dr. Zhang Xiaochun is resourceful in providing me information from time to time. Funding from the Research Grant Council, Hong Kong Special Administrative Region government (Project No. CityU 1053/00H) made the employment of these assistants possible. I thank the anonymous RGC reviewers whose opinions are incorporated in the strategies of research and the structure of the book. Some investigation activities were supported by the research funds from the Division of Building Science and Technology, City University of Hong Kong (03/04-05) and Sumitomo Foundation, Japan (Reg. Num.: 048029, 2004).

As my mental framework of Chinese architecture evolved, I had opportunities to present preliminary results in various conferences and journals, among which are *Journal of Architectural and Planning Research*, *International Journal of Housing and Its Application*, *Architecture and Urbanism* (Tokyo), *The Architect, Urban Design International*, *Time + Architecture*, and conferences organized by the University of Hawaii, National University of Singapore, University of Hong Kong, British Institute of Architectural Technologists Hong Kong Branch, and the biannual Architecture and Culture symposium in China. My thanks to all those associated with these publications and conferences for broadening my knowledge of various aspects of Chinese and world architecture. I am also grateful to my friends in Hong Kong, mainland China, and abroad for helping me to formulate my thoughts: Professors Stephen Lau, Gu Daqing, Jia Beisi, Wang Weijen, Arlen Ye, Li Lin, Joseph Wong, Raymond Fung, Xiang Bingren, Chang Qing, Zhong Dekun, Li Xiangning, Ma Weidong, Zhu Tao, Peng Nu, and Liu Jie, to name a few.

Many chapters would not be in their current state without the language editing by John Oliphant, Mee Ling Cham, and Neil Drave. Besides adding color and sparkle to the text, John Oliphant often provided critical comments and timely encouragement. My students Raymond Pit Hang Chan and Ki Wai Chan made an important contribution by designing the cover and drawing the maps. Several high quality color pictures were shot by Wong Wai Man, my friend and excellent photographer. Their help is much appreciated.

China Architecture and Building Press, *Architectural Journal*, *World Architecture* and *Time + Architecture* generously allowed me to use the pictures they hold copyright to. They have also been very supportive and cooperative in the past twenty years. My gratitude goes to Wang Boyang, Yang Yongsheng, Zeng Zhaofeng, Huang Juzheng, and Zhi Wenjun.

My thanks are due to the staff members of Hong Kong University Press, especially Colin Day, Dennis Cheung, and Ada Wan, for their enthusiasm, patience, and encouragement. I must also acknowledge the three anonymous readers who had read the manuscript and made valuable criticisms and suggestions for improvement.

Finally, I pay tribute to my wife Shiling and daughter Danyi for their support and tolerance during the long stretch of time that I spent on this project.

Charlie Q. L. Xue
Summer 2005

Huangpu District, Shanghai

PREFACE

In the 1980s, China adopted the open-door policy and unleashed a drive towards modernization. Twenty years later, after a period of intense activity, China's GNP was ranked sixth in the world. Together with a number of other Southeast Asian countries, China boasts one of the fastest developing economies in the world. From 1991 to 2000, the average annual economic growth was 10.1 percent, significantly higher than the world average of 1.8 percent (*World Development Report 2003*).

As one of the foundations of the Chinese economy, the construction industry continues to increase its output at an astronomical rate. During the period from 1991 to 2000, China's average annual growth in total building output in gross floor area (GFA) was 25.68 percent. The average annual growth in total floor area constructed was 16.3 percent. The average annual growth in GFA completed was 15.9 percent. In 2000 alone, the value of projects completed was 591.8 billion yuan (US$1 = 8.3 yuan in 2004), an increase of 6.2 percent from the previous year. The completed GFA reached 738.35 million square meters (Xue and Chen 2003). Entering the twenty-first century, China spent about US$375 billion each year on construction, nearly sixteen percent of its GDP. "In the process, it is using 54.7 percent of the world's production of concrete, 36.1 percent of the world's steel, and 30.4 percent of the world's coal (Pearson 2004). It is probable that nowhere in human history have so many buildings been erected in such a short time.

What happened to China's architecture during this "great leap forward" and impressive transformation? *Building a Revolution: Chinese Architecture since 1980* presents a picture of Chinese architecture in transition as

it shifted from being a planned, state-controlled enterprise to being market-led. This period saw China's architecture undergo a rite of passage from introversion to extroversion. Revolution is evolution made apparent. An astonishing architectural revolution has taken place in the past twenty years, one set against the monolithic passage of centuries.

THE COUNTRY

According to statistics for 2004, China's population of 1.3 billion accounts for almost one-quarter of the world's population, easily exceeding the combined total of Latin America and Sub-Saharan Africa. The territorial area comprises approximately 9.6 million square kilometers. More than two-thirds of the country is mountains or desert, resulting in the concentration of population and brainpower in the towns and cities along the east coast. Among the thirty-one cities with a population of over one million, thirty are in the eastern part (Xue 1999). As a result, development is unevenly distributed between east and west, urban and rural areas. Shanghai, Beijing, Guangzhou, Shenzhen, Hangzhou, Xiamen, Dalian, the Pearl River Delta, the Yangtze River Delta, and other coastal cities approach a level of development equal to that of Hong Kong and Singapore, whereas towns and cities in remote areas may lag twenty or more years behind.

In the mid-nineteenth century, the trade wars and opium wars perpetrated by foreign powers forced China to abandon its traditional and stable 5000-year-old feudal society. By the end of the century, China had become a semi-feudal and semi-colonial country (Mao Zedong

1963). Along with the colonialists' war fleets and civilization, Western architecture was introduced. Western-style buildings were constructed, using local materials and craftsmanship, in China's major coastal cities: Shanghai, Guangzhou, Wuhan, Tianjin, Ningbo, Qingdao, Dalian, and up to Harbin.

In 1911, after years of risky revolution, Dr Sun Yat-sen and his comrades overthrew the Qing Dynasty (1644–1911) and established the first republic in China. Ten years later, the Communist Party of China was secretly founded in Shanghai, a single spark that ignited the entire country decades later. In the coastal cities, conflicts between local warlords failed to hinder the pace of modernization. Shanghai experienced its most splendid period in the 1930s, as the glamorous star of East Asia.

Beginning in 1938, Japanese invaders conquered and exploited much of China's vast territory, and the nation was plunged into adversity. When the Japanese were finally defeated at the end of World War II, civil war broke out between the Nationalists (Kuomintang) and the Communists. The Nationalist Party and its troops, supported by the US government, fled to Taiwan and continued its regime. The Communist Party, bolstered by the then Soviet Union, seized control of mainland China in 1949, when China's population reached 400 million. Development and construction withered during these eleven years of war.

Fired with the ambition of building socialism, Mao Zedong and his Communists began a major reform of the economic system in 1950. Private land in rural areas was confiscated by the government, and the free market system was replaced by the centrally controlled state-owned system. Grand buildings in the classical-revival style were constructed in the capital and other cities, to symbolize the power of the dictatorship. In the successive waves of political upheaval, people were tortured and the country was wracked by crises and cut off from the outside world. This situation remained unchanged until Mao's death and the removal of conservative forces in 1976.[1]

Following Deng Xiaoping's rise to power in 1978, the open-door policy was adopted and China entered a period of rapid development. The past twenty or more years have witnessed the most vigorous economic growth and lasting peace in China's modern history. In 1978, China was an insignificant player in international trading, with total foreign trade of only US$20 billion. Only 500,000 tourists visited China that year. In 2002, the goods passing through China's ports had increased tenfold, and the number of tourists had leaped to more than 10 million (Zweig 2003).

The Bund, Shanghai

Economic liberation accompanied the freedom in culture and thinking. People walked out of the shadow of politics and power and started to embrace individuality and pluralism in culture and social life. The "end of history" — communism — that Karl Marx advocated in the nineteenth century and that was practiced by the Soviet and Chinese Communists in the twentieth century did not and will never come. Instead, as a result of the collapse of totalitarianism, the liberal state predicted by G. W. F. Hegel will write a full stop in the evolution of human society in China as well as the world (Fukuyama 1992). After a harrowing 150-year search for modernization and lessons learned from countless successes and failures, China has finally realized its destiny.

CHINA AND THE ASIA PACIFIC

The ascent of China followed the economic miracles of Japan in the 1970s and the four "Asian dragons" (Singapore, Hong Kong, Taiwan, and South Korea) in the 1980s. Asia is the most populous continent in the world, because it contains such densely inhabited countries as China, India, Japan, and Indonesia. Historically, the whole of East and Southeast Asia were influenced by Chinese culture: people spoke similar languages and had habits rooted in China. Such a tradition can be found in language, food, and other living habits. Confucianism and the concept of the family are considered unique Asian values that differ from those in other parts of the developed world.[2]

Modern Asia is a land of endless miseries and disasters. The long historic and cultural traditions did not bring prosperity to its modern era; on the contrary, Asian

China-Soviet Friendship Pavilion, Beijing, 1956

People in Asia, especially the younger generation, are eager to learn advanced technology and principles of management from the West. Over half of the intellectuals in the four "Asian dragons" received higher education abroad. Knowledge obtained from Western countries has been assimilated and integrated with Eastern culture and traditions. Japan, Korea, Singapore, Taiwan, Hong Kong, and Malaysia have successfully absorbed and utilized this knowledge for their own investment and experience. These countries and regions were listed as "high income" in the *World Development Report 2003*. Following their example, China opened its doors to investment. Its mass, acceleration and momentum, as well as its determination, have no equal in the world today. In surfing the wave of the open-door policy and modernization, China interacted with its Asian neighbors, and they benefited from their proximity, convenient trading, and exchange of ideas and personnel.

The ample supply of cheap labor, including inexpensive technical and scientific workers, and a gradually improving infrastructure have made China the factory of the world. Significant differences in the value of goods and services inside and outside China meant those who could move goods, services, or technology across China's borders could earn large profits. Products "made in China" occupy half of the world's middle-class and lower-class shops — from toys, shoes to television sets.[3]

The local governments and bureaucrats are active in enabling China's global integrations. According to Professor David Zweig's analysis, many foreign products faced limited competition in Chinese markets and could earn "extra-normal profits." Local government officials regulated these imports and harbored close relationships with business people overseas. They were therefore able to ensure themselves a piece of the profit, which gave them an incentive to be helpful. Thus, these bureaucrats emerged as facilitators of China's internationalization.

Hoping to control the process, the central government used various administrative units and legal institutions to create "channels of global transaction," empowering bureaucrats as gatekeepers of the state's global commerce. They had few incentives to block exchange. Facilitating flows, not stopping them, was the more profitable, strategy. As control over many of these channels was decentralized during the 1980s, they were able to proceed largely unsupervised. The central government's policies on tax also encourage local organizations to establish global links (Zweig 2003).

countries were heavily involved in and shaped by the colonization of Western imperialists. After World War II, Asian countries were gradually liberated from their colonial rulers and walked the path to independence. They initially seized the opportunities provided by labor-intensive industries and then expanded to the new and value-added industries, such as electronic appliances, automobiles, and computer hardware. In the tide of globalization, Japan led the way, followed by Singapore, South Korea, and Taiwan. During the period 1985–95, Southeast Asia recorded an average of 7.2 percent annual increase in GDP per capita, in contrast to the world average of 0.8 percent (*World Development Report* 1997). "The work ethic in many Asian countries is sustained not so much by material incentives as by the recognition provided for work by overlapping social groups, from the family to the nation, on which these societies are based" (Fukuyama 1992).

In some provinces, the Chinese government tried to promote the open-door policy by establishing special economic zones, coastal open cities, districts, export-processing or high-tech zones, which enjoyed preferential policies, cut transaction costs, and improved their comparative advantages. These "special" cities and zones seized the opportunity to link globally and quickly attracted both domestic and foreign investors in the 1980s. Their success inspired other areas to establish their own zones. The fever of special economic zones has swallowed large amounts of urban and rural land and brought problems. The "zone" experiences spread to Vietnam and North Korea.

Since 1990, China has gradually taken the lead in the Asia-Pacific region, becoming particularly prominent following the financial crisis of 1997. The "miracle" of East Asia was eventually proven by China's achievements. The Chinese leaders firmly believe that "development is the only truth" and "adjust during development, development during adjustment."[4] It has been predicted that, in a few years, if for no other reason, the increasingly vital and turbulent relations between China and the United States will ensure that the twenty-first century will continue to be called "The Age of the Pacific," an era that will both separate and unite these two world powers (Abel 2001).

Of course, China and other Southeast Asian countries face a series of challenges, both politically and environmentally. The alliance between state patronage and private interests, sometimes labeled "Asian values," allows privileged individuals and sectors to grow more powerful, while continuing to abuse their power on an even greater scale (Able 2001). The conflict among rapid development, explosion of population, and environmental responsibility has resulted in frequent floods, water shortages, sandstorms, and a drastic decrease in forests and arable agricultural land. What will the environmental consequences be of China's spectacular economic development? This problem will no doubt hamper or restrict China's development in the twenty-first century.[5] Moreover, the privatization of the original state-own property has become the primary capital accumulation of the people who possess or are close to power. Honesty and trust between people and in business activities are abandoned. The rate of unemployment and under-employment is over ten percent, if one considers the 100 million rural citizens who lost the land. The gap in social disparity is expanding in a policy favoring the rich. The Gini Coefficient, an index to reflect social disparity, is over 0.5, an alarming point that can trigger societal

Yu Hua Tai Memorial of Revolutionary Martyrs, Nanjing, 1987

upheaval at any time (He 1997). Suppression of dissenting voices — such as restrictions on gatherings and the media — is a typical measure employed by many Asian governments to maintain "stability" and ensure economic growth.

THE PURPOSE OF THIS BOOK

As China pursues the single-minded aim of rapid growth (*Government Report* 2000), the last decade of the twentieth century witnessed an unprecedented infrastructure and building boom. In quantity and scale, the construction that took place in China had never before been seen in the modern world. The title of this book therefore includes the word "revolution." The term refers to the impressive speed, quantity, and scale of its economy and building during a period of fundamental and dramatic change.

The country attracted an enormous number of talented professionals who competed in an increasingly fierce arena. In addition, scholars and students studied this remarkable burst of activity. The purpose of this book is to give a structured and factual picture of Chinese architecture as it has developed over the past twenty-five years, regardless of whether such a picture is positive or negative, pleasing or disturbing. The desired audience includes a broad range of students, scholars, and lay persons across the world. Cities, urban/building designs, and events are described and discussed in the vast

Hu Qing Yu Tang, Chinese medicine shop, Hangzhou, 2001

background of China's changing political and economic climates: the reform from the planned economy to the market economy, the system that gradually took the international norms, the increasing financial forces, the superimposition of globalization and localization, the conflicts between and excitement and anxiety brought about by international influence and indigenous consciousness, and, most importantly, the changing mindset of Chinese people. Such a picture itself can help readers to comprehend the hyperactive period in China's architectural history, and provide factual ground for the later research. Taking the pulse of all this, and conveying a sense of its historic moment to an audience unfamiliar with the country, is by no means an easy job. It would certainly be a challenge to any author to capture this subject in all its color, depth, and magic.

Born and raised in Shanghai, the author has worked extensively in mainland China, Hong Kong, the United Kingdom, and the United States. Through his experiences over the past decade working with colleagues in these countries and regions, he realized that most people are uninformed about China. There is also a general scarcity of English literature concerning China.

Modern Chinese architecture is neither well enough developed in itself nor well enough known elsewhere to draw great interest. In English, there are many books about delicate Chinese gardens, splendid ancient cities, and buildings, the practice of *feng shui* and so forth, but precious little touching the essence of contemporary China and its architecture. This book is intended to fill that void.

Why does this book cover architecture in China "Since 1980"? Building projects always lag behind the overall progress of society. The major buildings developed and designed after the Cultural Revolution gradually appeared after 1980, a date that marks the beginning of an "ongoing" process. In this quarter century, the obvious historic theme of China is modernization and high-speed development.

In describing Chinese architecture during this period, the author hopes to connect the old and the new, and to present the modern face of the nation.

RESEARCH METHODOLOGY

Most of the topics in this book have been addressed by authors whose publications are written in Chinese; for example, Gong Deshun *et al.* (1989), Zou Denong and Dou Yide (1999), Zou Denong (2001), and articles in *Architects* and *Architectural Journal* of Beijing. Zou Denong's writings give this book some factual references. However, there is still a gap between existing Chinese publications and what the author wishes to contribute.

A chronological treatise of modern Chinese history may not arouse the interest of an English reader. And the current standards of Chinese architecture are not so high that it can be studied as design model for young readers. But the discussions on some salient phenomena may have universal significance. Instead of using a chronological layout commonly seen in dynastic history, the author selects and focuses on prominent topics that can mostly represent the development of Chinese architecture in the twenty-five years. The chapters discuss issues raised by various seemingly disparate phenomena: some deal with popular theories; others address the system and practice. In these thematic chapters, chronological methods are sometimes used; for example, early development of housing, recent situations in urban design, etc. Some chapters do not use a chronological order because of their nature; for example, the portrait of the architects. To exemplify this era, the author includes not only the monumental and historically significant buildings, but also ordinary housing. These chapters delineate how the political/economic aspirations are communicated through building form and serve as another study of China in this drastically changing period.

The author and his assistants have visited almost all of the buildings discussed and have communicated with most of the architects and scholars mentioned in the book. Thus, the author has first-hand material, the necessary precision, interesting details, and the vividness of personal interpretation. An architect by training, the author also tries to take reference extensively from the views of technology, social science, and humanities, so that the readers can grasp the topic in a broader context.

This book includes more than 100 building examples and the names of many people. Most of the buildings and people represent a particular period and were widely discussed in China's architectural journals and magazines. They are familiar to readers in mainland China, and some have made an international début in the past few years. Some others are selected by the author according to the criteria discussed in Chapter One. However, the examples cited in the book are limited in number, compared to the numerous new buildings and new ideas emerging all over China every day: "blink for a moment and you are liable to miss something important" (Pearson 2004). It will be difficult for a written record, like this book, to keep up with the fast pace of development in such a vast country.

OUTLINE OF THE BOOK

The book is structured into three parts, namely cultural transformation, city and dwelling, and architects and creation. Part I starts by introducing China, discussing applied theory as illustrated by major design issues and case studies. It then proceeds to examine cities, housing, individual architects, the system itself, and, finally, to predict China's development and architectural directions.

Chapter One prepares a theoretical framework in which the architectural activities in China can be evaluated, and serves as an overview of Chinese architecture in the communist regime. The establishment and subsequent phasing out of "national form," discussed in Chapter Two, reflects the fundamental changes that have taken place. Chapter Three examines the works and influences by celebrated international architects in China since it opened its doors.

Part II shifts from architectural design to city planning, urban design, and housing policy. The new buildings in the three major cities — Beijing, Shanghai, and Guangzhou — are assessed in Chapter Four. Urban planning, theories, and trends of practice are explained in Chapter Five. And Chapter Six chronicles changes in housing policy and types of residential construction.

Cities and buildings are of course conceived by people. Part III focuses on active, young, and old architects, the design-institute system and private practice. Chapter Seven introduces the works by China's prominent architects. This is followed in Chapter Eight by a perusal of the new ideas that emerge from the younger generation of architects. Chapter Nine discusses the reforms underway in this socialist country and shows how practitioners have enthusiastically embraced private practice and the free market spirit.

The nine chapters cover the most important aspects of Chinese architecture. Chapter Ten serves as an epilogue and tries to predict possible future developments. The analysis is based on the clues of various statistical reports, including those conducted by the World Bank.

To provide a clearer background for readers unfamiliar with China, a chronicle of major events in Chinese architecture since 1980 is presented in Appendix I. Through the chronicle, readers can easily locate the discussions and building cases in a historic coordinate.

Education is an important part in the architectural industry; students and teachers are the key players and stakeholders in this revolution. Appendix II presents an overview of China's educational system as it applies to architecture. Several leading schools are highlighted and some special activities are described. This appendix also sheds light on the proliferation of books and magazines in China on the subject of architectural design, urban issues, and planning regulations and theories.

THE REALITIES OF CHINESE ARCHITECTURE TODAY

Observing the vast landscape of Chinese architecture, one can conclude that the entire country is feverishly pursuing modernity, the coastal cities obviously outstripping the others in obtaining funds and opportunities. The monotony of "national form" has given way to plural values and to the more superficial, commercial, and money-oriented forms that most clients favor. At present, there is no introspection or slackening of the pace. Chinese society lacks a serious contemplation of its social value and ultimate goal in the turbulence of globalization. The whole country appears to be swept up in the pursuit of short-term goals and the frantic rush for quick profits, speed of development being everything.

Although a handful of intellectuals voice environmental concerns in the light of China's enormous population and limited resources, these are seldom considered seriously when weighed against the need for instant profit. Provincial and municipal leaders, developers, architects, construction contractors, teachers, and end users are embroiled in this crazed production chain. Durable and lasting work in technology and the arts is rarely produced in such frenetic times.

Facing the relentless process of building, and "a unique and wrenching condition" created by an unprecedented intensity in Asia, Western architects and theorists feel perplexed, as Rem Koolhaas writes in the introduction to his Harvard team's book *Great Leap*

Forward. "The result is a theoretical, critical and operational impasse, which forces both academia and practice into postures of either confidence or indifference. In fact, the entire discipline possesses no adequate terminology to discuss the most pertinent, most crucial phenomena within its domain nor any conceptual framework to describe, interpret, and understand exactly those forces that could redefine and revitalize it. The field is abandoned to 'events' considered indescribable or to the creation of a synthesis idyll in memory of the city" (Koolhaas, in Chung *et al.* 2001).

Confronting such a scenario, the author does not wish to indulge in empty metaphysical "theories" but to present as realistic a picture or "events" as possible of the current situation in China. Theories about Chinese architecture — when there is a theory — should be broad-based and address China's development as a country, its economy, the range of its architecture, and the phenomenon of globalization. These topics and their implications are discussed throughout the text, although not at a philosophical level.

NOTES

1. From 1950, the Communists ruled China in the manner of the Soviet Union, cruelly suppressing dissenting viewpoints. The Cultural Revolution (1966–76) provided an excuse for the patriarchal Mao Zedong to extirpate his political enemies. During this period, the entire country was plunged into chaos. On October 6, 1976, one month after Mao's death, his widow and three henchmen were arrested in the Forbidden City. Thereafter, left-wing and radical political movements were gradually eliminated. See "Virtual Museum of Cultural Revolution" at http://www.cnd.org.

2. Confucianism is a significant driving force in Asian development. See the series of books edited and written by Harvard University professor Tu Wei-ming, including *Confucian Traditions in East Asian Modernity: Moral Education and Economic Culture in Japan and the Four Mini-dragons*, Harvard University Press, 1996; and *Confucian Thought: Selfhood as Creative Transformation*, State University of New York Press, 1989. "Asian values" as cited by Malaysian Prime Minister Dr Mahathir Mohamad are free from Western standards of human rights. See *South China Morning Post*, November 20, 1997.

3. As mentioned, severe social disparity exists in China. The large number of peasants, who gain little from their meager land or lose land in the so-called tide of "special economic zones," have to migrate to the provincial capital cities or coastal cities. Take Dongguan of the Pearl River Delta as an example. There are 1.5 million local residents and 5 million workers from other provinces, mainly Hunan and Sichuan, who work in the 150,000 private companies (according to the Municipal Government of Dongguan, 2002). They work an average of ten hours a day and six or even seven days a week in poor working environments under strict monitoring. Children under sixteen years old are also found in many factories.

   Take a shoe factory of a Nike contractor as an example. The workers work an average of 256 hours a month, and earn US$.28 an hour before deductions for personal and medical care (just for simple illness). The wage paid for producing a pair of Nike shoes is US$1.5, but a pair of Jordan Vs is sold for US$120 in the American market. Poisonous and harmful materials are used in the production process, and workers have little protection. A dormitory room of 25 sq. m. usually accommodates twelve to fifteen workers. There is no pension, unemployment insurance, medical, or maternity leave. This factory is only the tip of a huge iceberg. The local residents, who usually act as managers in those factories, know these facts. The local officials ignore the problem: they benefit from this joint-venture activity. The speed of China's economic development and the dumping of very low-priced goods are based on the exploitation of the Chinese rural labor class. See the report in *The New York Times*, October 2, 2003; Li Qiang, An investigation of workers' situation in China's joint venture factory — Nike and Adidas in China, www.cnd.org, www.chinanews.net, August 2003; Su Shaozhi, The blood and sweat factory in the twenty-first century, Free Asian Radio and www.cnd.org, October 2003. Some information is from the author's own observations.

   In the mid-nineteenth century, Friedrich Engels (1820–95) and Karl Marx (1818–83) exposed the miserable situation of British workers in early capitalism and primary capital accumulation (Engels, *The Condition of the Working Class in England*, 1845; Marx, *Capital: A Critique of Political Economy*, 1867). The situation has reappeared in twenty-first century China, which proclaims itself a "socialist" country.

4. This slogan has been iterated by Deng Xiaoping several times since 1992 and is seen extensively in China's mass media.

5. Since 1997, corruption in China has been highlighted by the imprisonment and even execution senior officials — including majors and provinical governors — and executives of state enterprises, striking example of corruption is Indonesia. Extensive reports concerning the collusion between privileged families and government officials, including student protests against this corruption, can be found in *Asiaweek*, *The Asian Wall Street Journal,* and other Asian news magazines from 1990 to 2000.

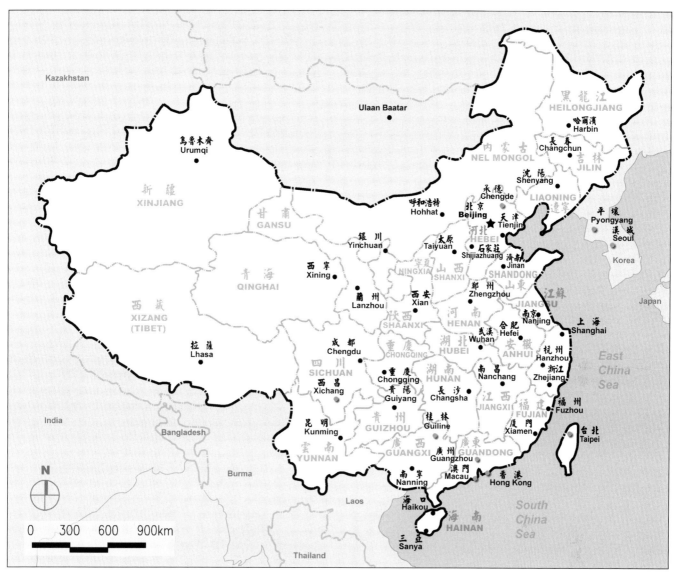

Map of China

Pearl River Delta

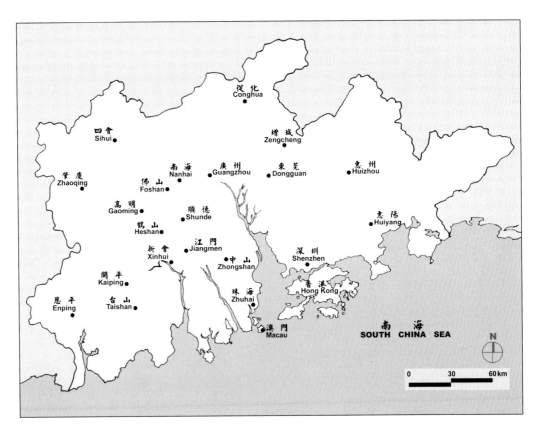

Yangtze River Delta and Bohai Bay

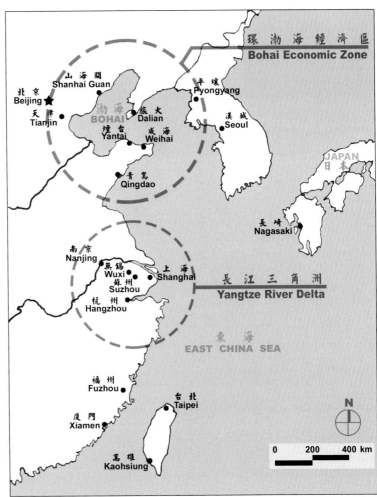

1. Huangpu River, Shanghai
2. Inner city, Guangzhou
3. Interior of Jinmao Building
4. Huaihai Road, Shanghai
5. Nanjing Road in the evening

6. Zhang Jinqiu, Restaurant of Tang Dynasty style, Xian, 1985
7. Lobby, Hotel of Tang Dynasty style, Xian, 1985
8. I. M. Pei, Fragrant Hill Hotel, 1981
9. Dr. Sun Yat-san University, Zhuhai campus, Guangdong Province, 2001
10. Old street of Zhong Shan, Pearl River Delta
11. Trophy buildings in Pudong, Shanghai
12. Restoration of the old lane house, Shanghai, 2000

13. Chang Qing, Renovation of Bund, Shanghai, 2002
14. Beijing Road, Guangzhou
15. White Swan Hotel, Guangzhou, 1984

16. Studio theater, Shanghai Drama Institute, 1986
17. Charlie Xue and Liu Tianchi, Taierzhuang Memorial of Anti-Japanese War, 1993
18. Mo Bozhi and He Jingtang, Museum of Nanyue King, Guangzhou, 1990

19. Qi Kang, Lai Juqui etc., Wuyi Mountain Village, Fujian, 1987
20. Qi Kang, Provincial Museum, Henan, 1998
21. Dai Fudong and Huang Ren, Architecture school building, Tongji University, 1988
22. Dai Fudong, Zunhua Hotel, Hebei, 1998
23. Lijiang old city, Yunnan
24. Xiang Bingren, Jiangning Residential Area, Nanjing, 2004

25. Lu Jiwei, Training center of Communication Bank, Taihu Lake, 1996
26. Foot bridge, Guangzhou
27. Cheng Taining, Dragon Hotel, Hangzhou, 1986
28. Guan Zhaoye, Tsinghua University Library, 1991
29. Guan Zhaoye, Science Building, Tsinghua University, 1997
30. He Jingtang, new campus of Zhejiang University, 2002

31. Miao Pu, Restaurant of Xiaolangdi Park, Henan Province, 2002
32. Miao Pu, Reception hall, Ecological Garden of Minhang, Shanghai, 2004
33. Park renovated from a shipyard, Zhongshan, Guangdong Province
34. Liu Jiakun, Disco renovated from an old factory, Chengdu, Sichuan Province
35. Zhang Lei, Student hall, Nanjing University, 2000
36. Kengo Kuma, Bamboo House, Commune by the Great Wall, Beijing, 2002

37, 38. Zhao Bing, Jade Culture Center
39. Zhao Bing, Museum of learning from Lei Feng
40. Liu Kemin/Yin Jia, Sculpture in Tongji University, 1999
41. Liu Kemin/Yin Jia, Mural at Graduate School, Tongji University, 2001
42. Zhang Lei, Student hall, Nanjing, 2000
43. Wang Shu, Xiangshan Campus, China Academy of Fine Arts, Hangzhou, 2004
44. Ma Qingyun, city center of Ningbo, Zhejiang

45. Li Linxue, Academic building, Sichuan University
46. Teng Kunyen, Warehouse studio in the bank of Suzhou Creek, Shanghai
47. PPDG, Reception center, Pudong, Shanghai
48. Fei Xiaohua, Public toilet, Shenzhen
49. City center of Shanghai

Part I

Cultural Transformation

Evaluation Criteria for Contemporary Chinese Architecture

"National Form" and Chinese Identity: Burden or Chance?

The Impact of International Architecture

From Vitruvius to Gropius, from Alberti to Giedion, the principles and theories of architecture are universal. In addition to the conventional assessment of architecture in form and function, social and cultural aspects are different in China, mainly because of its recent history of being behind the bamboo curtain and having a planned economy for almost thirty years. New criteria have to be sought and set for China's particular situation. In the future, Chinese architecture will have to pay greater attention to the market, technology, and the environmental requirements of the twenty-first century. A paradigm shift from traditional aesthetics to an ecological assessment of architecture is desperately imperative, given China's limited resources.

This chapter is written jointly by Charlie Xue and Zhang Xiaochun.

CHAPTER ONE

EVALUATION CRITERIA FOR CONTEMPORARY CHINESE ARCHITECTURE

The criteria for evaluating architecture are multifaceted and vary according to the social and cultural context, in China and in other countries.

It is widely accepted that social context has a profoundly important influence on architecture (Musgrove 1987; Rapoport 1969; Norberg-Schulz 1975). This chapter analyzes contemporary Chinese architecture from a variety of perspectives, including ideology, culture, and social values based on tradition, economy, the market, and technology. Environmental protection and sustainability are discussed, as they are global focal points in the twenty-first century. In this regard, they give new meaning to traditional aesthetic principles and play a special role in the evaluation of architecture.

By examining the prevailing architectural theories in China, this chapter poses questions about various aspects of China's architecture and serves as a general survey of Chinese architecture today.

ARCHITECTURAL EVALUATION: A RETROSPECTIVE

In his *The Ten Books on Architecture*, Vitruvius, an ancient Roman military engineer, asserted that "firmness, applicability, and delight" are the fundamental principles of architecture. He also defined and analyzed aspects of architectural design, such as site, orientation, column order, scale, and so forth (1999). From then on, his theories became the first set of criteria for how to judge architecture.

People's understanding of architecture as a symbol of culture has become increasingly influenced by almost all aspects of society, including aesthetics, religion, institutions, and social behavior. As a result, architectural design tends to be diversified; at the same time, the criteria for judgment have become more complicated and varied.

In ancient times, the practice, theory, and evaluation of architecture placed greater emphasis on aesthetic concerns such as scale, proportion, balance, and composition (Pevsner 1976). The Modern Movement and other "-isms" of the twentieth century not only gave further weight to architectural ontology but also endowed it with social and cultural connotations, adding human dimensions to architectural evaluation.

Modern architectural movements that emphasize spatial effects and "lightness," in contrast to the load-bearing walls and heavy forms of traditional architecture, have created a new set of architectural terms and language. This reform has changed both traditional formulations of architecture and ways of looking at architecture. In his book *Space, Time and Architecture* (1941), Sigfried Giedion argued that the concept of space should be regarded as a criterion to judge architecture. Other architects, for example, Bruno Zevi, continued to support and reaffirm the dominant role of the spatial model in architectural design and criticism (1980).

In the 1960s, Venturi suggested "complexity and contradiction in architecture" (1966) as an antidote to the "monotonous" singularity of Modernist architecture, while also advocating that popular culture be cited in design critique. Challenging the modernist orthodoxy, this so-called postmodern theory represented another significant milestone in architectural design and evaluation. From then on, Aldo Rossi conceived "city architecture" from typology (1972); Christian Norberg-Schulz put forward "architectural phenomenology," which injected the idea of *genius loci* into theories of space, place, and site (1980); and Peter Eisenman devoted himself to the explication of deconstruction architecture (2003). Geoffrey Broadbent explored the symbolic meaning of architecture from the perspective of semiotic theory, addressing minimalist architecture, which insists on rarefied techniques and concision of space and materials (1980). Moreover, architectural historian and theorist Manfredo Tafuri has referred to the importance of ideology, politics, and the economy in architectural critiques (1986), whereas Kostof understood and demonstrated historical architecture from "rituals and settings" (1985).

Among the thoughts about architecture mentioned above, some are aesthetic explorations of theories of space, whereas others analyze the meaning and cultural symbolic influences of architecture in depth, using the knowledge of such disciplines as philosophy, sociology, and linguistics as reference points. These theories complement, revise, and extend the original concepts and play an inspiring role in developing criteria for architecture.

CHINA IN THE 1950s TO 1970s: POLITICALLY ORIENTED ARCHITECTURAL DESIGN AND EVALUATION

Under the constraints of ideology, economy, and the social system, architectural creation was restricted to some extent. Chinese architects had to endure ideological and political pressures that might not have been apparent to observers in Western countries.

In the early 1950s, post-war construction was in full swing in China. With enormous enthusiasm, the Chinese people started to rebuild their socialist country under Mao Zedong's leadership. In 1953, a conference of architects' associations was held in Warsaw, Poland, at a time when the whole world was under the cloud of the Cold War. Architects from almost all socialist countries attended the conference. The participants agreed to "oppose structuralism" simply because structuralism was considered an expression of capitalism. In its stead, they advocated "socialist content, national form," a politically

colorful and appealing doctrine. This conference had a profound influence upon Chinese architecture.

In keeping with the harsh economic realities of the late 1950s, the government enunciated the guiding principles of China's architectural design, stating that it must be "functional, economical, and delightful if conditions permit," as well as serving to "create a new socialist architectural style in China." The principle essentially conformed to universally accepted evaluation criteria from the time of Vitruvius through to Gropius and reflected the economic and financial situation of China in that period. The principle was adhered to in the construction of the 1960s and is followed even to this day.

As far as aesthetics is concerned, the school of the Beaux Arts was the leading artistic style in those decades. In his article *Beyond Revolution: Notes on Contemporary Chinese Architecture* (1998), Zhu Jianfei looked at the subtle influence Beaux Arts exerted on architectural creation. "Despite the political changes and elaborate ideological theorization, the Beaux Arts model that was introduced in the 1920s had survived and was now serving a new political project". In 1956, Mao Zedong encouraged new ideas in social culture, arts, and science, with this proclaimation: "Let a hundred flowers blossom and a hundred schools of thought flourish." However, Mao's ideas were not carried out to any significant extent in architectural design during those years when the radical left wing prevailed.

During the 1950s, ideology, national form, China's weak economy, and the single Beaux Arts aesthetic model formed the criteria for architectural design and evaluation. In the late 1950s, "ten grand national projects" in Beijing powerfully embodied the policy-oriented content of Chinese architecture, epitomizing the climax of the style.[1] Construction activities stagnated during the years 1966–74 because of continuous political upheavals.[2]

FROM 1980 TO THE PRESENT: ARCHITECTURE AND SOCIAL TRANSFORMATION

A favorable development occurred in the late 1970s. In 1980, Deng Xiaoping, China's patriarch after Mao Zedong, issued a statement on construction and housing projects, pointing out that building construction should be one of the three pillar industries of the national economy. At the same time, the open-door policy was attracting new technology and materials as well as new architectural ideas to China. These trends broadened the perspective of Chinese architectural professionals. From then on, building construction, the mainstay of the national economy, grew rapidly. In the past twenty years, construction sites of every size and scale have been seen on almost every corner of the cities and towns of China. Standing at the base of a newly soaring skyscraper in Beijing or Shanghai, the question immediately comes to mind: how is one to evaluate Chinese architecture today?

Frampton stated that the development of Western architecture from 1750 to 1939 could be divided into three main streams embracing "cultural transformations, territorial transformations, and technical transformations" (1992). He also pointed out that these three streams were interwoven and developed in parallel. In fact, the progress of Chinese architecture exhibits similar features to what Frampton concluded. Great transformations in such areas as the natural environment, political systems, the economy, social culture, and technology interweave in parallel development, making the evaluation of Chinese architecture complex and multifaceted.

Chinese scholars also enumerate several models of architectural criticism; for example, models of value criticism, social criticism, cultural criticism, science and methodological criticism, science and technical criticism, form criticism, and so forth (Zheng 2001). It is only by integrating all of these models that one can achieve a comprehensive appraisal.

In this book, the success and failure of contemporary Chinese architecture and its possible role in the future is assessed more or less according to the preceding views. In the narration, three aspects are treated either separately or in sequence: form and function examined in architectural ontology, the social and cultural value of architectural texts, and the technological evaluation of architectural products.

It is not our intention to give a perfect evaluation but rather an individual observation of Chinese architecture for this period, its current situation, problems, challenges, possible strategies, and prospects.

FORM AND FUNCTION: CRITICISM OF ARCHITECTURAL ONTOLOGY

If architectural works could be regarded as self-contained texts, isolated from their social background, the appraisal could focus merely on the analysis of form, function, and aesthetic value. The widely accepted principles of architecture, such as space, scale, proportion, balance, hierarchy, rhythm, order, and so on, become the criteria. Consider, for example, Helou Xuan (literally, "Not a Simple Pavilion"), built in the 1980s in Songjiang Fangta Garden in Shanghai. Professor Feng Jizhong, the designer, employed pure language to create a small teahouse made up of flowing space and juxtaposed so harmoniously with the environment that it looks as if it is actually growing out of the earth (Figure 1.1).

Let us move to buildings in an urban environment. Individually, some of them are quite good; in shape, space, and function, they are full of creativity. However, architecture is such a complicated subject that aesthetic judgment and functional analysis are useful only in the most preliminary stages of assessment. A perfect individual building may not be successful when located in an urban context. In this regard, we may pay more attention to social and cultural critiques rather than to formal or functional judgments.

Figure 1.1   (a, b) Feng Jizhong, Helou Xian, "Not a Simple Pavilion," Songjiang, Shanghai, 1986

SOCIAL AND CULTURAL ASPECTS OF ARCHITECTURE

The Social Value of Architecture

In this section, we emphasize the essential purpose and significance of architecture. In our argument, the physical function of architecture is not equivalent to its essential purpose. In other words, form and function alone fall far short of telling whether or not a building possesses meaning, because architecture carries so much social and cultural information about our era. From this perspective, the purpose of building "for the people" is not only fulfilled by physical functions but by spiritual ones.

Take, for example, the projects in the 1950s–60s that pursued "socialist content, national form." When one discards the prejudice of ideology, one finds that these projects were created with the rationale of symbolizing the national dignity of dictatorship. Traditional

Figure 1.2 Office building of Ministry of Electrical Engineering, Beijing, 1999. In addition to the creative interior space, the building tries to capture the atmosphere of the nation's capital.

architectural vocabulary became an appropriate way of expressing that meaning. These projects embodied historic changes and became representatives of that special period (Figure 1.2).

However, "national form" gradually evolved into an extreme stylistic expression and became a kind of formal doctrinism. During the 1980s, especially in Beijing, contemporary buildings with traditional kiosks or pagoda-shaped tops were considered to have "recaptured the traditional style" and were the products of such extremism. These shallow imitations of ancient forms proliferated throughout China, but they were unable to "recapture the features of the ancient capital" (see Chapter Two). On the contrary, such parodies debased the traditional architectural language to that of a facetious and ridiculous label.

Some architectural slogans gained popular currency and reflect the psyche of many municipal leaders. Who hasn't heard proclamations such as "This building won't go out of date for at least fifty years" or "It will be a landmark of our city"? Or buzzwords such as "cyber city," "street in the Tang Dynasty style," "miniature world landscape garden," as well as the fabulous hyperbole of "tallest building," "longest bridge," or "largest convention center" in China, Asia, or perhaps the world. These superlatives reveal the ambitions of the developers or municipal leaders concerned and express the vainglory of their achievements. The buildings in question, which usually have important daily functions, are made to bear too heavy a burden (Figure 1.3).

The newly built Zhuhai Airport, which cost 69 billion yuan is a regrettable example. The government of Zhuhai was originally anxious to establish an "international first-class" airport to showcase the city's success. But things went dreadfully wrong and the airport that boasted "the longest runway" and "the most luxurious terminal lounge"

Figure 1.3 (a) People's Square, Shanghai, (b) Train Station in Shenzhen

sank into debt because of a dearth of business; it attracted few passengers and flights, primarily because of the city's geographic location. As a result, the Zhuhai Airport has become little more than an embarrassing "landmark." The design and function may be excellent, but the airport has lost its utilitarian value.

Social and Cultural Orientation of Architectural Text

Spiro Kostof once concluded: "Architecture, to state the obvious, is a social act — social both in method and purpose" (1985, 7). Architectural text epitomizes a society's culture and its time; consequently, a profound understanding of the culture and spirit of an era can help us to more fully evaluate its architecture. At this point, nothing else can replace cultural understanding as the basis for architectural critique (Figure 1.4).

During the 1980s, great transformations in Chinese society occurred: the economic system was shifting from a planned economy to a market economy. At the same time, theories from abroad flooded into China. As China began to emerge from the shadow of ideological domination, architectural professionals endeavored to escape from the straitjacket of "socialist content, national form." A revival of architectural creation began.

Pluralism in Architectural Design

In the 1980s, Chinese architectural circles started to appeal for pluralism in design as an alternative to "monotonous pattern." "Socialist content, national form" was replaced by "features of times, nationality, regionalism" (*Architectural Journal* 1980). At the same time, people were liberated from their long mental oppression, and their creative energies were unleashed. Like bamboo shoots after a spring rain, numerous high-rise buildings and huge mansions in a variety of styles shot up in the following two decades. A number of talented architects worked unremittingly to create new forms of Chinese architecture. Well-known projects such as the Beijing Olympic Sports Center, the Yanhuang Art Gallery, the China International Exhibition Center, and the Memorial Museum for the Nanjing Massacre of 1938 are only a few of these successful works.

However, an overreaction to the dictates of the "monotonous pattern" and a lack of understanding of the new architectural theories and critiques resulted in a one-sided approach to design "pluralism," and a farrago of vulgar, strange, and noisy buildings were thrown up in the streets of large and small Chinese towns.

Related to "pluralism" is the rich cultural connotation of architecture, which includes not only an understanding of traditional culture but also of foreign culture. In an article analyzing how foreign theories affected the development of Chinese architecture, Professor Zou Denong invokes the metaphor of "three tidal waves" to describe the interchanges between China and other countries that have occurred in different historical periods. According to Zou, we are now witnessing the "the third wave" (2001).

An enormous number of architectural theories, such as postmodernism, deconstruction, typology, and other philosophical, sociological, and anthropological "-isms" have flooded China. It was these exotic trends that enabled Chinese architects to contemplate architecture from more angles, and the new ways of thinking became the weapons of architects and students. Yet few had a real understanding of the social origins of the latest trends. In this situation, studying and applying these theories actually became only a kind of simple grafting or direct iconic imitation. As a result, the buildings with postmodern symbols or KPF decoration and SOM motifs that arose here and there were labeled "hybrid" buildings.

Figure 1.4   (a) Shekou (snake mouth), (b) Hotel of South China Sea, Shekou, 1986

It is necessary to mention the influence of globalization and Westernization on Chinese society. Given the global dominence of Western culture, Western ways of living and thinking, such as democracy, freedom, McDonald's, KFC, and Disney, quickly spread into mainland China. This kind of quasi-colonial discourse seemed to be a representation of advanced productivity and culture; Chinese people felt compelled to receive it but often did so inconsistently, both positively and passively. They surrendered to the pervasive force of this new social culture, which was so powerful that Chinese traditional customs and value systems were gradually overwhelmed. During this transformation of Chinese society, conflicting ideas and cultures clashed, resulting in abnormalities of social psychology. Worshipping the foreign style and having unquestioning faith in another culture, both in society and in buildings, was a reflection of the kind of dialogue and even struggles that ensued during this confusing time of transition. Chapter Three discusses the effect of international trends.

Regionalism and the Pursuit of Traditional Architectural Culture

"Traditional and national form" has haunted the Chinese architects for a long time. The description has varied from time to time; it was "national style" in the 1950s, "new socialist style" in the 1960s, and "of the times, nationality, and regionalism" in the 1980s; different slogans yet the same essence.

At the beginning, to inherit tradition was simply to imitate the physical form, which was superficial. In the 1980s, the contradiction between ancient form and modern function and materials became more pronounced, and people began to rethink how to best carry on the tradition. A "Chinese pitched roof" was not considered the only way to embody Chinese character. Indeed, traditional architecture is a source of unlimited inspiration. Take the Juer Hutong neighborhood project in Beijing, designed by Professor Wu Liangyong, as an example. The attempt to create a new relationship between traditional forms and modern life is highly commendable, although it has also generated controversy (2000). Chapter Two discusses tradition and innovation.

The continuity and innovation of regional architecture is worth mentioning here. For example, the "Lingnan style" of architecture rooted in southern China and led by Professor Mo Bozhi (see Chapter Seven) combines modernistic language and local context. Research conducted by architect Cheng Taining into territorial culture and local styles in architectural design is another persuasive example. We can also list the so-called "Shanghai school" of architecture created during the 1930s–60s, and various works designed by Xing Tonghe in Shanghai after the 1980s, as illustrative of such explorations. These new architectural styles are contemporary but possess Chinese characteristics. The achievements of these architects are discussed further in Chapter Seven.

Form Follows Finance: Commercial Culture, Media, and Form

In the mid-twentieth century, many architects and theorists were involved in a dispute over the relationship between form and function, a debate that continues even today. At present, the influence of commercial culture upon architecture has endowed the discussion with new content: does form follow finance?

During the recent transformation of Chinese society, the widespread and rapid proliferation of commercial culture has been a noteworthy feature. For architecture, there are both advantages and disadvantages to working within such an environment. On one hand, financial incentives and rewards will motivate designers to bring their initiatives fully into play. There will be more variety and creativity in the buildings constructed and greater design flexibility. The requirements of the public will be further satisfied as a result. On the other hand, the situation can have opposite and deleterious effects when commercial considerations are taken to the extreme.

The effect of commercial pressures in China has manifested itself in degraded city streets and urban spaces that lack character or humanity. The harmful influence of capital interests has taken its toll on traditional values, behavior, aesthetics, and taste, causing these cornerstones of Chinese society to almost collapse. The greedy "get rich quick" mentality and hunger for instant profits have spread throughout society, causing deterioration in moral standards and values. In building design, commercial considerations inevitably supersede artistic ones, and the profit motive becomes the sole *raison d'être* for development.

As a matter of fact, the two poles — commercial and artistic — coexist everywhere and at all times, but the two are not so contradictory that reconciliation is impossible. A commercialized architecture does not always conflict with the ideals of architectural form. Examples in both China and abroad provide ample proof of this contention.

Clients, Architects, and End Users: A Three-way Confrontation

Architectural space is ultimately designed for human beings. The parties in architectural projects are: clients, architects, and end users. As the building market gradually opens, architectural design is becoming an even more important commercial activity. Under these circumstances, direct communication among the three sides intensifies. But until now, the relationship among the parties has not been particularly harmonious.

The target of the client — be it the government, a developer, or a private individual — is to achieve maximum commercial and social benefit with a minimum outlay of resources. The expectations and demands of clients are not always easy to meet; they will often impose impractical requirements upon the architect, insisting that the building be "the most advanced," or "not become dated," or be constructed in a certain style, which might not be aesthetically or technically practicable. The client's desires can also be self-contradictory. A recognized architect in Beijing recently stated that few buildings in the capital were designed according to the ideals of the architects. Most were generated from the unreasonable ideas of local municipal officials and developers: awkward spatial relationships and a clash of icons are typical of the unfortunate results.[3] The municipal leaders, clients, or even construction contractors sometimes decided the materials of external walls, doors, or windows. The problem here is the low level and inferior quality of the "architectural education" of the clients who have commissioned the projects. In this case, the architect acts only as a "drawing puppet."

As far as architects are concerned, they serve both clients and users. According to a media survey gauging public perception of "golden collar professionals," architects ranked fifth (http://www.sina.com.cn, Sep. 2001). However, the ranking refers to income only; the social status of architects doesn't match this high rating. In China's rapid transition from a planned economy to a market economy, architects have not been immune to the blandishments of a profit-oriented culture. A client's commission is everything, no matter if the project is good or bad. The architect is not in a position to independently implement the responsibility to create a better society (Xue and Chen 2003).

The end users may be the majority of society, but they are ordinary people with neither power nor influence. From this point of view, the real needs of the users of architectural space are not always satisfied, because they must passively accept built environments. The concept of "public participation" is unfamiliar to most people. In addition, the ability of ordinary people to appreciate architecture is limited, and this affects the efficacy of such participation (Figure 1.5).

Figure 1.5 Rising from the old district, Shanghai

However, a new phenomenon is emerging. The government and private developers are paying increasing attention to the masses; at the same time, the awareness of the public's right to participate in architectural decisions is growing. For example, in Beijing, Shanghai, and other cities, more and more people have joined in activities such as choosing their ten favorite "celebrity" buildings. Public voting has become fashionable; for example, in the election of notable works from Shanghai's architectural heritage of the past fifty years, and in the public competitions held for the Grand National Theater of Beijing (1998), the Oriental Arts Center (2000), and the design for the World Expo in Shanghai (2002).

But it is unclear how significant public voting is in these activities. How did ordinary people's opinions influence the process of design revision and decision-making? It is reasonable to assume that such public participation is superficial.

Without a doubt, the three-way confrontation in China among clients, architects, and users is counterproductive. A healthy relationship among the three is an important parameter for evaluating the architectural design environment. Although the situation in China is gradually improving, the "social design" that Robert Sommer envisaged is just a matter of armchair strategy (1983). The subtle three-way relationship among clients, architects, and users remains a dubious factor in evaluating contemporary Chinese architecture.

EVALUATING THE TECHNOLOGY OF ARCHITECTURE

It is widely accepted that new inventions in the science of building and the improvement of architectural technology can create a revolution in architectural design. In the late nineteenth and early twentieth centuries, as a result of the invention of the steel structural frame and the elevator, the Eiffel Tower in Paris, the Crystal Palace in London, and the high-rise buildings of Chicago were constructed. These edifices dramatically illustrate the power of architectural technology to change our world.

Today, a century later, history seems to be repeating itself. The development of the computer, advances in digital and communications technology, and breakthroughs in structural and materials science are fueling the irresistible momentum of the building industry. It was the unprecedented computer power that enabled both Zaha Hadid and Frank Gehry to push the boundaries of space in their visionary projects. The construction of intelligent buildings and ecological buildings also requires the utilization of high technology. Some architects, such as Richard Rogers, would be unable to create the incisive details on the stressed skin of their buildings without tectonic and special material techniques.

Although China has made considerable progress in architectural technology, Chinese architects cannot congratulate themselves on their work in this area. Computer technology has not been fully used in design work, but only as a drafting and rendering machine. The understanding of ecological architecture is partial and incomplete, whereas research into intelligent buildings is only beginning. Moreover, an obvious disparity still exists between China and the developed countries in the matter of structural technology. One hears complaints from designers such as: "The concept could not be realized because of a lack of technology, and many details had to be changed on site." The construction personnel will often frankly admit: "We cannot do it."

THE ECOLOGICAL CRITERIA OF ARCHITECTURE

In addition to considering form and function, social culture, market, and technology, ecological aspects must not be ignored when evaluating contemporary Chinese architecture.

The rapid development of the economy is quickly depleting natural resources and threatening the ecological fabric of China. The conflict between people and the planet Earth is sharpened by the seemingly endless increase in population and limited and depleting natural resources. China's arable land accounts for only 6 percent of the world's total, but it must feed 25 percent of the world's population. One problem is that China's population continues to explode and will reach 1.7 billion in the mid-twenty-first century, although the strict one-child policy has been implemented since 1980; the areas of Beijing, Shanghai, Hangzhou, and Guangzhou doubled in the 1990s and urban sprawl is rampant. Another factor is that arable land is eroding at an alarming rate, sacrificed mostly in the name of the "Special Economic Zones" that the government is creating. Although a national "Land Management Law" was promulgated in 1986, farmland continued to decrease. From 1986 to 2002, farmland in China dropped 15 percent from 132 million hectares to 112 million hectares according to a very conservative calculation. This keeps China's farmland per person at the bottom of the world ranking.[4] The new movement of occupying rural land was launched in the Pearl River Delta and Yangtze River Delta, and this will affect more than 50 million peasants (*Mingpao Daily News*, March 2, 2004). The worry of "who will feed China?" was raised again (Brown 1995; *Mingpao Daily News*, Nov. 30, 2003).

Water resources is another area of concern. The water in China is 2,313 cu m per person, only one quarter of the world's level, and the number in northern China is even as low as 944 cu m (Zheng 2001). More than 300 cities, including some large municipalities such as Beijing, Tianjin, Shanghai and Xi'an are already regarded as areas with severe water shortages. Wastage of water can be observed in these cities. Water trucks in Beijing and Shanghai sprinkle plants, lawns, and asphalt roads when sandstorms from the north blow into southern China. China also needs to consider whether its limited water resources in western China can withstand the pressures of large-scale development (Figure 1.6).

To build a city — no matter how fabulous — at the sacrifice of energy and natural resources is self-defeating. Green architecture and ecological architecture take environmental protection and sustainability as their mandate; they can be of incalculable significance to a country that has a population of 1.3 billion and is short of natural resources at the same time. This is the reason that the voice of a developing ecological architecture has been

(a)

(b)

Figure 1.6 (a) Earth sheltered dwelling, Ganshu, 1988, (b) Interior of the earth sheltered dwelling

The criteria for evaluating architecture are multifaceted and vary according to social context, in China and other countries. After reviewing the historical standards used for evaluating architecture, this chapter analyzes the situation in China, addressing the economy, the social milieu, the population, and the natural resources, and indicates new criteria not just based on general principles of architectural judgment but on factors unique to China. Furthermore, the chapter emphasizes that sustainability and environmental protection will be the major concerns of the twenty-first century. In this regard, ecological standards applied to architecture will satisfy the demands of social progress, give new meaning to traditional aesthetic rules, and play a special role in how Chinese architecture is appraised.

China will have better opportunities and prospects in the twenty-first century than it did in the previous century. In this regard, the building industry in China, including relevant government departments and professionals, needs to understand how to turn challenges into opportunities.

NOTES

1. The "ten grand national projects" of 1959 include the People's Congress Hall (Great Hall of People), the Revolutionary History Museum, the Agricultural Exhibition Hall, the Fine Arts Museum, the Military History Museum, the Nationality Cultural Hall, the Beijing Train Station and the Workers' Stadium, the Nationality Hotel and Pavilion of Welcoming Guests, in a total area of 673,000 sq m. The decision to construct these impressive structures was made in October 1958, and all were completed before October 1, 1959, in time to celebrate the Tenth Anniversary of the People's Republic of China.
2. During the Cultural Revolution, from 1966 to 1976, most design institutes in major cities were dismantled and the architects and engineers sent to the countryside for labor and "brainwashing." See the Virtual Museum of the Cultural Revolution at http://www.cnd.org.
3. Interview with one of the project assistants, Dr. Zhang Xiaochun, June 2001
4. There are great discrepancies between the government's statistics and some scholars' studies. The author uses the figures from government's statistics. See Ye Yaoxian, *The process and prospect of China's urbanization, Architectural Journal*, No.1, 2002, pp.46–48, *Mingpao Daily News*, Nov.30, 2003. According to Zheng Yi, the farmland decreased 5% or more every year in the past ten years. And a large portion of forest and grassland was reclaimed to the new farmland at the same time, thus leading to more natural disasters. See Zheng Yi, *China's Ecological Winter*, Hong Kong: Mirror Books, 2001, pp.83–102.

raised more loudly in recent years. In regard to architectural design, the Ministry of Construction and some local governments have successively promulgated standards for energy saving and sustainability. For example, clay brick has been forbidden as a building material, heat loss through external walls (OTTV, overall thermal transfer value) must now be calculated; solar water heaters and passive solar building technologies are extensively used in north and south. Energy consumption, conservation, green areas, and innovative technology are emphasized as necessary in building plan and urban design submission.

The intensification of global warming indicates that humanity's efforts to prevent environmental degradation and collapse remain insignificant and ineffectual when weighed against the relentless ecological destruction that occurs daily. The future for China and the world is frankly bleak. To sum up, architectural principles based on ecology and sustainability will be an important component of Chinese architecture in the future.

2

The subject of "National form" is common in many developing countries, which usually have a long and proud history. Since the 1920s architects in China have struggled to adapt themselves to a succession of complicated international and domestic political waves. "National form" once cemented a fragmented nation, stimulated a weak nation, and earned foreign currency for an eagerly growing nation. This long and painstaking process reached its climax in the 1980s and 1990s, through arguments and building cases. Because of the proliferation of globalization, the requirement of "national form" has been gradually phased out, although local identities shaped by particular geographical, climatic, historical, and cultural conditions will never disappear. The positive and negative experiences of "national form" definitely hold lessons for the exponents of this style.

This chapter is written jointly by Charlie Xue and Zhang Xiaochun.

CHAPTER TWO

"NATIONAL FORM" AND CHINESE IDENTITY: BURDEN OR CHANCE?

In the early 1980s, following the Cultural Revolution (1966–76), two architectural projects captured the limelight and once again provoked considerable discussion and comment concerning "national form." One of these was the Fragrant Hill Hotel, designed by I.M. Pei and built in 1981; the other was the Queli Hotel, designed in 1985 by then deputy minister of construction Dai Nianchi.

The slogan "national form" was first used as early as the first half of the twentieth century, although its essential meaning has evolved over time and has varied with the circumstances of the particular era in which it was invoked. The simple intention originally expressed by the slogan has become increasingly complex and has been enigmatically influenced by social context, including ideological, economic, and cultural factors.

Long ago, humankind faced a wild world. In each group or, later, nation, people built shelters according to their needs, habits, land topography, weather and, most importantly, available materials and technologies. This material and technical availability was limited; therefore, we can appreciate the harmoniously uniform building styles in traditional European and Asian towns, for example, Siena of Italy and Pingyao Town of Shanxi, China. When people have more sophisticated building technologies and more choices, they still keep some traditional concepts, politically and architecturally.

National form, or perhaps more properly, nationality form, of architecture is the presentation of nationalism in the built form. Nationalism shows its function in modern society. According to some scholars: "The revolution of modernization has brought very considerable fragmentation, but also new modes of communication and integration based on the new electronic technologies of information and dissemination. In this unprecedented situation, nations and nationalisms are necessary, if unpalatable, instruments for controlling the destructive effects of massive social change; they provide the only large-scale and powerful communities and belief-systems that can secure a minimum of social cohesion, order and meaning in a disruptive and alienating world. Moreover, they are the only popular forces that can legitimate and make sense of the activities of that most powerful modern agent of social transformation, the rational state."[1]

What is "national form" in a Chinese architectural context? Of course, so-called "national form" has roots in traditional Chinese architecture, as a number of scholars have concluded.

China has developed a unique architectural system characterized by timber structure and distinguishing layout and decoration methods. Liang Si-cheng (Liang Ssu Ch'eng, 1901–72),[2] the "father of Chinese architecture," summarized the nine features of traditional Chinese architecture as follows:

(1) The individual building is commonly composed of three parts: podium, main body, and pitched roof.
(2) As far as layout is concerned, the main building and its auxiliary parts, such as porches and halls, are combined symmetrically along a north-south axis and enclose at least one private courtyard.
(3) The structural system is of timber.

(4) *Tou-Kung* is a kind of special bracket that acts as both a structural and decorative element and as a basic module for the traditional building system. In addition, *Tou-Kung* was regarded in ancient times as a symbol of hierarchical organization.

(5) *Ju-zhe* (*Ju-jia*), consisting of multilayered beams and short columns supporting the beams in between, is the system that determines the slope and curve of the pitched roof.

(6) The pitched roof plays a key role in traditional Chinese architecture.

(7) Buildings are ornamented boldly with different colors and vivid drawings and decoration; for example, red walls and green tiles.

(8) The structural system is exposed to the outside in an elaborate manner; in this case, these special joints contribute to the decoration in addition to their structural function.

(9) Some kinds of decorative element, such as colored glazed tiles, brick, and woodcarvings, are used on a large scale (Liang 1984, 2001).

It is clear that Liang's assertions are the physical aspects of "national form," although what we can inherit from tradition is far more than what the physical image alone can express, as scholars have remarked in recent years. For example, in *The Genius of Tradition* (Miao 1989), Miao Pu characterized Chinese traditional architecture in thirteen points; these are not ideographic descriptions but macroscopic analyses delineating traditional Chinese conceptions of the cosmos, including such concepts as the "mini-cosmos" and "two sets of scale within an interior space." Miao Pu's design work is discussed in Chapter Eight.

Moreover, Liang's summary of "national form" is the orthodox official form of the Han nationality, mainly in central China, regardless of the fact that there are fifty-three minorities located in the periphery of the country. In fact, the understanding of "national form" has varied according to times and circumstances. The term has been endowed to some extent with special political and ideological meanings that make it more complicated to interpret than it should normally be when treated only as a kind of description based on architectural ontology.

TIDES OF "NATIONAL FORM"

In most societies, nationalism is fuelled by past grievances caused by external powers (Pei 2003) and "the struggle for recognition" (Fukuyama 1992). China is no exception. Imbued with strong political color, the several tides of "national style" in architecture were formulated in the nation's humiliation and defeat.

The early twentieth century witnessed the ceding and devastation of territory in China by various foreign forces and domestic warlords. The stable agricultural and feudalist society that had run in its track for 5000 years was soon dismantled, and the new capitalist country was not yet established. Accompanying the decaying of the Qing Dynasty, the long continuation of cultural tradition was broken, especially after the May Fourth Movement of 1919. Science and democracy, as concepts of Western civilization, gradually replaced Chinese beliefs and world values. As both placebo and stimulant, the "national form" caught on with the government and intellectuals in the 1930s.

At the time, several overseas architects already had an appreciation of traditional Chinese architecture and the intention of making their designs "look like China." Examples of their work can be seen in Yenching University (now Peking University), designed by Henry K. Murphy (Cody 2001); Peking Union Medical College and Hospital (Shattuck & Hassey) and Wuhan University, designed by F.H. Kales (Figure 2.1). This "Chinese architecture" with missionary colors was neither fish nor fowl, and was laughed at by Chinese people and architects, who were determined to design buildings with real Chinese features.

During this period, the "National Rejuvenation" movement was initiated by the Nanjing National Government. Young Chinese architects who had been educated abroad soon joined this movement to revive traditional Chinese monumentality, and they designed a number of major buildings; for example, the Mausoleum of Dr Sun Yat-sen (Figure 2.1), built in Nanjing in 1929, and the Memorial Hall of Dr Sun Yat-sen, both designed by Lu Yanzhi (Lu Yen-chih, 1894–1929); university campus and buildings in Guangzhou, mainly designed by Lin Keming; and the buildings of the Academy of Science (Sinica) in Nanjing, designed by Yang Tingbao (Figure 2.2).

Figure 2.1 First tide of "national form" in China before 1940, (a) Nanjing University, (b) Yenching University, (c) Library of Wuhan University, (d) Peking Union Medical College and Hospitale, (e) Central Academy of Research, Nanjing, (f) Professor Liang Si-cheng, (g) Yang Tingbao, Music Stadium, Nanjing

(a)

(b)

Figure 2.2 Lu Yanzhi, Mausoleum and memorial hall of Dr Sun Yat-sen, (a, b) Memorial Hall of Sun Yat-sen, Guangzhou, 1931 (c-e) Mausoleum of Sun Yat-sen

(c)

(e)

(d)

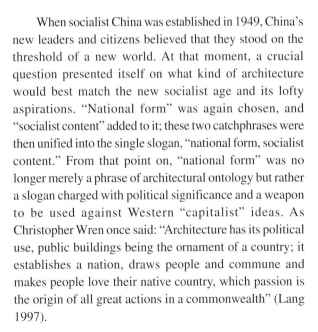

When socialist China was established in 1949, China's new leaders and citizens believed that they stood on the threshold of a new world. At that moment, a crucial question presented itself on what kind of architecture would best match the new socialist age and its lofty aspirations. "National form" was again chosen, and "socialist content" added to it; these two catchphrases were then unified into the single slogan, "national form, socialist content." From that point on, "national form" was no longer merely a phrase of architectural ontology but rather a slogan charged with political significance and a weapon to be used against Western "capitalist" ideas. As Christopher Wren once said: "Architecture has its political use, public buildings being the ornament of a country; it establishes a nation, draws people and commune and makes people love their native country, which passion is the origin of all great actions in a commonwealth" (Lang 1997).

In the early stages of the establishment of the new socialist China, the whole world was under the cloud of the Cold War. The grim confrontation between the two blocs of the socialist East and the capitalist West cast a pall over international relations. Architecture unfortunately fell victim to this ideological conflict. Combining socialist idealism with an uncertain economy, China's dictatorial government announced its intention of creating "a new socialist architectural style in China," and buildings with the characteristics of the modern movement, for example, a flat roof and strip windows, were criticized as the "bad taste" of capitalism.[3] At this moment, national identities were established with new characteristics — those physical forms associated with liberal democracy. It was obviously a negative use of national identity.

In an atmosphere dominated by ideology, many architects struggled to pursue socialist ideals and follow the commanding Communist Party, both practically and theoretically. For example, Professor Liang Si-cheng, who played a key role in investigating traditional Chinese architecture and was a pioneer in the study of Chinese architectural history, wrote a series of articles discussing the problem of how to inherit Chinese traditions and make them serve socialism. Professor Liang argued for the creation of an architectural language to be adopted by the entire nation. The nine characteristics or features of Chinese architecture that he articulated at that time can be regarded as his interpretation of such a language. At the same time, characteristics such as the pitched roof and certain other decorative details became emblems or motifs of the national style, regardless of whether the roof was timber or concrete. As a result, some famous projects embodied such a language (Figure 2.3). From the viewpoint of architectural aesthetics, the "national form" expressed by these projects is simply the imitation of traditional forms on a superficial level.

The essence of "national form" changed in response to shifting political currents. The year 1955 was a turning point. The use of this traditional vocabulary in architectural design drew criticism for reasons of economy and ideology. For instance, adding traditional roofs to contemporary multistory buildings led to higher costs, which the economy could ill afford. And colored glazed tiles were regarded as symbols of the feudalism that was to have been buried with the old society.

At the same time, the influence of the Soviet Union affected almost every aspect of Chinese society,

Figure 2.3 "National form" in the 1950s, Ministerial Building of Beijing

architecture being no exception. The "ten grand projects" constructed in Beijing in the late 1950s are illustrative (see note 1 of Chapter One); a number of them do not look particularly Chinese but more or less embody an eclectic style that expresses both Chinese and Russian traditions and the superb majesty of dictatorship (Figure 2.4). Such a "grand" style can be easily found in Hitler's Germany, militarist Japan in the 1930s, Stalin's Soviet Union in the 1950s (Wu 1997), and later in the communist regimes of North Korea and Romania (Leach 1999). They are delivered with a kind of xenophobic ethnocentrism. For example, Nazis fawned over traditional Bavarian buildings as a "pure" expression of the *volk*, untainted by globalizers and foreign influences. "This kind of architecture saw itself as ideological. Its politics stretched all the way from socialism to communism and all points in between. Great themes were adopted from beyond architecture, not from the imagination of the individual architect's brain" (Koolhaas 2000). Francis Fukuyama reveals the truth more relentlessly: "recognition is the central problem of politics because it is the origin of tyranny, imperialism, and the desire to dominate. But while it has a dark side, it cannot simply be abolished, because it is simultaneously the psychological ground for political virtues like courage, public-spiritedness, and justice" (1992).

During the 1960s and 1970s, China had to face the problems caused by a declining economy. At the same time, the political situation was undergoing a subtle transformation. The relationship between China and its former ally the Soviet Union deteriorated, and the cooperation that had been the hallmark of the relationship between these two socialist countries degenerated into its antithesis. In this case, "national form" became synonymous with "feudal sovereignty" and with drawing inspiration from history, as expressed by the phrase "back to the ancients," and came to be considered a waste of money. As a result, the slogan "national form" was replaced by another — "functional, economical, delightful if conditions permit"— which was promulgated by the government for two decades.

In the 1960s and 1970s, an unprecedented political calamity struck China. The Great Proletarian Cultural Revolution engulfed the entire nation, paralyzing the economy and causing society and culture to stagnate. "National form" was forgotten during this era of repression, during which some ordinary and sparsely decorated public and residential buildings were constructed.

(a)

(b)

(c)

Figure 2.4 Examples of "ten grand buildings" in 1959, (a) China Fine Arts Gallery, (b) Museum of Chinese Revolutionary History, (c) Great Hall of People

REVIVAL OF "NATIONAL FORM"

At the end of the 1970s, after almost twenty years of inertia, the revolution in Chinese architecture that had been percolating with the inauguration of the open-door policy swept across China with a vengeance. As a result of the government's new policies, significant investment capital, as well as a plethora of architectural theories from overseas, poured into a mainland China that had been isolated from the outside world for so many years. Numerous new buildings of various styles and composition designed by skilled architects from both China and overseas were constructed throughout China, enriching the traditional urban landscape with contemporary colors and vibrant new life.

But there are always contradictory facets to every phenomenon. On the one hand, Chinese cities became more modern; on the other, the Chinese national identity came under attack, as the influence of the West compromised ancient traditions. At this critical moment, the cry for "national form" was heard even more loudly, a strident outcry imbued with a sense of crisis over the perceived threat to national identity. For some, the mantra of "national form" was like clutching at a straw in the wind; for others, it was a rallying cry to restore the distinguishing national characteristics that were considered dangerously imperiled and even at risk of dying away completely (Figure 2.5).

During the 1980s, there were a number of reasons for the revival of "national form." At one time, a lot of simple,

(a)　　　　　　　　　　　　　　　　　　　　　(b)

Figure 2.5　Some examples of "national form", (a) Government building in Guangzhou, (b) Scenes in the city center of Beijing

matchbox-shaped buildings had been constructed because of the weak economy. Later, when political conditions changed, these monotonous boxes became an unharmonious blight on the city, especially in several traditional cities like Beijing and Xi'an. As a result, Chen Xitong, the former mayor of Beijing, expressed the opinion in a letter to veteran architect Zhang Kaiji that perhaps the city had no alternative but to place kiosks on the tops of buildings (*The Architect* 1992, 4). As an antidote to the mundane construction of that earlier period, the curved lines of the traditional forms were regarded as "good medicine" to improve boring views and enrich the skyline.

"National form" was also embraced as a reaction against the new architectural theories and technologies that had flooded into China along with the open-door policy. China swallowed these ideas and techniques too quickly to digest them, and the country's landscape felt the effect of this onslaught to such a degree that, in some cases, the identity of the local people all but disappeared. In this situation, "national form" was held to be a potent weapon against the depredations of the West.

Translations of postmodernist theory into Chinese gave the advocates of "national form" the theoretical basis for restoring traditional architectural models and venerating the past. The effect of such translations has been considerable. Charles Jencks's *Language of Post-Modernism* and Robert Venturi's *Contradiction and Complexity of Architecture* were introduced into China in the mid-1980s; the ideas were appropriated to suit the language and culture of the students and architects who studied them. Concepts such as the separation of a building's exterior from its interior function, the juxtaposition of historic icons, and two-dimensional

decoration were readily accepted by vulgar, fashion-seeking developers and obedient "productive" designers.

China's thriving tourism industry also feeds on "national form," as the instantly recognizable icons of Chinese culture channel tourist dollars directly into local economies. Beijing, Xi'an, and other historic cities have greatly benefited from the steady stream of foreign tourists eager to find the Eastern difference. The restoration of local identity likewise drives the use of traditional architectural vocabularies.

Examples from Masterpieces

Two well-known projects mentioned at the beginning of this chapter represent two different ways of treating traditional heritage.

I.M. Pei's design for the Fragrant Hill Hotel, built in Beijing in 1982, explored a way of integrating the southeastern vernacular building style with contemporary function. Having been away from his homeland for forty-three years, Pei wished to see if there were any valuable concepts in the Chinese tradition that were worth utilizing. The hotel is located outside Beijing in the picturesque Western Mountains that once served as the royal resort during the Qing Dynasty (1644–1911). The building complex has 35,000 sq m of gross floor area (GFA) spread over a landscaped site measuring 30,000 sq m. The building has 292 guest rooms, is divided into five wings, each not more than four stories in height, the organization of each wing determined by a series of courtyards. An atrium is topped by a trussed skylight similar to that of the just completed East Building of the National Gallery in Washington, DC. White walls decorated with patterns in gray brick convey a southern Chinese flavor, and classic window frames and ponds, popular motifs in traditional Chinese gardens, add to the charm. The design stresses the unique courtyard, proportions, and façade typical of the Chinese vernacular (Figure 2.6).

When it was completed, Fragrant the Hill Hotel attracted considerable interest from Mainland architects. Hundreds of articles discussing it appeared in the country's architectural journals. There was no doubt that it was an "élite" building, with an extremely refined treatment; however, some drawbacks were quickly pointed out. The site and hotel are too far away from the city proper, and the hotel is the center of attention in the traditional garden, destroying the garden's tranquility. The "garden" layout made the organization of the hotel too loose: the distance between a room and the reception counter could be up to 200 m. The large number of glossy white tiled walls and a

surface that was too reflective caused the building to lose some of the feel of the southeastern vernacular style that the designer had deliberately pursued. Pei's pursuit of a "vernacular" feel also came at a high cost in materials and craftwork. The gray brick veneer on the walls was ninety times more expensive than the price of ordinary brick at the time. The total cost of construction was double that of similar class hotels. But architects in China admired Pei's pursuit of high culture as well as the creative freedom he enjoyed in designing the hotel.[4]

The Queli Hotel, designed in 1985 by Dai Nianchi, the Deputy Minister of Construction at the time, also drew considerable attention. The hotel is adjacent to the Confucian Temple in Confucius' birthplace, Qufu in Shandong Province, a national Class I heritage site. It is a very sensitive matter to build anything near such an important historical monument. So, Dai's design for the

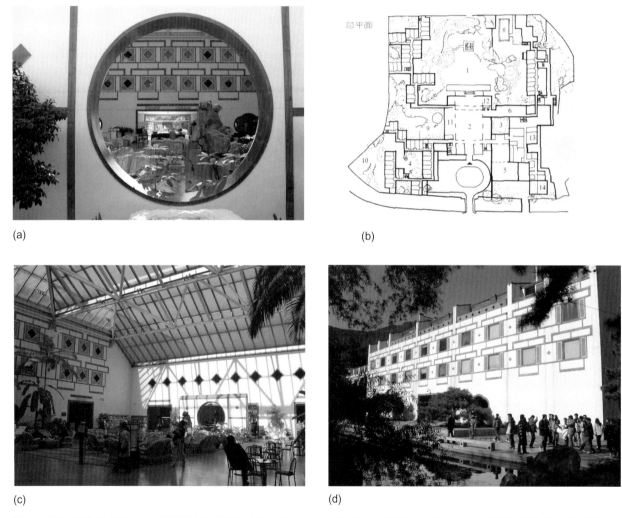

(a)

(b)

(c)

(d)

Figure 2.6 I.M. Pei, Fragrant Hill Hotel, 1981, (a) Scenic window, (b) Plan, (c) Spring Courtyard, (d) Hotel facing the hill

Queli Hotel borrowed the style of the ancients to subtly merge the Confucian Temple with the two-story-high hotel; the layers that form the courtyard are composed of black shingles, white walls, and gray skirting, providing a harmonious and unified tone. The relief patterns in the skirting stone subtly describe the Confucian rituals of the region. Dai's method acts as a bridge from the 1950s' "national form" to a more contemporary interpretation of Chinese tastes in the 1980s — cleaner and grander in general impression (Figure 2.7).

Figure 2.7 Dai Nianci, Queli Hotel, Qufu, Shandong Province, 1985

The Fragrant Hill Hotel and the Queli Hotel were lauded by many observers for their attempt to create a distinctive Chinese architecture for a new era. Pei's design did not use the pitched roof; instead, he used some Chinese spatial concepts and façade patterns, expressed by contemporary techniques. Dai's design directly used the "orthodox" traditional form. Just at a glance, people cannot tell the old from the new buildings in Qufu even at, say, 100 m away. Pei's design of the Fragrant Hill Hotel, together with his later works in Japan and Suzhou, actively shows how tradition can be incorporated in modern buildings. At the same time, a nationwide debate on this very subject was being carried out.

In November 1985, the Architectural Society of China held an important conference in Guangzhou. The primary topic of discussion was how China was to develop its architecture and make it flourish. Dai Nianchi, designer of the Queli Hotel, insisted upon the virtues of "national form, socialist content." He went on to argue that renovation and innovation in architectural design should take as their starting points traditional Chinese architecture in all its excellence; this foundation should then become

the basis for further elaboration (Dai 1986), a philosophy embodied in the Queli Hotel.

Meanwhile, at the beginning of this era of exciting change, many people did not fully accept the exotic ideas and styles from the West. For this reason, Dai's design for the Queli Hotel drew a great deal of enthusiastic applause from the public. It is undeniable that the Queli Hotel has a good layout and a harmonious dialogue with the existing historic location, in addition to being functional and efficient. At the same time, this project evinces a satisfying and rewarding attempt to combine traditional forms with modern technology and materials.

However, Dai's concept in this project could not suit all situations, especially in an urban landscape. The heavy roof was also criticized. Yet the imitation of the imperial system of traditional architecture displayed in the Queli Hotel has spread to other places in China; as a result "national form" has staged a comeback.

Historic Glory or Burden?

The dictum to "preserve and protect the face and atmosphere of the ancient capital city and promote creativity in architectural design," advocated by Beijing's Council of Urban Planning in the 1980s, has indeed been implemented, often with mixed results. Over the past 800 years, Beijing has been the capital city of several dynasties. The historic Beijing, especially in the Ming (1368–1644) and Qing (1644–1911) Dynasties, expressed its dignity and authority through its imposing city wall and the walled Forbidden City. In 1956, an advised choice of site for a new administrative center, coupled with human-made destruction and a lack of heritage protection, led to the dismantling of Beijing's city wall; unfortunately, the characteristic fabric of the old city has been altered in the drastic development of the past few decades. In the late 1980s and early 1990s, Beijing's municipal government vowed to "recover the style of the old capital." As a result, new buildings, regardless of their function or size, were crowned with a kiosk roof "cap." For example, the State Library, designed in the 1970s and completed in 1987, was rearranged to conform to a traditional layout and refurbished with a pitched parapet (Figure 2.8).

Another well-known project is the Beijing New (West) Train Station, completed in 1996, almost thirty years after the erection of the 1959 station. With a GFA of 720,000 sq m, the station is located on a 4-hectare site: the functional design innovations include a passenger terminal in both the upper and underground levels, thus

Figure 2.8 Beijing Library, 1987

shortening the walking distance. Because the main building faces north, the designers created a large opening 45 m by 50 m in the building's façade, making it possible for sunshine to flood the main north plaza during Beijing's cold winters. This 740 m by 180 m narrow plaza was divided into a main plaza and two secondary plazas. Building height and plaza-width ratios were controlled at 1:1.8 to 2.2 (Figure 2.9).

This new train station is a modern architectural work, but as the "gateway to Beijing" and the terminal of the Beijing-Hong Kong rail line, as well as the site of the capital of the Jin Dynasty (Beijing celebrated its 800th anniversary as a historic capital city in 1997), the station shoulders the burdens of being both a memorial and a celebration of contemporary transportation. Eventually, the main building was topped with a large functionless gilded roof that cost more than US$10 million! That sum is equivalent to the construction costs for eighty elementary schools, when 12 percent of China's population is illiterate (Xue 1999). The parapet wall, cornice, and other parts are ornamented with the language of traditional architecture, especially glazed terracotta. Looking from the plaza of the train station, people are unable to see clearly those ornamented details. Moreover, passengers with cumbersome luggage, and job-seeking peasants, who occupy the plaza all year long, may not be able to enjoy "traditional Chinese culture" in that particular place![5] Standing in front of this magnificent edifice, visitors will experience how small they truly are. The building's heavy ornamental and traditional architectural vocabulary seem incompatible with its function of quickly and efficiently dealing with the number of passengers who throng this crowded station.

A similar story can be seen in the famous city of Xi'an, the ancient capital of several Chinese dynasties, particularly the prosperous Tang Dynasty (618–907). In its built-up area of 200 sq km, there are 108 sq km of preserved heritage buildings spanning 3000 years of history. Traditional structures and relics can be found throughout Xi'an and its immediate vicinity. In this ancient city, there is a pervasive and overwhelming sense that one must "actively honor tradition," a force that finds

(a)

(b)

Figure 2.9 Landmark buildings in Beijing, (a) Beijing New (West) Train Station, (b) Xidan Department Store

expression in all culturally related activities and phenomena, architecture being no exception.

Zhang Jinqiu is the chief architect of the Northwest Design Institute of Architecture in Xi'an and a student of Liang Si-cheng. She made her name known through a series of designs inspired by ancient pagodas. The layouts are logically arranged and the shapes elaborated in accordance with the architectural features of the Tang Dynasty. These projects abstracted elements of traditional style, and her designs for hotels expand the resort concept using both old and new elements. The Shaanxi History Museum, designed by Zhang in 1991, strives to recreate the magnificence of a Tang palace. Zhang achieves this end to a remarkable degree. She characterizes her design

(a)

(b)

(c)

(d)

Figure 2.10 Design work of Zhang Jinqiu, (a) Tang Dynasty (618–907) style design hotel, restaurant, and theater, Xi'an, 1984. The ancient Wild Goose Pagoda is in the view of hotel guest room, (b) The garden, (c) Details of eave and wall, Shaanxi History Museum, (d) Professor Zhang Jinqiu, (e) Shaani History Museum, Xi'an, 1992

(e)

as "seriously emulating the classical school," rather than being merely "fake antiquity" (Zhang 1994) (Figure 2.10).

Looking at the situation strictly from the point of view of architectural ontology, the design process is simply a matter of seeking the most suitable answer for the question posed; theoreticians unanimously agree that there can be more than one solution for the various problems presented by each project. To imitate an ancient style is only one of many possible approaches; it may be quite suitable for certain traditional contexts but inappropriate in other environments.

But to a great extent, "national form" has turned out to be synonymous with "the style of the ancients," especially in building practice. In the special social context in China, it has been widely accepted as an infallible solution to solve intricate problems of architectural design and has been unquestioningly adhered to.

As a result, numerous buildings in "the style of the ancients," as well as streets in the style of the Tang, Ming, or Qing Dynasties, have sprung up throughout China, whether or not they were necessary or even reasonable solutions to specific architectural problems. A new type of "monotonous pattern" has come into existence.

The Beijing train station was criticized for its decorated kiosk, and the mayor who advocated "national form" stepped down from the political arena in 1997. The next year saw the radical egg-shaped national theater highly praised by the top leaders of the central government. These events are directly or indirectly related to the phasing out of "national form."

SOLUTIONS TO REGIONALISM

There is yet another architectural force that parallels the development of "national form" and has attempted to break away from its orthodoxy. From humble beginnings, this tributary of thought has gathered strength and has now flowed into and converged with the river of pluralism.

Southern China is well known for its "Lingnan" style of architecture, initially championed by Mo Bozhi. Resisting the severe pressures of ideology, Mo did not restrict himself to the doctrine of "national form." He concentrated on function, which he expressed through modern technology, while mirroring the local environment in both its natural and social aspects. We can view the result in his projects, such as the Beiyuan Restaurant, built in the 1950s, and the Guangzhou Hotel, built in the 1970s (Figure 2.11). The "Lingnan" style was further developed

(a)

(b)

Figure 2.11 Baiyun Hotel and other designs in Guangzhou, 1960s

by a group of architects in Guangzhou and the Pearl River Delta (see Chapter Seven for details).

Professor Qi Kang, of Southeast University in Nanjing, has significantly contributed to the exploration of China's new architecture. He adheres to the recognized elements of design, while stressing the picturesque and creative. Wuyi Mountain Village, a resort in scenic Fujian Province, was designed by Qi and his colleagues at Southeast University in the 1980s. The white stucco wall is divided by the brown wooden framing, and the wings

Figure 2.12 Meiyuan Xinchun Museum, Nanjing, 1987

of the building extend into the misty valley (Figure 2.12). The indigenous style is deftly and poignantly conveyed.

Professor Qi brings his unique concept to architecture in an urban landscape, especially in an ancient city like Nanjing. In two famous examples of memorial architecture, the Meiyuan Museum, the former residence of Premier Zhou Enlai, and the Memorial Museum to the Victims of the Nanjing Massacre, Professor Qi took great care with both the spatial layout and the utilization of materials, invoking the spirit of modernist architecture rather than simply relying on traditional labels. Although there is no grand roof, every visitor is still deeply affected by the artistic influence of these two buildings (see Chapter Seven for details).

Even in Beijing, the center of "national form," some nice works designed between the 1980s and 1990s have been erected that "recapture the old style." Two examples that relate at various levels and in different ways to traditional styles are discussed here.

The first one is Yan Huang Art Gallery, located outside of Anding Gate and opposite Yonghe Palace. Because "Yan Huang" is the old poetic name of a Chinese ethnic group and the site is adjacent to a historic palace, this project should have had plenty of reasons to adopt the ancient style. However, the designer, Liu Li, did not follow stereotypes but sought another solution. He arranged the entire building asymmetrically, at the same time simplifying the elements of traditional architecture and creating a kind of new abstract architectural vocabulary

with a contemporary feel. The result is not merely a perfect organization of function and space but a pleasant relationship with the existing historical urban milieu as well (Figure 2.13).

The second example is the Ju'er Hutong New Courtyard House project, directed and designed by Professor Wu Liangyong and his Tsinghua University team (Figure 2.14). Old Beijing is famous for its courtyard-style residential neighborhoods. But nowadays, the old single-family courtyard houses are usually occupied by dozens of households, and many are derelict and face the prospect of demolition by greedy developers. Wu's design was for the reconstruction and renovation of an old residential district in Beijing. In this project, he explored the juxtaposition of Chinese traditions and contemporary life. The courtyard style was retained in order to keep the unique texture of this traditional urban space. The bungalow-style buildings that enclose the courtyard were made multistory to accommodate the high density of the urban population. For the form of individual buildings, simplified architectural vocabularies were employed. This renewal project shows sympathy for traditional living style and strives to create a new neighborhood model in the city.

In Shanghai, renovating the old district and restoring the old lifestyle converged to start a trend of new usage in the old *lilong* house. The remarkable example is Xintiandi Square, an urban reconstruction and revitalization project in Shanghai. It is attracting attention in China because of its approach to both urban renewal and commercial

Figure 2.13 Yanhuang Art Gallery, 1988

(a)

(b)

Figure 2.14 Wu Liangyong and Tsinghua University design team, Ju'er Hutong new courtyard housing project, 1988–93, (a) Bird's eye view, (b) Inside the courtyard

management. The project is developed by Sui On Ltd. of Hong Kong. In Xintiandi Square, some old *lilong* houses are conserved, whereas some are partly conserved and partly rebuilt (the façade is retained but the interior is changed). As a result, visitors can experience the space of a traditional *lilong* house and a contemporary plaza in the same location (Figure 2.15). The success of Xintiandi proves the resilient life of regional culture.

INTERPRETATIONS BY OTHERS

Other important interpretations of "national form" came from overseas. After the open-door policy was implemented and China's construction market became accessible to those outside China, increasing numbers of foreign design firms began to venture into the country. To some extent, in order to operate effectively in China, given its unique social and cultural context, they had to follow the maxim, "When in Rome, do as the Romans do."

Perhaps someone who is not Chinese can never fully understand the spirit of Chinese tradition. Furthermore, to most non-Chinese, "national form" means a kind of special traditional architectural category, one that is quite different on the level of artistic form from the categories of one's native country. But for this reason alone, those who arrived in China during this period were free to create with an unburdened conscience. In the design of Shanghai Center (1989), for example, John Portman used the red column and simplified *dougong* (a Chinese column bracket) to express his understanding of local tradition. The eighty-eight-story Jin Mao Building was inspired by the ancient Chinese pagoda, and the design-director Adrian Smith created a sparkling contemporary version of the traditional pagoda utilizing new technology and materials.

To some extent, foreign interpretations of Chinese traditions may be superficial, yet they provide important and valuable insights for the further exploration of local identities and Chinese regionalism. Compared with their predecessors in the early twentieth century, for example, Henry K. Murphy and F. H. Kales, the foreign architects at the turn of the twenty-first century showed more respect to Chinese culture and fewer missionary colors.

"NATIONAL FORM" AND CHINESE IDENTITY

During the evolution of Chinese architecture in the modern era, the slogan of "national form" and the discipline of architecture have always been closely linked. What is discussed here is the extent to which "national form" relates to national identity and how much weight it must bear when the relationship between the two is considered.

(a)

(b)

(d)

(c)

Figure 2.15 Xintiandi (new horizon) in Shanghai, a renovation of old lane houses, (a) The old lane becomes popular gathering place, (b) Lane interior, (c) Open space is wider than before, (d) Old houses find new usage, (e) Bird's eye view of the whole area

(e)

In the late 1950s, the word "identity" was unknown at that time, but under the socialist system, the authorities decreed that the primary function of culture and art, including architecture, was to define and describe "socialist reality." At the same time, China's ordinary citizens, the "new hosts" of the socialist country, also wished to express their sense of pride and dignity.

Given the political imperatives that prevailed and the ideology-saturated moment, the most viable way to satisfy and celebrate the values of both the authorities and the common people were the traditional vocabularies, to wit "national form, socialist content." Augustin Ioan pointed out in his article, "A postmodern critic's kit for interpreting socialist realism" (1999), which analyzes the transformation of architecture during political movements in Russia, that "its language could be both elitist and popular; both utopian and forward-looking as well as realist and retrospective." In this regard, national identity expressed through "national form" is related to the policy and ideology of the time.

When China opened its doors to the outside world in the early 1980s, and in the years that followed, many changes were wrought. Original traditional features disappeared in the rapid growth of urban construction, but concepts such as "identity," *genius loci*, and "context" became topics of discussion in artistic and architectural circles throughout China. Because its traditional language was suitable for both refined and popular tastes, "national form" experienced a revival, exhibiting its vital force again. During that period, "national form" was regarded as a panacea that could "recapture" the distinctive features of China's ancient capital, harmonize new buildings with old landscapes, and ultimately create a definitive sense of national identity.

In practice, as so often happens, the good and the bad are inextricably intermingled. In the worst situations, the pitched roof or other classical icons of Chinese architecture were used indiscriminately on a superficial level; the resulting style cheapened traditional architectural language, reducing it to a shallow and facetious parody of itself. From the view of postmodernism, "national form" in China has already turned out to be a kind of postmodernist semiotic emblem.

On the question of "national form" versus modern style, many relevant issues have been raised. For example, some theorists have pointed out that one must not only consider the hardware of Chinese tradition but also the software, such as spirit, culture, and similar related elements; despite their subtle and intangible nature, these influences must also be recognized (Hou 1990). Others have indicated that tradition and modernity do not contradict each other (Zhang 1987). Such thought-provoking ideas have been marshaled by theoreticians who are rethinking the idea of "national form" and its related concerns that have puzzled China's architecture circles for so many years. Such deliberations may correct some of the more extreme misunderstandings of "national form" that persist; for example, "national form" is not equal to "national identity," as the latter term has a much more profound and colorful meaning.

Another focus that has emerged during the debate is that it is more valuable to design in a modernist style than to artificially imitate old forms. As an Asian companion, Japan and its road towards modernity may serve as reference for Chinese peers. The development of Japan is a history of Westernization, following the rules and path laid down by Western developed countries (Wu 1997; Bognar 1985; Sha 2001). Kenzo Tange and Tadao Ando never deliberately pursued any "Japanese style," but critics, for example Professor Kenneth Frampton, can clearly see their shadow of indigenous Japanese influence (Ando 2002). Similarly, the buildings designed in China or by Chinese people are no doubt Chinese architecture. Of course, this topic of comparing China and Japan should be discussed elsewhere than in this book.

Scholars have also strived to release "national form" from burdens that it should not have to bear. Dr Ken Yeang, a world-renowned Malaysian architect, succinctly made this point: "Pursuing a kind of national architecture is a dilemma imposed by foreign architects. ... I can also ask you what is today's British architecture: the classical Palladian, Tudor or vernacular thatched roof? You will find it is extremely difficult to describe British national architecture. It is similarly difficult to conclude what is American, Japanese, German, Swiss, and Swedish architecture. Therefore, why should we define a national architecture, but these developed countries cannot?"[6]

In conclusion, "national form" or "national style" should not become the touchstone or mainstay of architectural creation in China, although one must give up tradition. However, by divesting themselves of the burden imposed by "national form," Chinese architects can move briskly and confidently into the future and heed the dictates of their own inspiration, taking up the challenge of creating a new architecture that will belong to the entire Chinese nation and to the world.

NOTES

1. This view was expressed by several authors such as Edward Carr, Karl Deutsch, and Anthony Giddens, and summarized by Anthony D. Smith in his book, *Nations and Nationalism in a Global Era*, Cambridge: Polity Press, 1995, p. 4.

2. In 1900, the allied forces of eight countries invaded and looted Beijing. As a defeated nation, China gave money and land to the eight countries. The Americans used this money to establish a foundation for Chinese youth studying in the United States. The talented young people were selected through rigorous examinations all over China. They were first trained in Tsinghua School (later Tsinghua University; see Appendix II) for two years, and then sent to various American universities. Most of the first group of students who studied architecture went to the University of Pennsylvania in the 1920s. Liang Si-cheng was one of them. The graduates became the main forces of the first generation of Chinese architects. Anecdotally, American architect Louis Kahn was a schoolmate of this group of students.

    After returning to China, Liang Si-cheng acted as chair of architecture at Northeast University in Shenyang. Later, he and his wife, Lin Huiyin, who also studied in the UK and US, joined the China Institute of Architectural Research, whose mission was to survey, investigate, and document traditional Chinese architecture. His views on Chinese architecture were formed during this period and is embodied in a series of his writings.

    In 1946, he established the Department of Architecture at Tsinghua University and lectured at Yale and Princeton Universities. He also represented the Chinese government in the design of the United Nations building in New York. His English manuscript *A Pictorial History of Chinese Architecture*, written in the chaotic and turbulent years of the Anti-Japanese War, was brought to the US and stored at Yale University Library. The manuscript thus escaped a series of political storms in Liang's motherland. After many years of tribulations, the book was published by MIT Press with the help of his lifelong friend Wilma Fairbank in 1984, twelve years after Liang's passing from depression and regret in China.

    See Denis Twitchett and John King Fairbank (eds.) *The Cambridge History of China* (Cambridge University Press, 1978), and Wilma Fairbank, *Liang and Lin: Partners in Exploring China's Architectural Past* (foreword by Jonathan Spencer), Philadelphia: University of Pennsylvania Press, 1994.

3. The criticism of the "bad taste" of capitalism was launched from the central government through the local design institute. *Architectural Journal*, the official journal of Architectural Society of China (ASC) published more than ten articles on this topic in its 1954–57 issues. Political ideology overwhelmed academic discussion.

4. For Pei's speech on traditional Chinese forms and the direction of Chinese architecture, see *The Architect* (No. 1, and No. 2, 1979 and 1980) and *Wenhui Bao* (Shanghai, December 18, 2001 and March 17, 2003). In these speeches and interviews, Pei reiterated his exploration of harmonizing with the local environment and finding the third way out for Chinese architecture, including the exploration in his "last work," the Suzhou Museum.

5. Beijing, Guangzhou, and other big cities have been filled with millions of job-seeking peasants in the past ten years. This migration provides endless cheap labor for the cities but causes more social instability.

6. Ken Yeang is quoted from his article "Asian Design" published in *World Architecture* (No.4, 1996, p. 27). The English translation is my own.

3

In the nineteenth century, Western imperialist powers had to use superior weaponry to force open China's doors to world trade. In the post-Mao era, however, China has willingly opened its own doors, embracing foreign investment and technology. This open-door policy has led to a liberalization of ways of thinking, a true Chinese "Renaissance." Since 1978, the importation of international architecture has increased dramatically. Exotic buildings and the lifestyle that goes with them have expanded the vision of ordinary citizens, and Chinese architects have learned new technologies, styles, and management practices along the way. Today, major civic projects are really the province of international architects. But behind the excitement, pride, and admiration are serious tensions and ongoing arguments about the proper relationship between indigenous architecture and its foreign counterparts.

This chapter is written jointly by Charlie Xue and Zhang Xiaochun.

CHAPTER THREE

THE IMPACT OF
INTERNATIONAL ARCHITECTURE

Chapter Two presents the story of how China's identity and architecture have developed in tandem over the past century. The desire for a strong Chinese national identity has been spurred by worries about losing the country's distinctive cultural heritage to globalization and internationalization. In Chinese, China is *zhongguo*, literally "country at the center of the earth," and this precisely describes the attitude of China to the outside world until the late nineteenth century. China was self relivant, with little interest in trade with other countries. Invasions by Western powers hastened the decay of the feudalist kingdom; ironically, the invaders' main purpose was to open China's doors.[1]

When the People's Republic of China was established in 1949, it adopted the Soviet Union's socialist model in everything, from the all-pervasive "socialist content and national form" to individual building technologies, as mentioned in Chapter Two. However, this conduit for overseas ideas was closed in the 1960s, when the two countries clashed ideologically over their interpretation of communist doctrine. From the 1960s to 1977, China cut its political and economic links with the rest of the world to such an extent that the Chinese word for "foreign" became synonymous with "crime."[2]

After China implemented the open-door policy in 1978, overseas influences started trickling into the country. Anything and everything from abroad was deemed innovative and fashionable. For China's architects, the liberation from the old-style communist ways of thinking coincided with the influx of imported international

architecture. When Chinese architects intended to pursue individual expression, they immediately looked to the imported buildings. New foreign ideas, both technical and cultural, dazzled the Chinese architectural and building industries. These influences came mostly through a number of highly publicized projects as well as through books, journals, and magazines that offered tantalizing glimpses of architecture abroad. The international architecture and imported building activities are inevitable developments of globalization in China.

To continue the rapid economic and infrastructure development that China had experienced over the previous two decades, the central government had to be resolute in upholding its market-centered reforms and in sustaining enthusiasm for learning from international examples. As the country's economy grew, the architectural design field began to rejoin the global architectural community. It did not unquestioningly embrace foreign influences, though, but tried to seek its own identity. This chapter assesses the influence of imported architecture by focusing on foreign-designed projects.

THE FIRST TRENDSETTERS

When China began opening up to the rest of the world in 1978, the first foreign influences came from overseas Chinese and from ethnic Chinese areas, such as the British territory of Hong Kong.

Figure 3.1 Jin Lin Hotel, Nanjing, early design of Hong Kong architects in mainland China

Figure 3.2 City Hotel, downtown Shanghai

Figure 3.3 Great Wall Hotel, Beijing, 1983, the first curtain-wall building in China.

In the late 1970s and early 1980s, foreign architects were commissioned directly by mainland Chinese authorities, invited into China as guests of the nation. They helped China's modernization and its international image, as the country was eager to give the impression of being more open. In Beijing, I.M. Pei and his Fragrant Hill Hotel (1979–82), and Jianguo Hotel, partly financed and designed by Chinese-American Chen Xuanyuan, based in Hong Kong, serve as examples. Fragrant Hill Hotel is an example of a modern interpretation of a traditional Chinese architectural style by a "foreigner," as discussed in Chapter Two, and introduced American working practices, as Pei's company collaborated with Beijing's design institutes.

Jianguo Hotel, completed slightly earlier than Fragrant Hill Hotel, is located on Beijing's main east-west thoroughfare, Chang'an Street. This hotel consists of five buildings aligned irregularly along the edge of the quadrate site, most of them less than ten stories high. The atmosphere is informal and comfortable, much like a mid-range American-style motel or Holiday Inn. A strip of garden lies between the buildings, containing a water and miniature mountain feature, making guests feel as if they have entered a southern Chinese town. The scale of the project is relatively small, having a GFA of less than 30,000 sq m. Such hotels partly eased the shortage of modern accommodation for overseas tourists.

Viewed from afar, Western ideas in general were attractive to Chinese people; yet for all their desirability, they were considered ultimately unreachable by communist China, both physically and psychologically. But the neighboring Asian dragons of Singapore, Hong Kong, Taiwan, and Korea successfully absorbed Western experiences and services into their market economies. Hong Kong in particular has become China's gateway to the West, so much so that learning from the West means first learning from Hong Kong.

In the 1970s, while the Cultural Revolution was wreaking havoc in mainland China, Hong Kong started to take off economically. The city's active building industry, which had been shaped by British rule and methodologies, and the territory's emergence as a trading hub combined to fuel a boom in construction that helped to promote architectural diversity.

Architecture in Hong Kong has greatly influenced architecture in mainland China, beginning in the southern part of the country. Because of relatively large financial investments from Hong Kong, or overseas investments via Hong Kong, architects and building professionals based in the city have long been able to land commissions in mainland China, mainly in Guangzhou, Shanghai, Beijing, and some coastal cities. Practitioners from Hong Kong are not renowned for extravagant or avant-garde designs, but they are trained to international management and operational standards and share enough of the Chinese language (written, at least) to facilitate effective communication with the mainland.

Palmer and Turner (now the P & T Group), an old British firm that built many commercial landmarks in Shanghai's Bund and Hong Kong's Central area in the early twentieth century, designed Nanjing's Jin Lin Hotel (1980–83). This hotel set a modern standard for mainland architects. The 68,000 sq m GFA building consists of a thirty-seven-story, 111 m high tower containing 760 guest rooms. A rotating restaurant is located on the thirty-sixth floor, one full revolution taking an hour. The hotel's bold, straight profile brought immediate admiration, and the hotel became an instant icon; it had the most stories and best facilities in China in the early 1980s and was the first project to be partly funded by foreign investors and co-designed by an overseas party (Figure 3.1).[3]

Designs by Hong Kong architects often went hand in hand with financial investments from Hong Kong. City Hotel, located on the "old-style" Shaanxi Road in

Shanghai, was jointly developed by Sui On Ltd. of Hong Kong and the Shanghai branch of the China Youth Travel Service. It was designed by Sui On and completed in 1986. The building is laid out compactly, using a series of triangular shapes that vary in scale to solve the problem of a site area of less than 1500 sq m. The plot ratio is about 12:1. This economical yet effective design has made the building a lasting presence in the cityscape (Figure 3.2).

In 1983, Ellerbe Becket from Los Angeles designed the first curtain-wall building in China, the Great Wall Hotel in Beijing. The hotel has 982 guest rooms and is 84 m high, with a GFA of 83,000 sq m. The curtain wall cost about US$200 per square meter, almost twenty times more than any other type of external cladding used in China at the time. A decade later, buildings with curtain walls began appearing all over China, as a glass envelope came to be regarded as sophisticated and modern, if environmentally unfriendly (Figure 3.3).

IS FOREIGN ALWAYS BETTER?

China's own particular brand of communism still dominates the political climate, but the country's enthusiasm for importing the features of international architecture has never abated. To most Chinese throughout the 1980s, anything foreign was always thought to be inherently superior.

An example of how foreign designers were received is the Shanghai Center, developed and designed by John Portman, from Atlanta, in the late 1980s. His hotel and atrium designs in Atlanta and Los Angeles were admired in China long before his building was actually constructed. The layout spreads symmetrically along an existing axis that is also the central line of the Tower of Friendship between China and Russia, another important Shanghai landmark. Its main façade facing busy Nanjing Road West and featuring a half-enclosed front courtyard and exclusive boutiques, the Shanghai Center became an iconic landmark for the new Shanghai. The building, with 180,000 sq m GFA, was constructed on a site of 18,000 sq m. The plot ratio of 10:1 is unusually high for Shanghai at the time. The retail outlet floors on the podium, the central five-star Portman Ritz-Carlton Hotel, and two wings of service apartments are efficiently arranged. The building is situated on what was once the site of the house of Silas Aaron Hardoon, a Iraqi Jewish capitalist and speculator in the 1930s. The area is fashionable and has a historical, romantic ambiance. In handling the details, the designer employed such classic elements as the moon gate, red columns, column caps, and railings, features taken from ancient Chinese architecture and that endow the entire complex with a Chinese flavor. Shanghai Center helped bring glamour back to Shanghai's "upper corner" neighborhood and is quite popular with both professionals and ordinary citizens of Shanghai (Figure 3.4).[4]

(a)

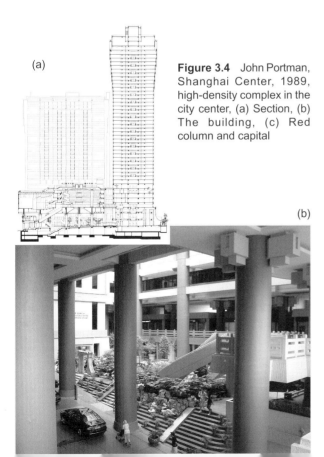

(b)

Figure 3.4 John Portman, Shanghai Center, 1989, high-density complex in the city center, (a) Section, (b) The building, (c) Red column and capital

(c)

At the end of the 1980s and beginning of the 1990s, foreign design firms started to participate in the Chinese government's most significant projects in Beijing, China's cultural and political center. A clear example of this is the China International Trade Center on East Chang'an Street. The winning design, by Sober/Roth Design Co., was chosen from entries prepared by foreign firms, including those from the US, Japan, and Hong Kong. The building raised the bar for luxury hotels and office complexes in Beijing. It dominates the skyline of Chang'an Street, and its simple but strong profile has changed the atmosphere of the area. The 95,000 sq m complex consists of a thirty-eight-story office tower, a six-story office block, two hotels and two thirty-story luxury serviced apartment towers, an 8000 sq m exhibition hall, and a 13,000 sq m shopping center (Figure 3.5). The China International Trade Center is not decorated with any overt symbolism of traditional Chinese culture, but its efficient arrangement and bright curtain wall have made it both an economic and visual focal point on Chang'an Street. The cooperation between American and Chinese architects and the process of design were documented and disseminated to architectural circles.

In a time when monetary exchange and foreign currencies were strictly controlled, Beijing, as the capital city, received special treatment. Foreign investment trickled in through various channels, including government ministries, joint ventures, foreign trade and international airlines.[5] The Lufthansa Center, finished in 1992, is an example of the influence of international aviation. The building has a GFA of 165,000 sq m and is located east of the third ring road in Beijing, not far from the Great Wall Hotel and Kunlun Hotel, an area of busy trade, commercial, and residential buildings. The Center, designed by the German firm Novotny Mahner & Assoziierte GmbH Philipp Hdzmann AG Bilfinger Berger Ban AG, is composed of a shopping center and restaurant, the Kempinski Hotel, and a residential and office block. The complex does not include a high tower, which would be out of character with nearby buildings. Spaciousness is created by the shopping center and restaurant and the residential and office block being dispersed around the site, with the Kempinski Hotel standing in the middle of a courtyard. However, the most striking aspect of the Lufthansa Center is its bold, Western play of color: a dark-red solid wall is juxtaposed with a cool dark-blue curtain wall. Though the red and blue building was an instant architectural breath of fresh air in Beijing's urban fabric, it has also drawn praise from locals and become a symbol of first-class service and elegant environment (Figure 3.6).

Figure 3.5   China International Trade Center, Beijing

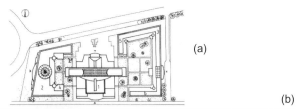

Figure 3.6   The Lufthansa Center, Beijing

The Lufthansa Center was the first joint project between Chinese and German architects and was a prelude to increased cooperation between the two countries. A recent notable addition is the German School (2001), designed by another famous German firm, von Gerkan Marg & Partners. The project consists of a red school building and two yellow apartment blocks for diplomats and their staff. These three buildings look simple at first glance, but they function well, given the complicated demands of use: as education facilities and classrooms for all grades from nursery school to high school, library, multipurpose hall, gymnasium, administration offices, restaurant, kitchen, and garage. Although red and yellow were commonly used in traditional Chinese palaces and temples, any use of bright color in a modern building in the mainland is now thought of as a foreign, usually Western, practice. Local architects received a lesson on the effectiveness of simplicity in design, showing that sophistication is not always appropriate. The design also means being able to view a pleasing addition to Beijing's cityscape (Figure 3.7). "Architecture as opposed to any other art form is irredeemably mixed up with the life-world" (Frampton 1999), and these imported buildings have taught Chinese people something of the lifestyles and civilization of the modern world.

The steady demand for international education in major Chinese cities has resulted in several new teaching facilities that also try to blend Western and Eastern styles, for example, the China Europe International Business School in Jinqiao in the Pudong district of Shanghai. The site area is 39,995 sq m and the GFA is 36,000 sq m. The

Cooperation between overseas experts and their mainland Chinese counterparts has increased in the field of architectural design. The same can be said for the fields of building and civil engineering; for example, in the design and construction of the subway system, light rail and inter-city mass transit rail.

But not all instances of cooperation have been smooth. The aesthetically inspiring China-Japan Youth Exchange Center in Beijing was a wake-up call for local architects in the capital. The center is principally composed of a hotel tower and theater, connected by a "bridge of friendship." The collaborative work of designing the project, as well

Figure 3.7 (a, b) The German School, Beijing

Figure 3.8 (a,b,c) Henry Cobb, China Europe International Business School, Shanghai, 2000

(b)

(a)

(c)

first phase of the project was completed in 1999 and had a floor area of 18,000 sq m. The design was led by Henry Cobb of Pei Cobb Freed & Partners.

The project consists of an academic center, lecture hall, bookstore, dormitory, sports facilities, and restaurant. These are arranged along two edges of the site, creating an L-shaped central courtyard. Several verandas connect at various points, forming smaller, more informal courtyards. The white walls with black brick strips are reminiscent of traditional architecture in southern China. The courtyards, individual buildings, verandas and distinct façade combine spaces and forms of China and the West (Figure 3.8). The school has played an important role as a business and academic bridge between China and the European Union.

as the symbolism of the bridge, implied a new relationship between the young people of the two countries. The sculptural, flower shape of the tower was derived from a deep vertical concave, skillfully based on the tower's plan and elevation (Figure 3.9). After completion in 1990, the complex became an important cultural facility in Beijing, but it also stirred up debate among China's architectural professionals. Disputes between the center's Japanese designer Kisho Kurokawa and the Chinese designer Li Zongze (from the Beijing Architectural Design and Research Institute) were reported in several local architectural journals. The building design was mainly undertaken by the Chinese party, but in various publications and on public occasions, credit went to the Japanese side. The media criticized the Japanese architect and other Chinese parties involved in the design process, which led many local architects into a wider discussion about their responsibilities and rights as architects. As a result, local designers became more conscious of their role in joint projects.

TOWARD BIG AND SPECTACULAR

In the early years of China's open-door policy, many cities and clients could not afford overseas architects. However, now every major city in the country typically invites international participation in prominent or technically complicated projects, providing a chance for foreign firms to get involved in projects that might not even be possible in their home countries. At first, hotel or office projects that were partly funded by overseas investment were the only plans designed by foreign firms in conjunction with

Figure 3.9 China-Japan Youth Exchange Center, Beijing, 1991

local design institutes. Gradually, the variety expanded to include government office buildings, schools, health care facilities, residential buildings, cultural facilities, landscaping and urban planning, and even urban renewal and conservation. The overseas firms able to contribute to these sectors are likely to have more design opportunities in these areas in the future.

The long list of international firms that have worked in China includes such renowned names as SOM (Skidmore, Owings & Merrill); HOK (Hellmuth, Obata + Kassabaum); KPF (Kohn Pedersen Fox); RTKL; Robert Venturi; Michael Graves; Steven Holl; Norman Foster; Richard Rogers; Zaha Hadid; Jacques Herzog and Pierre de Meuron; Rem Koolhaas, MVRDV; Cox, Nikken Sekkei; Kisho Kurokawa; Isozaki Arata; Tadao Ando; and Ken Yeang. Many other lesser-known overseas firms also conduct business in mainland China. They have close ties with China's design institutes and are intimately involved with their projects; many of these firms have set up branch offices and employ mainly local staff (also see Chapter Nine). In these circumstances, the foreign firms were able to handle larger-scale projects such as the trophy buildings in Shanghai.

In 1998, the Shanghai Grand Theater proudly rose from People's Square, next to the municipal government, in the heart of Shanghai. The opera house, designed jointly by French architect Jean-Marie Charpentier et Associés and the East China Architectural Design Institute, offers a contrast to the gleaming glass-clad skyscrapers adorning the Shanghai skyline. But the symmetrical pose of the new opera house shows little respect for surrounding buildings, and the original design, especially the auditorium, had to be altered for audience line-of-sight and acoustic reasons (*Time + Architecture*, Shanghai, Apr. 1998) (Figure 3.10). Charpentier was responsible for the schematic design, and the East China Institute of Architectural Design completed the rest of the project, from construction documentation to site supervision.

In 1999, the 421 m high Jin Mao Tower in Pudong, Shanghai, became the tallest building in China. The lower fifty floors of the tower are used as office space, the upper thirty-eight floors as a hotel. The podium, with retail outlets and other public functions, is decorated in a contemporary style. SOM, the designer, was inspired by the traditional pagoda. Numerous theoretical setbacks in the mass of the tower are countered by cladding the delicate stainless steel bars and rods in an envelope. The rhythm of the height change is a nod to the form of a traditional pagoda. Unlike the ethereal illusion that a curtain wall creates, the Jin Mao

Figure 3.10 Jean-Marie Chapentier, Shanghai Grand Theater, 1998, (a) The grand theater in People's Square, (b) Lobby

Tower's busy spread of metal components recreates both delicacy and strength. In the upper hotel part, a central circle tops off an atrium thirty-four stories high — another symbol of a pagoda and a good way to reduce the dead load. This immense atrium was inspired by another competition entry, John Portman & Associates, and forms a surprising interior effect (Figure 3.11).

Next to the Jin Mao Tower, the Global Financial Center, designed by Kohn Pederson Fox, is 460 m high with ninety-five stories. This project was postponed for several years because of the Asian economic crisis in 1997 but has been given the green light again and is scheduled to be finished in 2006 — despite concerns about the wisdom of constructing very tall skyscrapers in the wake of the 9/11 terrorist attacks in the US (Figure 3.12). The 335,420 sq m GFA cuboid volume is "diagonally" dissected by a beautiful curve from top to bottom. In order to reduce the wind load, the design includes a circular opening at the top, recalling the traditional moon gate used in classical Chinese gardens. There will also be a bridge in the opening, a metaphorical "world bridge." A coffee shop, a gallery and retail stores will be beside a 400 m high viewing terrace that will offer grand vistas of the whole city. The center's simple shape, smooth glass, and metal mullion façade conveys a sense of the industrial yet is easy on the eye from any perspective.

By 2002, Shanghai's profile was already enhanced by two other high-rises: Tomorrow Square at People's Square, and Plaza 66 located on Nanjing Road West. It is interesting to note that, together with the Jin Mao Tower, these three skyscrapers reside on reclaimed land, where the Lujiazui trade and business center, People's Square, and the Nanjing Road shopping and commercial area are sited. All three also stand almost in line, and all were designed by American architects. A similar example can be found in Raffles Place near People's Square, which was funded by Singapore companies.

Tomorrow Square, designed by John Portman & Associates, has sixty stories and a GFA of more than 80,000 sq m. The complex comprises a podium shopping mall and a tower, which houses hotel, office, and service apartment space. The upper part of the tower is set at a 45° horizontal angle to the lower square-plan base. Tomorrow Square looks as if it is a rocket ready for launch, an optimistic gesture to Shanghai's prosperous future (Figure 3.13).

Kohn Pedersen Fox's Plaza 66 is slightly taller than Tomorrow Square, and is currently the tallest building on the west bank of the Huangpu River. The original design proposed two towers, and the first office tower was completed at the end of 2001. (The second tower has been penciled into the second phase of construction.) The podium boasts the highest-quality shopping center in Shanghai, and many multinationals have been attracted to

(a)

(b)

(c)

(d)

(e)

Figure 3.11 Jin Mao Tower, proudly standing in Pudong, Shanghai, 1998, (a) Jin Mao standing in Pudong, (b) Details of the external wall, (c) Top cafe shop, (d) Exhibition hall, (e) Entrance

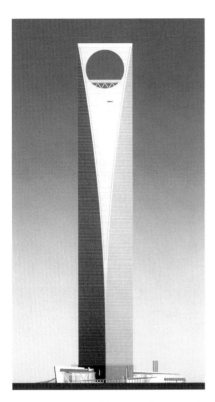

Figure 3.12 KPF, The Global Financial Center, scheduled to be completed in 2006

Figure 3.13 John Portman, Tomorrow Square, 2004

the office space by the supporting infrastructure and good location of the Nanjing Road West commercial environment. The huge spotlight on top of the tower lights the sky above Nanjing Road, adding a sort of "Chinese" character to the American-designed Shanghai landmark (Figure 3.14). The pace may be too fast and retail prices too high, as the shopping mall has seen very few customers since opening.

Foreign architectural firms have also been involved in mega-form projects, such as the Shanghai New International Exposition Center designed by Murphy & Jahn, Inc. The triangular site area in Pudong measures 850,000 sq m. Internal exhibition halls will offer a total of 200,000 sq m, and the area available for open-plan exhibitions is about 170,000 sq m. The design was inspired by the concept of a town, the seventeen exhibition halls to be arranged in a triangular plan.

In the heart of this "town" there will be a large courtyard, where open-plan exhibitions can be held. An arcade will be employed to link all the halls and their entrances to form a coherent entity. A circular tower is to be placed on the 90° apex, to emphasize the main entrance. All the exhibition halls will have the same vault shape and structure, the repetition of the vault form creating an

(a)   (b)

Figure 3.14 KPF, Plaza 66 in Nanjing Road, Shanghai, 2002, (a) Outlook, (b) Atrium

undulating wave. In this clean-lined, efficient building, high-tech materials and components are to be used. When the center is finished, it will become a new landmark in Pudong and Shanghai.

I.M. Pei was at the forefront of the trend towards American architects working in China. He and his two sons designed the Bank of China headquarters in Beijing after he set a successful precedent with the Bank of China Tower in Hong Kong in 1989. The treatment of the volume of the headquarters distinguishes the building from commercial buildings nearby, which are full of decorative gimmicks. In a way, the headquarters is a retrospective showcase of many of the distinctive design elements Pei has employed during his decades-long career. The atrium in the Fragrant Hill Hotel and the curtain wall façade of the Bank of China Tower in Hong Kong are all evoked in some way in the Bank of China's Beijing headquarters. In the atrium is living bamboo from southern China, which is changed every two months, just as in the Fragrant Hill Hotel. Bamboo is a symbol of southern Chinese culture and cannot normally survive in the harsh, northern climate of Beijing (Figure 3.15).

In 2002, Pei and his sons were commissioned to design the Suzhou Museum in the ancient city 80 km north of Shanghai, near the traditional gardens of the Ming Dynasty (1368–1644). Pei actively undertook the design task, concerned that his sons could not understand the implications of the local context. Because Pei is aging, this might be his last major design, but for the young Peis and many other overseas Chinese of the next generation, the twenty-first century is full of opportunities in the East.

At the same time, more and more Chinese architects educated abroad are returning to China and entering local design institutes or starting their own firms. They will help to close the gap in design quality between foreign and local architects. They were directly exposed to overseas architectural styles and operations when they were abroad. After they return and participate in China's projects, their role will be more active — affecting design and management decisions. From this perspective, they have more control over China's projects than foreign architects have at the moment.

Some of these returned architects work for foreign architectural design firms and become their local delegates in China; others have set up their own firms and want to develop their business at home. Beijing WSP Architectural Design Consulting Co. Ltd., whose principals were once young students in Germany and elsewhere in Europe, is an example of the latter type (also see Chapters Eight and Nine).

(a)

(b)

(c)

Figure 3.15 Pei Architects, Bank of China headquarters, Beijing, 2000, (a) Seen from the Chang'an Street, (b) Lobby, (c) Skylight

Many overseas companies choose to staff their China offices with mainland chinese; thus they are international only in name, for the purposes of design tendering. An obvious advantage of a foreign brand name is that it attracts a higher design fee than does a Chinese firm (also see Chapter Nine).

EMBRACING AND CONFRONTING THE INTERNATIONAL

In November 2001, China formally entered the World Trade Organization (WTO) after fifteen years of intense international lobbying. China's markets, including the building industry, became more open to foreign trade and participation. China's situation complements those countries that actively export their concepts of consumerism and technology, for example, the United States. As pointed out by Professor Jeffery Cody, "In the early twenty-first century, as the United States has become a political and military superpower, it also sits at the center of global popular culture and corporate capitalism … One of the chief selling points of American architecture abroad concerns building technology and the efficient ways in which U.S. designers, builders and architectural practitioners can help clients achieve a high-quality spatial and formal solution" (2003, xvii). China now welcomes not only the United States but also other developed countries.

Since 1998, design competitions have been held frequently in China. The Ministry of Construction and local governments have issued a series of regulations on the submission of design tenders. In some cities, for example, Shanghai and Shenzhen, potential buildings of more than 3000 sq m GFA require an invited design competition in order to select the winning proposal. Design schemes from at least three design companies should be submitted. This is also called "design tendering" in China (Xue and Shi 2002).

The highest-profile design competition to date in China has been for the National Grand Theater in Beijing, which occupies 260,000 sq m and a land lot of 11.8 ha adjacent to the Great Hall of People, with a 166 m frontage facing the east-west thoroughfare, Chang'an Street. From 1998 to 1999, sixty-nine entries from around the world were received and assessed by an eleven-person international jury of renowned figures from China and overseas. Five entries made it to the second round: ADP of France, Terry Farrell of the UK, Isozaki Arata of Japan,

HPP of Germany, and Design Institute of Construction Ministry, China. Another four were invited to the second round: Beijing Institute of Architectural Design, Wong & Ouyang (Hong Kong) Ltd., Tsinghua University, and Shenzhen University (Zou 2001, 603–4).

The winner was French ADP architect Paul Andreu, designer of the new Shanghai Pudong Airport and Guangzhou's sports center. The opera house, concert hall, main theater, small theater, with 5463 seats, and auxiliary facilities are covered in a huge glass-titanium curvilinear structure, giving rise to an urban landscape which encompasses Tiananmen Square. The audience will walk through a transparent underwater tunnel before entering the grand sky-lit lobby, enjoying the crystalline ripples of a pond in the plaza.

Andreu's egg-shaped theater, to be located on Chang'an Street and opposite Tiananman Square, aroused fierce debate among the public, architects, engineers, and intellectuals, both citywide and countrywide. Hundreds of commentary articles and interviews appeared in the mass media and professional bulletins, magazines, and journals. Public interest in architecture has remained strong since I.M. Pei's design of the Fragrant Hill Hotel, and reached a climax in the debate about the Grand National Theater, which is in a very sensitive historic location.[6]

Fellows from the Academy of Science, Academy of Engineering, and 114 influential architects, engineers, and scholars signed several letters to the central government, claiming that the design had "first-class cost, second and third-class function, it was irrational and not in harmony with its surroundings," "completely ignoring China's actual situation and Chinese culture, going against architectural and scientific principles." This kind of opposition to a building had never been seen in China since 1949. The "opposing" reasons included "not being harmonious with its surroundings," and being "an alien in the historic city of Beijing." As the theater strongly embodied the ideology and symbolized the hopes of the time, expectations were high. The architects from southern China posed several questions, for example, "can we evaluate the grand national theater? Can ordinary citizens enter such a glamorous theater?" As the building is inevitably associated with such concepts as "nation" and "monumentality," the discourse of "national form," which had obsessed China for decades, returned to prominence.[7]

Of all these worries, technical concerns seemed most pressing. Andreu's design was challenged because of potential technological and construction difficulties and went severely over budget because of its "roof on roof" system and an entrance under water (Figure 3.16). Critics asked whether winter's freezing temperatures and insufficient exits would lead to a disaster, forcing people to escape from the underwater tunnel.[8]

However, quite a number of comments praised the scheme as "poetic," "forward-looking in the twenty-first century," "hinting at a traditional Chinese musical instrument, the 'wood fish'" and even "best embodying traditional Chinese philosophy."[9] Paul Andreu argued that what he wanted to do was to discard history; rejecting the national theater would not make poverty go away, he

argued.[10] Due to the disputes, work on the project had to be halted in the summer of 2000, but it restarted in June 2001. The project remains controversial. The superstructure, 20,000 titanic boards and 12,000 glass panels, was finished in 2004 and the building is expected to open in September 2005.

The National Grand Theater in Beijing cost 4 billion yuan (around US$50 million), an average of 700,000 yuan per seat, compared to 500 million yuan for the Shanghai Grand Theater. Another 300 million yuan is needed for the annual operation. It is estimated that the ticket price

(a)

(b)

(c)

(d)

(e)   (f)

Figure 3.16 Grand National Theater, Beijing, (a) Sketch by Paul Andreu, (b) Article in *South China Morning Post*, (c) Lobby, (d) Section of theater, (e) Lobby new construction, (f) The shell

would need to be 1000 yuan, on average, to recoup the investment. To put this in perspective, 1000 yuan (around US$120) is the half-yearly income of a peasant family, and 60 percent of Chinese people live on 2000 yuan per year. The investment in the National Grand Theater could have been used to build 20,000 rural schools and educate four million children. According to one source, as more people receive education, fewer crimes would be committed and so fewer prisons would be needed (www.cnd.org, May 27, 2004). For these reasons, the National Grand Theater is not only interesting from an architectural point of view but also as a topic of social debate.

Another project that has caused controversy is the headquarters of China Central Television (CCTV). CCTV is a national-level state-owned television station with fourteen channels that sends signals to the world. Traditionally, a television station was seen as a communist party and government organ and placed under heavy surveillance. The international design competition for CCTV headquarters was a gesture of openness by the government, which demonstrated China's desire to share in, and even lead, a global culture, instead of confronting it as it had done previously.

At the end of 2002, CCTV announced that Rem Koolhaas, laureate of the 2000 Pritzker Architectural Prize, and his Office of Metropolitan Architecture (OMA) had won the project. The other short-listed firms included Dominique Perrault of France, KPF, SOM of the US, and East China Design Architectural Institute of Shanghai.

Juggling a busy schedule and traveling around the world, Rem Koolhaas picked up the Beijing challenge and gave up the "Ground Zero" project in Manhattan (*Time + Architecture*, No. 2, March 2003). His design of CCTV headquarters includes news, production, broadcasting, and administration sections, a performing hall, service building, hotel, and other facilities, totaling 550,000 sq m over an area of 10 ha. Instead of a soaring skyscraper with an ornamented crown, the 230 m high CCTV headquarters is presented as two twisted Z shapes, the top a flat ring. The twisted Z shapes are sheathed in a supporting mesh that must be adequately rigid against Beijing's windstorms but flexible enough to withstand earthquakes. People in the city can appreciate the building from various angles, and people in the building can have a panoramic view of the central business district. No two of the fifty-five stories have the same floor plan. It is a realization of Koolhaas's "L" (large) and mass consumption theories in China (Koolhaas and Mau 1995). The very individualistic

Koolhaas style is a sharp and heroic "figure" against the vast generic "ground" of Beijing high-rise buildings (Figure 3.17). The designers fully understand the psychology of the Beijing authorities, which vow to surpass Shanghai and other Asian cities, and will make a magnificent building. The Dutch architect said: "We are engaged with an effort to support within the current situation the forces that we think are progressive and well-intentioned ... We have given them a building that will allow them to mutate" (Jakes 2004, 34) The proposal was 30 percent higher than the budget, but it won, partly due to the strong recommendation of jury member Charles Jencks (*Time + Architecture*, No. 4, 2003).

As in the Grand National Theater debate, letters of opposition signed by prominent architects and scholars and stating concerns over structure, location, and budget were sent to the central government. The 70 m cantilever makes some key parts vulnerable structurally but also stretches the travel distance in fire. When it stands in Beijing's central business district (CBD), it will attract 10,000 cars and a huge number of people each day, bringing great pressure to the already congested CBD. The 5-billion-yuan (more than US$60 million) budget is also not a small sum for a developing country. Professor Wu Liangyong pointed out that "delight" is necessary for architecture; the question is why so much money is spent to create this kind of "delight" (www.abbs.com.cn, May 2004).

Even as the debate about the Grand National Theater and CCTV projects continues, the 2008 Olympic Games in Beijing are providing yet more opportunity and money for architectural imagination. The "water cube," a swimming pool designed by PTW of Australia and Arup, the "bird's nest" national stadium, designed by Herzog & De Meuron, and the top hyperboloid-lit Wukesong Cultural and Sports Center, designed by Bruckhardt + Partners AG are only three of many innovative projects. Herzog & De Meuron's imaginative scheme was selected by jury member Rem Koolhaas (Figure 3.18). The contrast with the 1964 Olympic Games in Tokyo is striking. The Japanese games accompanied the expansion of the domestic economy and trained a group of homegrown architects like Kenzo Tange and others; however, the 2008 Olympic Games in Beijing are providing opportunities mainly for foreign architects.

No matter how much praise the Herzog & De Meuron scheme receives, the proposal was US$150 million higher than the design of Chinese architect Ma Guoxin and his team. Andreu's design for the National Theater was double

(a)

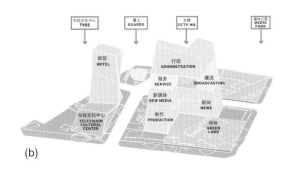

(b)

Figure 3.17 Rem Koolhaas and OMA, CCTV Headquarters, (a) The winning scheme, (b) Accommodation, (c) Standing in Beijing's CBD

(c)

the original budget (Peng 2000). The "bird's nest" scheme was recalculated by the structural engineers in Beijing, two-thirds of steel components were removed, and stadium was made "thinner" (www.abbs.com.cn, Jan. 2004). When the Beijing train station was installed with a functionless kiosk crown in 1996, people fiercely criticized the waste of investment. Now that the problem of running over budget on these imported buildings is more severe, questions are being raised about whether the use of Chinese taxpayers' money is justified. Moreover, these projects use a lot of immature technology, not fully tested, and consume too many materials and energy: they are inappropriate for a developing country, with an average annual GDP of just US$900 per person.

Learning from the capital city Beijing, other major cities such as Chongqing, Shenzhen, Guangzhou, Hangzhou, and Nanjing held similar international design competitions for their own concert halls, exhibition and other civic centers. These large-scale civic buildings, plazas, and expansive surroundings help nurture a communal atmosphere in the modern, urban areas of Chinese cities. The country's status in the architectural arena has also been enhanced by international activities held in China, for example, the Shanghai International Residential Design Contest 1996 and the Shanghai International Residential Conference 2000. The most prominent events to date have been the Twentieth UIA (International Union of Architects) World Congress of

Architects held in Beijing in June 1999, the design competitions for the 2008 Olympic Games in Beijing, and for the 2010 World Exposition in Shanghai.

Setting up international competitions and related activities, especially inviting such stellar figures, is undoubtedly costly. However, it can be viewed as necessary and worthwhile for Chinese authorities and professionals to pay this "tuition fee" in order to learn the latest architectural technologies and techniques from overseas experts. Chinese architects are experienced in small and medium-sized projects and cultural and public buildings, but they desperately need to become familiar with large complexes incorporating complicated technology such as super-skyscrapers, intelligent and green architecture, central business districts, and integrating new technologies and materials. Joint ventures between overseas designers and Chinese design institutes have proved successful in past years as cultural and technical exchanges.

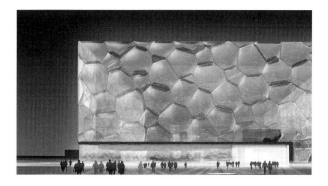

(a)

(b)

(c)

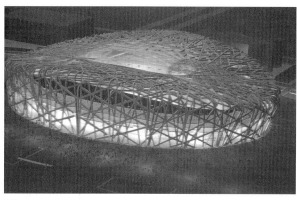

(d)

(e)

Figure 3.18 Winning sports building for 2008 Olympic Games, (a) and (b) Swimming Hall, (c) Wukesong Sports Center, (d) and (e) National Stadium

As Chinese architects encounter the methods, techniques, and vocabulary of international architecture, which increasingly permeates China, the knowledge and skills gained become feasible options in the repertoire of the country's architects and architectural students. Many Chinese architects began to arbitrarily imitate these forms and exploit the novel ideas. Unfortunately, this adoption of styles was mostly based on scant knowledge of these fashionable "-isms." In the late 1980s, Richard Meier's distinctive architectural signature was much lauded and copied in China; in the mid-1990s, books illustrating Kohn Pedersen Fox's portfolio sold very well and became almost like manuals for many designers of high-rise buildings. In some cases, a lack of technical resources resulted in absurd situations; for example, using concrete members as substitutes for metal elements when imitating the Kohn Pedersen Fox style.

LEARNING FROM EXPERIENCE: A TRANSITIONAL RETROSPECTIVE

International planners, architects, contractors, and building materials exporters have marketed their architecture overseas, including to China. "In part they have profited because American standards have often been the norm by which other places have been judged to be 'modern', 'progressive' or 'developed'. International clients have emulated American buildings such as skyscrapers, they have followed patterns of American urbanism such as suburban residences, and they have adopted American concepts of form and space for eating and shopping such as fast-food restaurants and shopping malls" (Cody 2003, xvii). Professor Cody's words apply perfectly to China, which has accepted the lifestyle of the developed world, from sneakers to skyscrapers.

In this process of exportation, foreign architects have realized their career dreams. Raimund Abraham, most of whose buildings exist only on the pages of a book titled *(un)-Built*, eventually had his work constructed in Beijing. He said: "There's no way I could get a design like this built in America, but in China, one starts to feel that anything is possible." Another American architect, Christopher Choa, from the New York City-based firm HLW, said of his two years in China: "I've built four skyscrapers and designed millions of square feet of urban landscape. In New York, I'd have been happy to do as much in my entire career" (Jakes 2004, 34).

Some commentators have pointed out the problems of exporting architecture indiscriminately to Asia and China. Deborah K. Dietsch, editor-in-chief of *Architecture*, has said: "These overscaled designs represent only a sampling of the tall buildings sprouting up all over Asia, despite the fact that many Asian cities lack the necessary infrastructure, materials, or skilled labor to build them. In most cases, little thought is given to the environmental and social consequences of high-rise development, which is increasing the density, pollution, and congestion of cities that are already growing faster than any others in history. Such rapid growth, especially in agricultural countries where land is at a premium, may require high-rise housing and offices, but where is the sensitivity to site and context American architects proclaim so loudly at home?"

"Despite the profession's growing awareness of sound planning, sustainability, and preservation, these issues seem to be ignored by American architects working in Asia, who are leaving their consciences stateside. Many of the skyscraper exports in Asia seem recycled from the 1980s

(a)

(b)

Figure 3.19 Shanghai Science and Technology City, (a) Overview, (b) The court in front of science city

— design that got shelved during the recession, now gussied up with minarets and pagoda tops" (Dietsch 1994, 15).

Western architects and academics familiar with Eastern architectural styles and architecture in former colonies are beginning to re-examine whether Western-oriented concepts of modernity and civilization are appropriate for China's new urban landscape. As Asia and China emerge internationally as economic forces, a key question that deserves more consideration is how to make Asian countries aware of and able to retain their own cultural identity in the age of globalization.

As in the "critical regionalism" advocated by Kenneth Frampton,[11] after twenty years of learning from and adopting Western architectural styles, China's architects are becoming conscious of the fact that the exact copying of Western forms is a short-sighted dismissal of the country's own rich architectural heritage and runs counter

(a)

(b)

(c)

Figure 3.20 Other examples of overseas design in 2000 (a) Oriental Plaza and its 500-m.-long elevation in Beijing's east-west thoroughfare Charg'an Street, (b) Vehicular entrance of Oriental Plaza, (c) Paul Andreu, Pudong Airport, Shanghai

to the meaning of architectural ontology. The renewal of interest among China's citizens and architects in the mainland's own architectural traditions is becoming stronger, with the result that more and more of them are

Figure 3.21 East China electricity Management Tower, 1986

(a)

(b)

(c)

Figure 3.22 Examples of parody, (a) A district court of Shanghai imitating the US Congress, (b) Yuhua District government building, Nanjing, (c) "Ronchamp Chapel" in Zhengzhou

beginning to question the idea that "foreign is always superior." The aforementioned public debate that erupted over Beijing's major projects is a good example. Along with a further deepening of cooperation between local architectural design institutes and foreign architects, the institutes have come to recognize that it is more sensible to study new design concepts, operating procedures, and management models, rather than to simply copy them in a fragmented, ultimately meaningless, manner (Figure 3.20).

During twenty-five years of reforms and a gradual opening up to the outside world, China has witnessed not only a radical and rapid development of its economy but a dramatic transformation of its once isolated culture and concepts. The perceived professional and financial threat

Figure 3.23 Pei's contributions in China, (a) Tianfu Square and Chengdu Museum, Sichuan, (b) Shopping center, (c) Suzhou Museum, Suzhou

from foreign architects entering the Chinese market has been alleviated by gradual, mutual understanding. At the same time, Chinese architects recognize that they have to improve standards and hone their skills by working with and competing against their overseas counterparts in design concepts, management, and organization.

It is widely believed that the international standing of China will grow and that exchange of ideas, knowledge, and skills between China and the rest of the world will further develop, following China's entry into the WTO. The already overt presence of foreign architecture and its influence on modern architecture in China will not be limited to architectural forms but will spread to construction technology, materials, and techniques, as well as management and operation procedures and standards.

NOTES

1. The defeat of the Qing Dynasty (1644–1911) in a series of wars with imperialist countries resulted in a succession of "unfair treaties," including the Nanjing Treaty of 1841 in which China ceded Hong Kong Island to Britain and opened the ports of Guangzhou, Fuzhou, Xiamen (Amoy), Ningbo, and Shanghai; the Beijing Treaty of 1857 in which China gave Kowloon Peninsula to Britain as well as a huge amount of money in compensation; and other treaties leasing Chinese territories to France, Germany, Russia, and other countries. See Yang Bing-de (ed.) *City and Architecture of Modern China* (China Building Industry Press, 1992).

2. During the 1960s in China, any contact with a foreign country was deemed a severe crime. For example, in 1969, a nineteen-year-old man in Shanghai wrote an anonymous letter to Voice of America about the situation in the city as a result of the Cultural Revolution. He was subsequently tracked down and executed.

3. Yang Yongsheng and Gu Mengchao (eds.) *Chinese Architecture in the 20th Century* (Tianjin Science & Technology Press, 1999, p. 321).

4. In old Shanghai, the "upper corner" referred to the west part of the city, the most desirable and classy district with the best living conditions; it included Bubbling Well Road (now called Nanjing Road West) and Avenue Joffre (now known as Huaihai Road). The "lower corner" referred to the lower-class zones in the north and east with their poor living environments.

5. In the early 1980s, the Chinese government introduced Foreign Exchange Certificates for the use of foreigners in China. Foreigners were able to change their US dollars, British pounds sterling, etc. into this certificate in airports or hotels. It could be used in high-class hotels, restaurants and Friendship Stores, those open only to foreigners. This system was abolished in 1994. Such a system was once popular in the iron-curtained communist countries and

can still be seen in Cuba and North Korea. Up to the time of writing, the Chinese Renminbi (RMB) is still not a freely exchangeable currency.

6. Public interest in architecture is shown by the burgeoning publication of various popular books on architects and their works, both in China and abroad. Some influential newspapers, like *Wenhui Bao* of Shanghai, have columns on architecture, with contributions from writers, critics and architects.

7. The views of southern Chinese architects are reflected in Shenzhen-based He Chengjun's article "Grand National Theater facing the Beijing citizens" (*Building News*, July 28, 1998, p. 7), among others.

8. The anti-Andreu-scheme alliance included several top scholars, including the vice president of UIA, Professor Wu Liangyong. Alfred Pei-gen Peng, an architect and professor who had returned from Canada, published several articles challenging the design and technology of the Grand National Theater. A representative article is, "Why do we strongly oppose the French architect's scheme of Grand National Theater?" *Architectural Journal*, No.11, 2000, pp. 11–2.

9. The favorable articles outnumbered the opposing voices. The quotations here are mainly from Yu Jun, "Defense for Andreu and discussing with Mr Peng Pei-gen," *Architectural Journal*, No. 3, 2001, pp. 31–3.

10. Paul Andreu has talked with China's ambassador in Paris and was interviewed by the media in mainland China and Hong Kong. His words were widely quoted in the Chinese media. This quotation is from Zhou Qingling, "The difference of east and west culture in the Grand National Theater schemes," *Architectural Journal*, No. 1, 2001, p. 21. Some views are given in Andreu's article, "Defiant Design," *South China Morning Post*, Hong Kong, July 10, 2000.

11. Frampton is quoted in Cheryl Temple Herr, *Critical Regionalism and Cultural Studies: From Ireland to the American Midwest* (University of Florida Press, 1997).

Part II
City and Dwelling

Survival Strategies: Beijing, Shanghai, and Guangzhou

Urban Design as a Tool for Better Living

Form Follows Policy: The Evolution of China's Housing

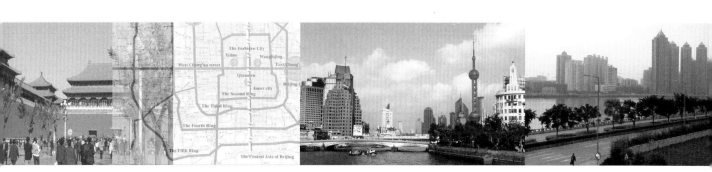

4

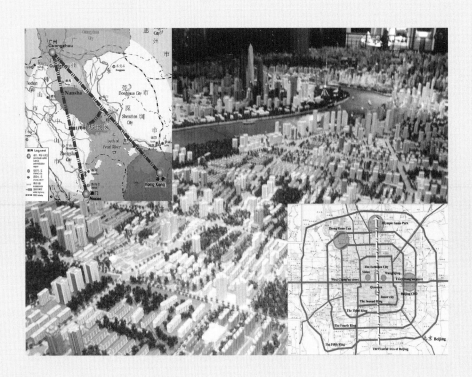

Development in China is uneven. If the entire country is viewed as a staircase, the coastal cities are undoubtedly the highest step. They absorb the greatest majority of the investments, materials, and brainpower from overseas as well as from within the country, as these various contributions are more handsomely rewarded there. These influences gradually spread to central and then to western China. In this situation, Beijing in the north, Shanghai in the east, and Guangzhou in the south most typically represent their respective areas and embody the highest achievements that cities in China can manifest. The tale of these three cities is about contesting and survival in the keen inter-city competition by their natural, geographic, and historic resources. Beijing is China's capital and administrative center; Shanghai and Guangzhou represent the two engines of mainland China's economy — the Yangtze River Delta and the Pearl River Delta.

This chapter is written jointly by Charlie Xue, Chen Xi and Wang Hongjun.

CHAPTER FOUR

SURVIVAL STRATEGIES:
BEIJING, SHANGHAI, AND GUANGZHOU

The international influence and the eminent trophy buildings discussed in Chapter Three usually appear first in the coastal cities. This proves a phenomenon in modern China: development has always proceeded unevenly in its territory, gradually spreading from the coastal cities of the east to the undeveloped interior of the west. In any ranking of Chinese cities, Beijing, Shanghai, and Guangzhou undoubtedly occupy preeminent positions. In addition to their special origins and growth in ancient and modern times, these three cities play a pivotal role in the politics, economy, and culture of China. Their development history and the nature of their growth and associated experiences exemplify three distinctly different and instructive trajectories.

Today, these three cities are facing similar challenges as they adapt to globalization and confront issues such as city expansion, urban sprawl, population pressures, traffic problems, highways and ring roads, historical preservation, social continuity, and urban renewal. How will they cope with these problems? How can they excel against the regional and global competition? And how can they maintain their sustainability and identities in the mutation? These questions are of pressing urgency for China's cities and reflect the challenges that confront other major cities in the world today.

This chapter analyzes the development record and prospects of these three cities, based on their history, development process, and spatial structure, in order to present an overview of China's cities in the last two decades of the twentieth century.

BEIJING: FROM WALLED KINGDOM TO MEGACITY

A Brief History of Beijing

As the capital city of the Liao Dynasty (916–1125), the Jin Dynasty (1115–1234), the Yuan Dynasty (1271–1368), the Ming (1368–1644) and the Qing Dynasties (1644–1911), Beijing was always the center of political power in a feudal country ruled by a monarchy. Established in the mid-sixteenth century, this great city is a famous example in the history of the world's cities because of its precise grid layout and splendid city axis on which a series of spaces and buildings are arranged with order and rhythm.

From the very beginning, Beijing was constructed to serve China's ancient rulers as the emperor's ideal capital. The traditional principles of building a city, particularly from the ancient book *Kao gong ji* (roughly translated "system of construction") of the Spring and Autumn Period (770–476 BCE) were adopted; for example, the city had four sides, each wall of which contained three gates, streets laid out in a grid, a royal palace, ancestral temple, and public market. The strict rules of design dictated that there be a central axis, a palace in the center, three to four layers of walls, and other precisely located ceremonial buildings. The physical form of the capital city expressed the official values, religion, and hierarchy of Chinese culture (Figure 4.1).

By the time of the Qing Dynasty, Beijing already had four layers of walls and a 7.5 km central axis from

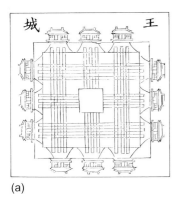

(a)

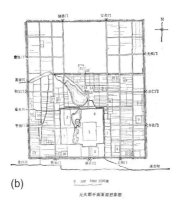

(b)

Figure 4.1 Plan of Beijing, (a) The ideal model of city planning according to the ancient book "Kao Gong Ji," in Spring and Autumn Period (770–476 BCE), (b) Beijing's plan in Yuan Dynasty

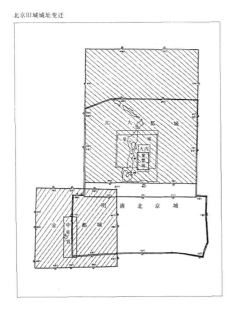

Figure 4.2 Evolution of Beijing. From Jin Dynasty (1115–1234), lower left-hand side, to Yuan Dynasty (1271–1368), upper part, then gradually southward, lower part, in Ming (1368–1644) and Qing (1644–1911) Dynasties

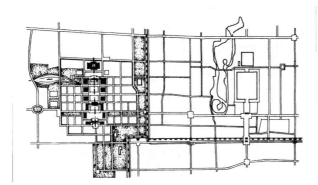

Figure 4.3 Scheme of Liang Sicheng and Chen Zhanxiang in 1956 moves the administrative and business center to the west

Yongding Gate in the south to the Bell and Drum Towers in the north. The changes that have been made to the city over the years are described in Figure 4.2.

The central and dominant position of the royal palace was a statement about the supreme power of the empire. This design motif can probably be traced to the Chinese idea of "central" and "respected." Such traditional ideas and cultural beliefs still play an important role in today's planning, as Beijing's central axis has been doubled and tripled in length for important structures, most recently for construction projects related to the Olympic Games.

In the early twentieth century, the Qing Dynasty declined and Beijing became influenced by new technology and culture. The walls of the imperial city were breached by foreign invasion. In 1906, Beijing began to construct a railway around the city. Industrial and workers' residences were built. In 1913, the palace wall between the Great Qing Gate (*da qing men* or *zhong hua men*) and the Gate of Heavenly Peace (*Tiananmen*) was demolished, and this formed part of today's Chang'an Avenue. The blockage between the back gate of the Forbidden City and Jin Shan was removed, making possible eastbound and westbound traffic.

After the communists seized power in 1949, vigorous discussions about a "master plan" for Beijing took place. Professor Liang Si-cheng and Chen Zhanxiang (1916–2001), once assistant to Sir Patrick Abercrombie in London after World War II proposed that a new administrative center be built in the west, keeping the ancient city and walls intact. But the central government eventually adopted a proposal submitted by experts from the Soviet Union. The political and administrative center remains in Tiananmen Square. The ancient city wall was demolished and the location broadened to become the second ring road. The traditional *pai-lou* — a Chinese arched gate usually constructed of wood — was also demolished. The ring road was created at the expense of 38 km of ancient wall

Figure 4.4 Traffic analysis of Beijing

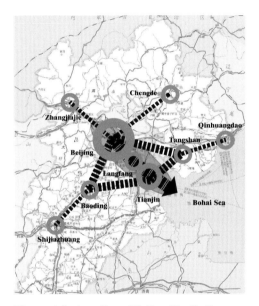

Figure 4.5 Location of Beijing-Tianjin-Tanggu

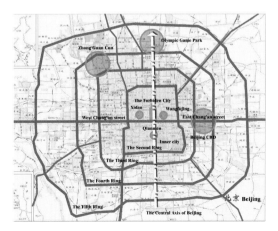

Figure 4.6 City of Beijing and its ring roads

and sixteen gates, only four of which remain standing (Figure 4.3). Professor Liang Si-cheng, as well as other preservationists, was heartbroken; as he said, "demolishing the wall is like peeling off my skin!" However, the intellectuals' cry did not impede the pace of bulldozers in the 1950s.[1]

Beginning in the 1950s, the second ring road was connected; it was completed in 1979. The square checkerboard streets of the inner city joined the ring roads, the third, fourth and fifth rings being formed naturally through the years. Between the ring roads are the radiating roads that sprawl outwards like a huge web.[2]

Regional Influence

Greater Beijing presently occupies an area of 16,800 sq km. The city is divided into eighteen districts and has a population of 12.5 million. According to the plan for a greater Beijing conceived by Professor Wu Liangyong, the city will act as the heart and driving force of a much wider zone to include Tianjin, Tangshan, Baoding, and other adjacent areas. Beijing's development will undoubtedly stimulate the economy of the surrounding region, although a number of environmental and ecosystem concerns, including water resources and unbalanced development, will need to be addressed.

The eastern part of greater Beijing has been the focus of the city's most recent development. The Bo Hai region to the east has been an important developing zone in northern China. Of the five Beijing expressways, three lead to the east. The Beijing-Tianjin-Tangshan expressway in particular has become a major spine for development by means of which people and goods from Beijing are moved quickly to the sea. The Beijing airport expansion and the future subway from Shi Jinshan to Tong County, east of Beijing, will also facilitate the rapid movement of goods and people (Figures 4.4 & 4.5).

Spatial Structure and Focus of Development

In planning structure, Beijing can be read in three layers: the inner city inside the second ring road, the area outside the second ring road, and the ten peripheral groups. The three layers are connected by six ring roads (expressways), a number of radiating roads, and subways and railways (Figure 4.6).

No single place better represents China's political power than Tiananmen Square. Since its construction in the 1950s, it has been China's political center and the site of a series of historic events. After being added to and expanded a number of times and witnessing numerous political and societal dramas and upheavals of the twentieth century, this square along Beijing's central axis has become imbued with even more meaning. Chang'an Avenue, which crosses Tiananmen Square, links Fuxin Men in the west and Jianguo Men in the east. It is the main east-west axis of the city. The various governmental, institutional, financial, and cultural buildings are located along this axis, including the disputed National Grand Theater (Figures 4.7 & 4.8).

The traditional commercial centers of Beijing are in Wangfujing, Xidan, and Qianmen. New sub-centers have recently sprung up in the city. In the northern part, the university district of Haidian and the Zhong Guan Chun Science Park form a high-technology district, Beijing's "Silicon Valley," which generates billions of dollars a year. The central axis extends northward, where the Olympic Games Park and Sports Center are being built.

In the years to come, Beijing's urban construction will focus on the following:

(1) The stadiums, gymnasiums, and related facilities of the Olympic Games, located in the Olympic Games Park and three other Olympic centers in Beijing. The Olympic Park in the north gives the historic central axis "international" meaning, whereas the poor southern half of the city is significant. In some new proposals the south is turned into a new residential, office, cultural, and green area, balancing the increasingly important north. A new central station, mainly catering for the Shanghai-Beijing Transrapid, will be located in this new south (Albert Speer & Partner 2003).

(2) Urban infrastructure, including traffic engineering projects such as urban rail transit, expressways and subways, as well as ecological infrastructure and information networks.

(3) Three functional districts that are focal points within the city: the Beijing CBD, Zhong Guan Chun Science Park, and Olympic Games Park. Far from the old city center, the CBD lies in the east of Beijing on the extension of Chang'an Avenue, although it is still controversial whether China needs a second "financial center" after Shanghai (www.cnd.org, October 2003). Having the advantage of a great location, this 4 sq km area has been a new hub of investment. In addition to these functional districts, some major buildings will be completed soon, such as the Grand National Theater, the Capital Museum, and the expansion of the National Library.

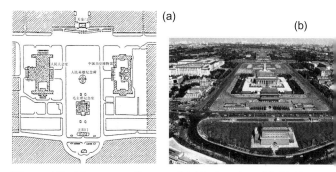

Figure 4.7 Tiananmen Square, (a) Master plan, (b) Bird's eye view

Figure 4.8 The Forbidden City, Beijing

(4) Concentrating on developing housing for ordinary people, especially for those in lower-income brackets, including construction and financial assistance. This will accelerate housing construction and the renovation of structurally dangerous buildings.

(5) Improving the overall layout of the city by accelerating the development of marginal areas, satellite towns, and small towns, as well as establishing a hierarchical spatial structure within the city itself to include green belts, marginal areas, satellite towns, and small towns.

Goals and Problems

After 1949, the amendments made to Beijing's master plan attempted to represent the city as "a famous historic and international city, with a prosperous economy, a safe and stable society and first-class public services, infrastructure and sustainability" (*Master Plan of Beijing* 1996). To achieve this idealized goal, Beijing still needs to successfully address the following four problems:

(1) Land Use and Population: A rapidly increasing population continuously demands more urban land, causing serious land-use problems related to housing and traffic, problems that can be seen in every major city in the world today. One possible solution for Beijing is to limit the immigrant population while improving traffic flow to the neighboring urban centers. This may have a two-fold benefit, also serving to revitalize these adjacent areas.

(2) Environment and Energy: In addition to severe industrial, heating fuel and automotive pollution, Beijing is attacked every year by increasingly severe sandstorms. In 2002 alone, sandstorms struck the city seven times. Moreover, drought conditions in northern China are worsening. The world standard of critical water storage is 1000 cu m per person. The standard for Beijing and its environs is one-third of this standard (http://www.cnd.org, July 2002). The prospect of being without water looms over Beijing like a Sword of Damocles. A project to carry water from southern China is under construction, but this will cause additional environmental problems because it will deplete the water resources in that region. In addition, there are plans to pipe natural gas to Beijing from Shaanxi Province, Gansu Province, and the Ningxia Hui Autonomous Region.

(3) Preservation of the Old Capital City and Urban Renewal: It is vitally important that the inner city of Beijing

(a)

(b)

Figure 4.10 New buildings in Beijing (a) Chang'an Street, (b) Wangfujing, pedestrian shopping street

be preserved. A law that controls building heights has been enacted so that visitors to the Forbidden City will not see modern high-rises. Such restrictions always conflict with the commercial interests of developers, and the law was waived for several projects, such as the gigantic Oriental Plaza in Wangfujing, which was developed by Hong Kong's Cheung Kong Ltd. (Figures 4.9 & 4.10).

Beijing's traditional *hutongs* were once found throughout the inner city. These one-story quadrangular courtyard houses consisting of numerous lanes and passageways typify the ancient fabric of the city. Since the 1980s, due to severe population pressures, many of these old *hutongs* and lanes were demolished and replaced by opulent multistory and high-rise hotels, office buildings, and residential buildings. Because of their redevelopment potential and the high profits they represent, *hutongs* are coveted by developers, who often act in collusion with the municipal authorities to evict the residents, usually elderly people who have lived in the *hutongs* for most of their lives.

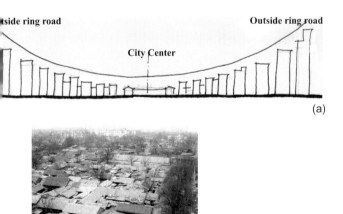

Figure 4.9 Height control of Beijing city , (a) Height control, (b) Seen from the old city

Some venerable buildings deemed to be of historical value have been saved from the bulldozers, but most courtyard houses with their intimate dimensions and atmosphere have vanished forever. The vociferous outcries and demonstrations of local residents and heritage activists, though publicized by media still hobbled by strict government censorship, have been largely ignored. On the one hand, Beijing uses *hutongs* as a tourist attraction to reap foreign dollars; on the other, a short-sighted municipal government in league with developers lacks the political will or patience to retain these fine old heritage buildings. Urban renewal and the process of displacing residents are not transparent. Thousands of residents who had lived in the old city for decades were evicted in a night and removed to a remote suburb, with little compensation.[3]

(4) Urban Sprawl: The mega-scale of Beijing, with its six concentric circle roads, has caused the same kinds of problem faced by other major cities in the world. Unrestrained urban sprawl erodes the suburbs, leaving them deserted, with poor infrastructure and a host of social problems. They also become unappealing because of their monotonous nature. The newly established satellite towns, for a population of 300,000 to 500,000, are only for living; people have to commute several hours to the city to work. This costs a huge amount of energy and money. To curb this kind of unrestricted sprawl, Beijing must change from being a single-center system to a multi-center net system, following the example of other international cities, and establish a more coordinated and desirable spatial structure. This has been partly embodied in the revised planning of 2004 (*Wenhui Bao*, Feb 23, 2004).

SHANGHAI: FROM FOREIGN CONCESSIONS TO METROPOLIS

From Rural Town to Modern City

Unlike large cities such as London, which evolved from traditional inner cities, or cities that developed entirely

Figure 4.11 Map of Shanghai, (a) Shanghai County in Ming Dynasty (1368–1644), (b) Shanghai in 1900

under the control of colonialists, such as Hong Kong, Shanghai is a huge commercial port created by immigrants from all over the world. It took Shanghai less than fifty years to evolve from an insignificant rural town to the largest city in the East during the 1930s.

Shanghai is located on the southern bank of the Yangtze River estuary, where the deep waters of the Huangpu River, which flow through the city, make a natural harbour. Shanghai County was established in the Southern Song Dynasty (1127–1279), and the walls of the city, now in Nanshi District, constructed in the Ming Dynasty (1368–1644) survive today. After the Nanjing Treaty of 1843, Shanghai was opened as a trading town and foreign colony. From 1845 to 1937, the British, American, and French concessions, which occupied a large amount of land on the west bank of the Huangpu River, continued to expand while the Chinese government established shipyards in the Nanshi District. Most lower-

Table 4.1 Division of Land Use Compared with That of Other Cities, 1985 (%)

City	Industrial land	Commercial land	Housing	Roads	Green spaces	Other
Paris	8.0	4.0	30.0	27.0	12.0	19.0
London	3.9	5.2	36.3	22.2	19.4	13.0
Chicago	6.9	4.8	24.1	7.4	29.0	17.9
Shanghai	24.36	8.43	30.6	10.5	2.63	25.27

Source: *Comparison of Pudong Planning and Other World Cities*, Shanghai Committee of Science and Technology and East China Normal University, 1994

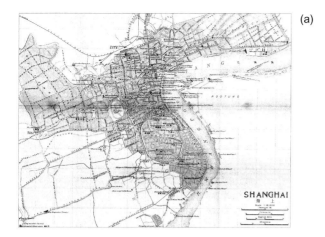

(a)

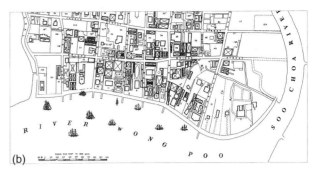

Figure 4.12 Expansion of foreign concessions in Shanghai, (a) Map of British concession, (b) The Bund in the nineteenth century

and middle-class Chinese gathered in the dense blocks and districts along Suzhou Creek. The contemporary layout of Shanghai took shape at this time (Figures 4.11 & 4.12).

In 1849, shrewd British colonialists began to build their consulate and docks at the juncture of the Huangpu River and Suzhou Creek, the strategic neck of water transit. From then on, numerous docks, warehouses and firms were built along the Huangpu River to the south. Gradually the Bund and the cradle of modern Shanghai, came into being. In 1923, the headquarters of the Hongkong and Shanghai Banking Corporation was completed, one of the most beautiful buildings on the Bund and a symbol of that epoch. To the colonialists, the 1920s was the golden age of Shanghai. The construction of Shanghai followed on the heels of other major cities in the world.

In the first half of the twentieth century, the invasion of Japanese troops and the Chinese civil war forced people to escape to the safety of the foreign concessions. The construction of housing and other public buildings increased sharply in the concession areas, known as the

"upper corner" of the city. At one time, the Japanese and the post-war Chinese government created a set of plans for Shanghai, but these were never implemented.

Once the largest city in the East, Shanghai owed its prosperity to its well-developed trade and industry; prior to 1949, over 50 percent of all factories in China were located in Shanghai, and more than half the cargo processed through China's ports went through Shanghai's teeming harbor. In 1949, Shanghai's population reached 4.2 million and the city covered an area of 86 sq km.

The city took Nanjing Road and the old Bund as its center, developing southward and northward in concentric circles. From 1950 to 1980, Shanghai was primarily constructed to function as a manufacturing center. In 1985, industrial land accounted for around 24.36 percent of the city's land use, or 14.39 sq m per capita (Yang 1988). As an economic pillar of China, Shanghai contributed 90 percent of its revenue to the central government each year, and 8 percent of the central government's income was from the city before 1990.

Table 4.2 Comparison of Urban Built Land and Gross Domestic Product (GDP)

	Population (million people)	Urban built land (sq km)	GDP (US$100 million)	GDP generated from the built land (million US$/sq km)	Urban built land per capita (sq m/ person)
Paris (Greater Paris)	10.95	2395	3952 (Euro)	165(Euro)	219
Tokyo (capital)	12.06	1304	6937	532	108
Seoul	10.61	606	872	144	57
Shanghai	13.21	1503	598	40	113

Source: Ye Guixun, Xu Yisong *et al.*, *Strategies of Shanghai Urban Development*, China Architecture and Building Press, Beijing, 2003

The planning authority of Shanghai has tried to enhance land efficiency economically. In Tokyo, every square kilometer of land can generate US$53,000 million a year, but Shanghai is one-twelfth that (Ye, Xu *et al.* 2003). If Shanghai hopes to reach the standards of a developed city while also using less built-up land, it has to change its mode of land use and take a more sustainable and comprehensive way (Table 4.2).

Regional Influence

The group of cities in the Yangtze River Delta, a traditionally rich area in China, includes Shanghai, Suzhou, Wuxi, Changzhou, Yangzhou, Zhenjiang, Ningbo, Hangzhou, Jiaxin, Shaoxin, and other small towns in Jiangsu and Zhejiang Provinces. This group of cities benefits from a good investment environment, convenient traffic network, concentration of manufacturing, and technological innovation and mutual cooperation. Shanghai's development is bolstered by the Yangtze River Delta, and the city's progress will effectively radiate outwards to this area (Figure 4.13).

As shown on the map, Shanghai is supported by two wings. One is Jiangsu Province, including the cities of Suzhou, Wuxi, Zhangjiagang, and others. The other is Zhejiang Province, including the cluster of cities located in Hangzhou Bay. In this large area of the Yangtze River Delta, Shanghai, Nanjing, Hangzhou, and Ningbo are four central cities, and they lead the surrounding cities and towns. Shanghai is often colorfully described in promotional literature intended to encourage local people as an arrow in a bow facing the Pacific Ocean.

The Layout of Shanghai

Influenced by its early urban development, the Bund and Nanjing Road constitute Shanghai's core, the city expanding outwards in concentric circles. The waterways naturally divide the districts, Zhenru, Jiangwan, Hongqiao, and Zhangjiang as scattered sub-centers.

The Bund and Nanjing Road, landmarks from the 1930s, remain the proudest expression of Shanghai. The majestic colonial buildings of the Bund contrast with the soaring contemporary skyscrapers built on the opposite

(a) (b) (c)

(d) (e)

Figure 4.13 Yangtze River Delta and regional influence of Shanghai, (a) Map of Yangtze River Delta, (b) Suzhou, a city 80 km north of Shanghai, (c) Suzhou garden, built in the eighteenth century, (d) and (e) Hangzhou, a city south of Shanghai. Both Suzhou and Hangzhou are called "heaven" in China

(a)

(b)

(c)   (d)

Figure 4.14 Historic Shanghai, (a) The Bund (b) The Huangpu River and Suzhou Creek, (c) The terraced lane house (*lilong*), (d) The old post office

Figure 4.15 The master plan of Pudong, New District, Shanghai

side of the river. People's Square (the racecourse before 1949), several kilometers from the Bund, is the largest open space in the city center (Figure 4.14).

The old manufacturing industries have gradually relocated to the suburban districts of Jiading, Baoshan, and Jinshan, as Shanghai implements its multi-core development plan. The original peripheral districts of Xuhui, Changning, Putuo, Zhabei, Yangpu, and Pudong have gradually absorbed more residential and industrial pressures. Government and commercial offices have also moved to the original peripheral districts (Figure 4.15).

The inner ring road and a cross-shaped expressway place any point in the city only a few kilometers from the elevated highway. Within the ring road, main thoroughfares extend in north-south and east-west directions. The continuously expanding subway, light rail and inter-city and state expressways are connective skeletons, along which develop new districts.

Interestingly, the center of Shanghai has shifted through the years. In the late Qing Dynasty (before the twentieth century), it was within the walls of Shanghai county, the later Nanshi District; then the commercial Bund took the lead in the city's splendid 1920s; and the National government could only plan the city center in the northeast Wujiaochang when the prosperous banks of Huangpu River were occupied by foreign concessions. The communist party built its center in People's Square in the 1950s, the old racecourse and geometric center of the city proper; and eventually, the government yielded the Bund again to the financial sector; and the city center partly moved to Lujiazui, Pudong, the east bank of Huangpu River.

Development Unleashed in Pudong

Since 1980, the focus of Shanghai's development has been to improve the city center and to construct satellite towns. The 1986 master plan included preliminary research on Pudong, located on the eastern bank of the Huangpu River. In April 1990, the new district of Pudong was formally established. During the ten-year period from 1990 to 2001, the shape of Pudong was largely defined. The development of Pudong includes the 1.9 sq km central business district and administrative area of Lujiazui, the new technology district of Zhangjiang, the manufacturing district of Jinqiao, the tax shelter district of Waigaoqiao, two bridges over the Huangpu River, and Pudong International Airport. To facilitate the development of Pudong, several other projects were carried out simultaneously, for example, an

(a)

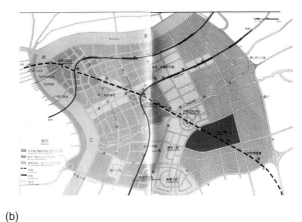

(b)

(c)

(d)

Figure 4.16 Lujiazui CBD, Pudong, Shanghai, (a) Seen from the west, bank of Huangpu River, (b) Master layout plan, (c) Puxi looking out, (d) New trophy buildings

inner and outer ring road, a new harbor, a gas plant, a sewage treatment plant, a water plant, and a communications station. The new Pudong has an area of 522 sq km which makes it almost the same size as Singapore. Its development resulted in a dramatic face-lift to both sides of the Huangpu River and stimulated the economy of the Changjiang (Yangtze) River Delta and its population of almost 100 million people (Figure 4.16).

Pudong's ten-year development constitutes another "golden age" for Shanghai. In addition to Pudong, the infrastructure of the whole city was greatly enhanced and excellently prepared for additional development. The central government has decided to develop Shanghai to the standards of an international city and a leading economic, financial, trading, and transportation center. The blooming 1990s, no less than the 1920s, will be regarded as a milestone in the history of Shanghai.

The development of the city proper is along both banks of Huangpu River, which flows to the Yangtze River

and the East China Sea. Except for the Bund, most parts of the riverside are occupied by docklands, warehouses, and factories, now mostly deserted. These deserted areas are mainly located in Yangpu District, which connects the mouth of river and the prosperous Bund. Professor Chang Qing of Tongji University proposes to renovate this part to a 15 km long and 500 m wide park, similar to Stanley Park in Vancouver, renovating and maintaining some old industrial buildings in the park. In Fuxin Island, located at the junction of the East China Sea, Yangtze River, and Huangpu River, a sculpture of an angel, originally in the Bund, will be built to meet the visitors from the sea. Chang's proposal was adopted as part of the 2010 World Exposition plan (Chang 2003).

Shanghai's successful bid for the 2010 World Exposition will give the city further impetus. Early in 2000, before the voting of the International Exposition Bureau took place, Shanghai started to plan for the event. In September 2001, a conceptual design competition was held, drawing entries from such firms as Philip Cox of Australia, Luca Scachetti & Partners of Italy, Architecture Studio of France, Marcia Codinachs of Spain, Albert Speer of Germany, RIA of Japan, DGBK + KFS of Canada, and Xing Tonghe Design Studio (see Chapter Seven) of Shanghai. The entries were exhibited for a year in the Shanghai Exhibition Hall of Urban Planning and attracted many viewers. Like Beijing's National Theater, a voting scheme by ordinary visitors was also conducted for the exposition of Shanghai in 2002.

Most participating firms had experience in World Expo design and had been involved for a long time in the construction of Shanghai. Ecological and environmental by aspects were highlighted. Among the designs, those by Philip Cox and of the Architecture Studio of France were the most striking. In Cox's scheme, a steel and glass pedestrian bridge of several stories was used to express his concept of the city, together with wedge-shaped green space open to the river. In the scheme of the French architects, a huge oval canal was designed to define the World Expo boundary and to integrate the water and land. The French architects also designed a "flower bridge" 600 m long, 50 m wide, and 200 m high, across the Huangpu River, as a landmark. This scheme was eventually selected for implementation (Figure 4.17).

Of particular note is that, in 1999, the Shanghai government built a five-story high Exhibition Hall of Urban Planning, symmetrically balancing the Grand Theater designed by Charpentier of France at People's Square, the very heart of Shanghai. The huge models, videos, pictures, and motion pictures make it almost a theme park for tourists and local people alike (Figure 4.18).

(a)

(b)

Figure 4.17 World Expo 2010 in Shanghai, (a) Scheme by Architectural Studio of France, (b) Scheme by Cox

(a)

(b)

Figure 4.18 Shanghai Exhibition Hall of Urban Planning, (a) The building, (b) The model of Shanghai city proper

Goals, Problems, and Other Factors

Shanghai is determined to become an international economic center of finance, trade, and transportation. To achieve this goal, Shanghai faces several challenges.

The high population density creates constant pressure in Shanghai. In 1990, density in the city proper was 25,428 people/sq. km. but reached 39,057 within the inner ring road. The per capita figures for highway, greenery, and trash treatment capacities were far from the acceptable international levels. The land per capita was also lower than that of Beijing and Guangzhou.[4] If Shanghai's central districts hope to continue to function efficiently, the population density will need to be adjusted by moving residents and industry to other areas (Figure 4.19).

Shanghai used to be a multi-functional Asian economic center. After 1949, the city gradually focused on its manufacturing industry to meet the needs of civic development. The manufacturing system is now in the process of being adjusted to become an integrated part of a comprehensive international economic, financial, and trade center. This process is almost complete but has resulted in some pain for the affected parties.

The rapid drive of urbanization in the twentieth century made Shanghai, like other cities, into an endless sprawl. The planning authority noticed this and tried to replace "high speed" and "large scale" with "high quality" and "much dignity." Up to 2003, there were 2800 buildings over eighteen stories, and construction consent had been given to another 2000-plus skyscrapers. The development density and high-rise buildings will be strictly controlled, partly to ensure living quality and partly to slow the continuous land sink.[5] To curb the urban sprawl, Shanghai proposed building "one city, nine towns." This means building ten satellite towns on the outskirts of Shanghai. In the near future, each town will have a further ten smaller towns around it. The park will be introduced between the city proper, the satellite towns, and smaller towns. The objective is for 30 percent of the area to be forested by 2020 (*Architecture + Urbanism*, No. 399, Dec. 2003).

The economic ascension of Shanghai relies on the support of surrounding towns such as Suzhou, Wuxi, Changzhou, Yangzhou, Zhenjiang, Ningbo, Hangzhou, Jiaxin, Shaoxin, and others. It is in the interest of the rural towns of suburban Shanghai to form a better network to link with the above towns in other provinces (Figure 4.20).

From the end of the twentieth century, Shanghai has become a magnet for investment and brains from all over the world. Two-thirds of the world's top 500 enterprises set up branches or offices in Shanghai, 400,000 Taiwanese moved to the city from across the Taiwan Strait. These new residents are all professionals and capitalists in their thirties to fifties, with energy, wisdom, and high consuming power (www.cnd.org, October 2003). Fueled by strong demand, the price and rental of properties in Shanghai escalated; in some areas they even approached levels in Hong Kong and New York. The brighter nights in Shanghai are partly at the expense of dimmer Taipei, Hong Kong, Singapore, and other envious Asian cities.

Compared with Beijing and other historic cities, Shanghai does not have a long history, but it is unique in the history of modern China. The old Bund, Nanshi, Huangpu, Xuhui, Jinan, Hongkou, People's Square, and others have their own story and uniqueness. How to exploit the story and create a unique Shanghai style poses a major challenge. Compared with its rapid economic developments and eagerness to be an international

(a)

(b)

Figure 4.19 Scenes in Shanghai, (a) West Nanjing Road, (b) Northeast part

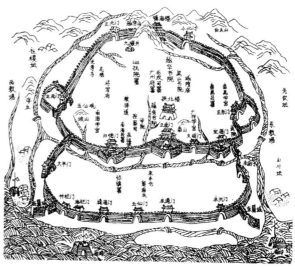

Figure 4.21 Ancient Guangzhou in Qing Dynasty (1644–1911)

Figure 4.20 Shanghai in the twenty-first century

metropolis, Shanghai is quite awkward in positioning itself culturally. In the globalization tide of the 1990s, Shanghai had no hesitation to discard its Chinese attributes represented by Longhua and Yu Garden and return to the nostalgia of the illusive 1930s when it was called the "Paris of the Orient." The semi-colonial history is the city's pride today (Li 2003). The new town planning in the twenty-first century generally adopts various European styles, and this seems easy to justify in modern Shanghai history.

GUANGZHOU: ALWAYS A SOUTHERN WIND

Origin and Path

Further south, we arrive in Guangzhou, the earliest city in China to trade with foreigners. In the Qin (221–206 BCE) and Han (206 BCE–220 CE) Dynasties, Guangzhou was already trading with Southeast Asia. In the Song (960–1279) and Ming (1368–1644) Dynasties, the maritime Silk Road started in Quangzhou, a port for exporting china and silk, and importing spices from southern and western Asia. The city was expanded almost ten times during the Song Dynasty. In the Ming Dynasty, the privileges of trading cities were revoked, with the exception of Guangzhou.

In 1757, the Qing Dynasty opened China to foreign trade. The "thirteen factories," which included foreign warehouses, hostels, and wharves, were constructed along the Pearl River. In 1860, Shamian was ceded as British and French Concessions. The city reached 15 to 20 sq km in size (Figure 4.21).

Guangzhou's characteristic feature is the harbor. Its development has been closely linked with this geographical feature. Because of the silt, the city had to grow towards the west and the south. Land use is in a concentric mode. Modern industry grew and the functions of the city became comprehensive. When Liwan, Yuexiu, Dongshan, and Haizhu were part of the city, the southwest became the commercial area. The higher education and science areas were formed in the east. Zhuhai Bridge was built, and public transportation through the south bank of the Pearl River was opened in 1933. Guangzhou's influence gradually waned as Shanghai's rose (Figure 4.22).

Spatial Evolution and Structure of Guangzhou

After 1949, Guangzhou gradually became a center of textiles and trade in southern China. Its master plan, after many revisions and amendments, oversaw the development of the city eastward along the north bank of the Pearl River.

(a)

(b)

Figure 4.22 Shamian, Guangzhou, (a) The office buildings of foreign trade were constructed in the nineteenth century, (b) Waterfront

In the 1950s, the city grew simultaneously in several directions, its manufacturing functions located primarily in Xicun, Chigang, and Nanshitou. In the 1950s and 60s, other areas were used for a variety of functions; for example, schools and universities were built in Wushan, Huangpu Harbor, and the Dasha industrial area. In the 1960s and 70s, after completion of the highway, the city developed along the northeast axis. After 1978, when Tianhe Sports Center and its auxiliary facilities were built, another linear axis was formed.

Since 1978, Guangzhou has been an open experimental laboratory, both in economy and architecture, because of its proximity to Hong Kong. However, the rising of Shenzhen, Zhuhai, and other coastal cities has gradually replaced Guangzhou. But the city still has ambitions to be an international metropolis in the region. In the strategic plan for 2002, the airport of 260,000 sq m GFA is located in the north end, and the southern border is pushed to Nansha, which makes Guangzhou directly face the sea. Greater Guangzhou today is 7434 sq km in

area, making it larger than Shanghai. The current population is 8.5 million. The area of the city proper is 3718 sq km, or about three times the size of Hong Kong (Figure 4.23).

As a harbor city, Guangzhou possesses the essential geographic feature for it to become a hub of commerce. People use words like "fresh and vital" to describe the city. It is also a big market. Shops are found in every street. The integration of the harbor, airport, railway, and expressway attract increasing numbers of trade fairs and manufacturing exhibitions and conventions.

Currently, the administrative center of Guangzhou is in the old Yuexiu District, which has been functioning as such for 2000 years. The modern commercial office buildings stretch from Liuhua to Tianhe Districts. The retail outlets are scattered throughout every corner of the city; particularly famous are Shangjiu and Xiajiu Roads, which were restored in a traditional style in the late 1990s. The wholesale markets are located in a fan-shaped area from Liwan to Xinchun.

Guangzhou is a good example of a city laid out in a typical linear pattern. White Cloud Mountain and the Pearl River bless the city not only with a wonderful landscape but also with spatial restrictions. For some time, Guangzhou had no clear spatial direction in which to grow, and sprawled aimlessly. City planning lagged far behind the rapid economic growth. In 2000, two nearby towns, Panyu and Huadu, were rezoned as districts under the administration of Guangzhou. This greatly enhanced Guangzhou's development potential and converted the city planning from a linear mode to that of a multi-centered group city mode with a clear southeast spatial development.

When Guangzhou's urban areas were expanding, many old rural villages became surrounded by the new city's roads and zones. These villages were called "villages in town." They were most often located in high-density areas with bad environments and were usually rented to low-income laborers who had poured in from other provinces. Houses in these villages are maximized in size, as a larger size can bring in more rentals, and more areas can get more compensation before demolition for new development. Consequently, the public space is hard to find. "Villages in town" have become a special phenomenon in Guangzhou and other expanding coastal cities.

Historically, Guangzhou was far from the central government and political center of China. The unique geography and natural conditions of Guangzhou nurtured

(a)

(b)

(c)

(d)

(e)

Figure 4.23 Architecture of Guangzhou in 2000, (a) Old retail streets were revitalized in the 1990s, (b) and (c) AXS, Japan, Guangzhou Exhibition and Convention Center, 2003, 400,000 sq m GFA, (d) and (e) Parson Group, URS Greater International Ltd. USA, Guangzhou Baiyun Airport in the north end of its new territory, Phase I, 280,000 sq m, Phase II, 320,000 sq m.

a culture distinctively different from the traditional culture of "central China." Its gardens, painting, food, clothing, and other arts and crafts are special. As mentioned in Chapters Two and Seven, the architecture of Guangzhou once expressed itself freely according to its own manner, whereas the other parts of China had to follow the so-called national style and other political slogans. At one time in the 1980s, Guangzhou was synonymous with a free and open style.

The Pearl River Delta

The Pearl River Delta extends its two wings along the Pearl River, in which Guangzhou occupies the top position in a large A-shaped triangle. In the past twenty years, this area has been the generator of China's economic development. Zhuhai, Zhongshan, Guangzhou, Dongguan, and Shenzhen, the major cities along the river, are actually manufacturers to the world, and each has its own characteristics.

For example, the city of Dongguan has 150,000 private companies and contributes 50 percent of computer hardware to the world. World-class companies like Dupont, General Electric, Nestle, Phillips, Sony, Samsung, Nokia, Swire, and Hoechst have opened factories in the city (Municipal Government of Dongguan 2002).

The area of Nansha, now a district of Guangzhou, forms a horizontal stroke of an A shape by its geographical location and Bridge of Humen. The proposed ocean bridge in Ling Ding Yang, around 30 km in length, will further physically link Hong Kong, Macau, Shenzhen, and Zhuhai. The Pearl River Delta, together with Hong Kong and Macau, is determined to stay ahead in China.

The Pearl River Delta can be further stratified into several layers. The bottom layer is the factories in the countryside. The manufacturing workshops and plants are scattered among the village houses and farmland. They form the basic operation of this so-called "world factory." The second layer is towns that have already established their identities, for example, furniture making and exhibition in Shunde, lighting fixtures in Guzhen, garments in several other towns. Their GDP increases by double digits every year. In these towns, luxurious restaurants, clubhouses, golf courses, first-class hotels, massage parlors, (illegal) brothels, and various entertainment venues occupy the town center to serve the newly emerging class of factory owners and affluent residents. The top layer is the central cities in the Delta; for example, Guangzhou, Shenzhen, and Zhuhai. They are the arenas where the incumbent leaders try to showcase their achievements by constructing huge city plazas, infrastructure, and landmark buildings (Feng and Yang 2004). The Delta is a gold-mine ridden by crime prostitution, gambling, and drugs.

As mentioned, the development of Shanghai's Pudong district in 1990 will stimulate the economy of the Yangtze River Delta. China's two deltas will compete fiercely in the drive towards modernization. Table 4.3 shows a comparison of the two areas.

The Goals and Way Out

The annexation of Panyu and Huadu strengthened the status of Guangzhou as a central city in the Pearl River Delta and in southern China. On its way to becoming a "scenic and sustainable international city," a goal the city embraces, Guangzhou faces challenges and opportunities, as does any other coastal city.

As an old city, Guangzhou is severely hampered by the vast number of old areas and derelict buildings. This is a problem faced by all historic cities. Haphazard city planning, rampant urban sprawl in the city proper, and confusion and disorder in the supply of land have worsened the situation (Figures 4.24 & 4.25).

Compared with the thirty-seven universities and colleges in Shanghai[6], the ten-plus universities in Guangzhou make it seem backward in higher education. In 2000, Dr Sun Yat-san University opened its new 330-ha campus in the city of Zhuhai, about 80 km to the south of Guangzhou. The other ten universities in the city proper were assigned land to construct new campuses in the original rural county, Panyu, thus partly alleviating the cramped environment in the old city campuses.

Guangzhou has always benefited from its neighbor, Hong Kong. The economic downturn in Hong Kong after 1997 affected Guangzhou's business.

The rapid development of other cities in the Pearl River Delta and outside the region resulted in both strain and stimulation. From collaboration and further connections, the cluster of cities in the Pearl River Delta of Hong Kong-Shenzhen, Macau-Zhuhai, plus Dongguan, Zhongshan, and of course Guangzhou, will, it is hoped, become a strong international bay area. Their mutual help and shared benefit will no doubt raise Guangzhou to new heights.

Table 4.3 Comparison of Two Important Deltas in China

	Pearl River Delta, Guangzhou in the center	Yangtze River Delta, Shanghai in the center
Population Percentage in China	40 million 1.8%	75.34 million 5.9%
Land Percentage in China	50,000 sq km 0.45%	90,000 sq km 1%
GDP Percentage in China	1055.6 billion yuan 8%	1698.1 billion yuan 17.7%
Exports to other countries Percentage in China	US$ 176.4 billion 40%	US$73.9 billion 27.8%
GDP per capita	30,000 yuan	22,537 yuan
Personal savings in banks	1000 billion yuan	unknown

The above statistics are for 2001 and are taken from *Mingpao Daily News*, Hong Kong, January 3, 2003. The figures for the Pearl River Delta do not include Hong Kong and Macau.

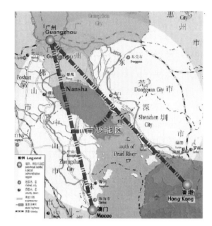

Figure 4.24 Relationship of various cities in the Pearl River Delta

(a)

(b)

(c)

(d)

(e)

(f)

Figure 4.25 Scenes in the Pearl River Delta, (a) The city of Dongguan, (b) Exhibition Center of Dongguan, (c) Nansha, outside Guangzhou and geometric center of the Pearl River Delta, (d) Zhongshan City, native town of Dr Sun Yat-sen, the first president of Republic of China, (e) Old street of Zhongshan, (f) New city of Shunde

There is a historic urgency to form such integration in the situation of globalization and localization. The proposed bridge linking Hong Kong, Macau, and Zhuhai Bridge will no doubt intensify and cement this unity. From September 2003, the central government allowed citizens from Guangdong, Beijing, and Shanghai to travel to Hong Kong individually without having to join a tourist group. The more flexible entry to Hong Kong for the Mainlanders gives further motivation to the personal, monetary, and logistic exchanges.

In August 2003, both the Hong Kong and Guangdong governments announced the vision of vowing to turn the Pearl River Delta region into one of the world's economic super-zones. Under the blueprint, Hong Kong will continue to be a center for logistics, shipping, trade, finance, and high value-added services, whereas Guangdong will be a manufacturing hub (Cheung and Leung 2003). In the blueprint, Guangzhou-Nansha-Humen-Shenzhen-Hong Kong will be a spine linking three areas of Greater Guangzhou, and the eastern and western parts of the Pearl River Delta (*Mingpao Daily News*, Feb 24, 2004). In 2004, led by Guangdong Province, a pan-Pearl River Delta "9+2" cooperation was formed. "Nine" means the nine southern provinces: Guangdong, Guangxi, Fujian, Hainan, Yunnan, Guizhou, Sichuan, Hunan and Jiangxi; "two" are Hong Kong and Macau. It is planned that any location within this "9+2" area can be reached by one day of travel. The various provinces and parties expect to gain from this regional cooperation (*South China Morning Post*, June 2, 2004).

The current competition among Chinese cities is fierce. Beijing represents the historic cities that carry the heavy heritage burdens, and walks towards modernization. Shanghai leads the coastal commercial cities that intend to be reincarnated in the process of globalization. The situation is somewhat similar to the scenes in today's Europe, as described by Lord Richard Rogers. The European countries are dissolving, and the individual cities form the new Europe. The competition among cities is an old civilization phenomenon in Europe (Rogers 1992).

NOTES

1. Professor Liang Si-cheng's laments appear in several articles and books. Typical is Yang Yongsheng (ed.) *Hundred People's Memoir in Architecture* (China Architectural and Building Press, 2000).

2. Nowadays, the road system in Beijing is knitted by square checkerboard, ring roads, and radiating roads. The hierarchy is expressway, main road, secondary road, and branch road. The road density is around 1.7 km/sq km The road accounts for 5.21% of the urban land use. See Wang Bing, Chen Xiaoming, Liu Kanghong, Olympic Games and Beijing: Opportunities and Challenges in Urban Development of Beijing, *Time + Architecture*, No. 3, 2002.

3. The quick prosperity of Chinese city centers is mostly based on the barbarous eviction of the original residents, in the name of "renovating the old derelict inner city area." The inner city renovation usually ends with the fabulous commercial buildings or classy high-rise apartments; for example, Oriental Plaza in Chang'an Street of Beijing, and the Jinan Temple area of Shanghai.

   In most cases, the local residents can no longer return to the "renovated" places they lived in for decades. They are moved to remote suburban areas, with bad living conditions, insufficient community services, and four to five hours of daily commuting. The large-scale development in the city center lifts the face of the city but demolishes the old city fabric, like the *hutongs* of Beijing, and creates much corruption. Many such projects are the results of collusion between the greedy developers and government officials. They trigger numerous conflicts and litigations of local residents versus the developers or government. To facilitate the "urban renewal," the courts usually decline such litigation cases in Beijing and Shanghai. In August 2003, more than ten affected residents protested in the "eviction office" in Nanjing that they were forced to leave their home in the city center with meager "compensation," by burning themselves. Eventually, eight people died, and the event shocked the country.

   Also See Fang Ke, *Contemporary Redevelopment in the Inner City of Beijing — Survey, Analysis and Investigation* (China Architecture and Building Press, Beijing, 2000); Craig Simons, "Wrecking crews take gold — redeveloping Beijing" (*South China Morning Post*, August 15, 2003); and the reports about Shanghai real estate tycoon Zhou Zhengyi (*Mingpao Daily News*, Hong Kong, June 2003). For the event in Nanjing, see *Singtao Daily*, Hong Kong, August 26, 2003, and www.cnd.org, August 26–29, 2003.

4. In the late 1980s, the land use per person was 30 sq m in Shanghai, 82.8 sq m in Beijing, and 60 sq m in Guangzhou. The standard of the Ministry of Construction is 60 to 120 sq m per person. See Peng Zaide, *The Sustainable Development of Big Cities: Theory and Practice* (Ph.D. dissertation, Research Institute of West Europe and North America, East China Normal University, 1997).

5. The land sink was found in Shanghai in the 1970s, mainly because too much underground water was piped. It was worsening, as too many high rise buildings were erected in a short time. The city's land sinks 1.5 cm each year. A YMCA building near People' Square, built in 1931, was

found to be sinking 6 cm a year. The land within a 100 m radius of Jin Mao Tower sinks 12 to 15 cm a year, and the process has accelerated in recent years. *Singtao Daily News*, Hong Kong, August 6, 2004, www.cnd.org, August 9, 2004.

6. There were fifty-one universities and colleges in Shanghai before 1997. To compete for the honor of being the top universities, a wave of university mergers appeared in the last five years of the twentieth century. For example, four universities, including the original Hangzhou University, a medical school, and agricultural college in Hangzhou, formed the new Zhejiang University. Independent medical schools were swallowed up by comprehensive "research" universities. Eventually, fifty-one institutions became thirty-seven.

5

The progress in China can be measured not only by the physical form of its buildings but by the people's ideas and concepts. In the 1980s, what is known as urban design evolved simultaneously in both Western and Chinese cities. Today, urban design often supersedes architectural design in the thinking and discussions of academics and municipal authorities. Urban design partly embodies the thrills and wonders of the architectural revolution of new China in the past quarter of a century. "Big, fancy, and magnificent" central plazas are the coveted goal of ambitious mayors throughout China. Provincial capital cities were transformed into vast construction and demolition sites. Because of China's determination and the pace of urbanization, this intensive urban design and renewal will last another twenty years.

This chapter is written jointly by Charlie Xue and Chen Xi.

CHAPTER FIVE

URBAN DESIGN
AS A TOOL FOR BETTER LIVING

The fundamental changes in the cityscapes of Beijing, Shanghai, Guangzhou, and other Chinese cities are a result of numerous projects of urban design, which have been part of the urban renewal movement since the 1980s.

Most traditional Chinese towns had only linear, straight streets. Even in China today, major cities such as Shanghai, Beijing, Nanjing, and Wuhan are mostly composed of linear streets and alleyways, with the primary function of moving people and goods. Chinese culture traditionally did not allow for public gatherings (Xue and Manuel 2001). After the open-door policy was implemented in 1980, civic life gradually became a part of people's needs. Strolling in a park in Shanghai, Guangzhou, or Nanjing today, one sees promenades and wide pedestrian walks and observes people doing Taiji, dancing, and exercising. These activities require suitable public environments (Figure 5.1).

Although concepts of urban design have been strongly promoted in China for only twenty years, ideas about how to design a city originated a long time ago. Even at the beginning of human history, people constructed their dwellings consciously, showing that they had some design concepts. Thousands of years later, the city building experiences and achievements of various peoples in various cultures have resulted in a series of theories about "city planning" or how best to support the behavior of human beings in city constructions. Compared with these disciplines, urban design — a discipline between, or combining, building design and city planning — is really quite new.[1]

Urban design in this chapter refers to "a complex art for it strives to attain a multitude of ends simultaneously. These ends range from the provision of shelter for activities, to the creation of a sense of place, to the technological soundness of the built environment, to the health of the fiscal and biological environment" (Lang 1994, ix). Urban design is intended to serve the interests of the public and should embody public consciousness instead of the values of individual clients. The scope of urban design combines building design and city planning (Moughtin 1999). Contemporary urban design pays more attention to the value and behaviors of human beings (Lang 1994).

In the past twenty years, China has undergone a drastic upsurge of urbanization. Between the census of 1990 and of 2000, the number of residents living in urban areas jumped from 26 percent to 36 percent (Chan and Ying 2003). That can be roughly translated as 120 million people moving to the towns. Urban areas are continuously sprawling in all directions and greedily eroding agricultural land. Streets are widened, the old districts razed, and fashionable skyscrapers erected. The strong social demands appeal for a more rational order in the city and better living conditions. Urban design emerged in response to this need. Since the 1980s, along with the gradual increase of urban planning strategies, the theory of urban design has played an increasingly important role in city planning and construction in China. It is therefore necessary to review the development of urban design theory and practice as it has occurred in China.

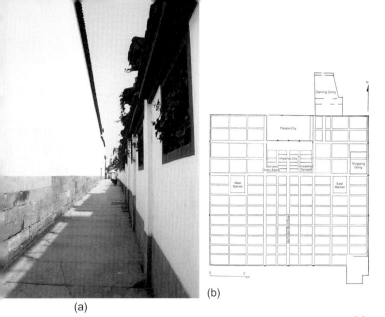

(a)

(b)

(c)

Figure 5.1 Traditional Chinese towns have only linear space, (a) Traditional alley in Hangzhou, (b) Plan of Chang'an in Tang Dynasty (618–907), (c) Open space widely utilized by citizens

At the end of the 1940s, Liang Si-cheng, the "father of Chinese architecture" (also see Chapters One and Two) initiated the idea of built-form design. Liang had visited several universities in the United States — including the Cranbrook Art Institute, whose architectural school was led by Eliel Sarinnen — and saw the importance of the city planning departments in those universities. He realized that everything, from a grand and sprawling city to the drinking cup in one's hand, was part of a built form and should be better designed.

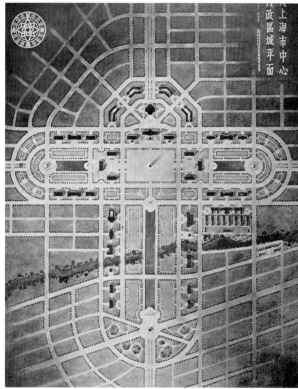

Figure 5.2 Plan of Shanghai showing influence of beautification movement, 1930s

STAGES OF URBAN DESIGN IN CHINA

The development of urban design in China can be divided into the following two stages: before 1980 and after 1980, the latter date marking the introduction and development of contemporary urban design theories.

Early Ideas of Urban Design

The idea of urban design was introduced into China as early as 1927, when Shanghai was designated a special city by the national government and began its urban planning process. The organization given this responsibility was a design committee. The new downtown and central area in Shanghai that it came up with in 1929 inherited the idea of the "City Beautification Movement," the prevailing urban design model between the end of the nineteenth century and the beginning of the twentieth. The result was both a city plan and a civic design (Figure 5.2).

During the 1950s, city planning in China, including master planning or detailed planning, followed the practices of the then Soviet Union. As the roots of this planning came from the aesthetics of Beaux Arts and the ideology of the City Beautification Movement, popular in the United States at the beginning of the 1920s, urban planning in China in the 1950s contained the thought of city design. During this period, China promulgated *The Provisional Law Regulating the City Planning Process (1952)* in which it identified the first step in city planning as that of "master planning and design," implicitly establishing through this principle that the entire process must be integrated. In October 1954, the founding of the Building Engineering Ministry and the China Institute of Planning Research marked the beginning of China's commitment to urban planning.

At the end of the 1950s, the development of city planning in China gradually stagnated as a result of the endless political movements that wracked the country. In 1958, the "fast planning" slogan adopted at the Symposium of City Planning in Beijing simplified the processes and content of city planning and confined planning to land use zoning. In November 1960, China's planners announced their decision "not to do any city planning for the following three years" and to shut down city planning organizations throughout the country, a move that brought all city planning activities to an abrupt halt.

In general, the development of city planning in China before the 1980s was very much exploratory; it was marked by the limited introduction of the theories and practices of city planning. City planning in China utilized the ideas of the Beaux Arts movement and civil engineering practices in the United States in the 1920s.

After 1980

After 1980, along with internal reforms and the open-door policy, many kinds of architectural theory were introduced into China (see also Chapter Three). Modern urban design theories, which had arisen in Europe and the US after World War II, spread rapidly throughout the country.

From 1980 to the present, urban design in China has taken place in two stages: the early stage (from the 1980s to the early 1990s) and the more recent period (after 1990), which was characterized by China's booming economy.

In the early 1980s, urban design theories from overseas, primarily Europe and the US, began to be zealously introduced into the field of architecture; translations of the relevant literature was published throughout China. From May 1980 to July 1981, in its No. 3–7 issues, the journal *The Architect* published *The Design of External Space* by Japanese scholar Ashihara Yokonobu. And from 1983 to 1989, the following influential books were translated and published: *Downtown Design* by F. Gibberd; *The Image of the City* by Kevin Lynch; *The City: Its Growth, Its Decay, Its Future* by Eliel Saarinen; *Design of Cities* by Edmund N. Bacon; and books by Christopher Alexander and his students: *Timeless Way of Architecture*, *A Pattern Language: Towns, Buildings, Construction* and *A New Theory of Urban*

Design. These theories in these books have been widely quoted and applied in design practice.

In the 1990s, a number of experts and scholars in China published academic papers about urban design. Examples include *Modern Urban Design Theory and Method* by Wang Jianguo (Southeast University Press, 1991); and *Introductory Theory of Urban Design* by Xiu Sishu and Zhou Wenhua (China Architecture and Building Press, 1991).

After the 1980s, national professional meetings and conferences put more effort into city planning and design, and some well-known Chinese specialists and scholars published a number of serious and thought-provoking papers and articles. For example, in October 1980, "Comprehensive Urban Design Work" and "Preserving the Characteristics of our Cities" by Zhou Ganzhi and Ren Zhenying were presented at the Fifth Congress of the Architectural Society of China. In the same year, the First National Conference of City Planning Work promulgated *The Provisional Approval Method of City Planning*.

In June 1984, the Ministry of Construction sponsored an academic conference on architectural design and the city. During the conference, Wu Liangyong gave a major presentation, "Important Ways to Improve the Quality of City Planning and Architectural Design." In 1988, when the Ministry of Construction published a *Compendium of City Planning (1989–1993)*, urban design was given an important role in the new guidelines. According to the compendium, the government should build comfortable and beautiful communities that reflect the specific features of both super-size and historic cities.

At the same time, an increasing number of development projects throughout China applied the ideas of urban design. For example, at the end of 1983, the Shanghai Institute of Civil Architecture and the Shanghai Institute of Planning were responsible for the urban design of New Hongqiao District, near the old airport. In this project, planning principles and urban design theory were experimentally combined. High-class hotels and exhibition centers were erected. In addition to this landmark project, several feasibility reports regarding urban design have been produced. An example is Shenzhen's Urban Design Research Report, produced in 1987 by the Shenzhen Planning Bureau and the Llewelyn-Davies Planning & Design Company, England. In 1988, Liaocheng (in Shandong Province) published a planning report concerning its cityscape. Following that, a number of provinces, including Liaoning, Heilongjiang, and Jilin, followed suit. Furthermore, Shandong and Heilongjiang

Provinces codified their local technical standards to guide their planning and urban design practices.

After 1990, an increasing number of worthwhile academic papers in the field of urban design were published, and theoretical research became even more impressive. In December 1997, the Architectural Society of China (ASC), the Planning Society of China, and the ASC Shanghai Chapter held an urban design conference in Shanghai. It received more than 150 papers and subsequently published the conference proceedings. One year later, a collection of 118 urban design research papers was published by the editorial board of *City Planning*.

In practice, the city of Haikou in Hainan Province saw the first design firm specifically devoted to urban design, in 1991. An urban design session was established in the Planning Bureau of Shenzhen in the same year (Zou 1999). Some projects in large or historic cities have been gradually introduced. The Bell and Drum Tower Square in Xi'an began construction in November 1995. It is an excellent example of urban design. Zhang Jinqiu, the chief architect of the China Northwest Design Institute, headed the project, which explored several aspects of traditional and contemporary design, preservation and renewal concerns, and other facets of urban planning and design.

The Bell Tower and Drum Tower, major historical relics in China, are located in the old town of Xi'an in a crowded and run-down environment. Zhang's design connects the Bell Tower and the Drum Tower with a group of new buildings and a civic square, the sunken part of which provides the entrance to an underground shopping center, while also separating the square from the street. The design is harmonious with Xi'an's historical character and provides sufficient commercial floor area. There is one obvious design failure: the lack of street furniture and the absence of greenery make it hard for people to remain comfortably in the square for any length of time, and the sunken shopping lane beside the new building discourages passers-by (Figure 5.3).

Because of the development of Chinese cities, increasing numbers of foreign design companies and firms have participated in major urban projects. From January to August 1996, four foreign companies were invited to submit designs for Shenzhen City Center: SCAUIM of France, Yabenko Architecture Planning Consultation Company of Singapore, HuaYi Design Consultants of Shenzhen, and John M.Y. Lee of the United States. Eventually, the design submitted by John M. Y. Lee was awarded first prize. In the same year, two foreign companies, HOK of the United States and RIA of Japan,

(a)

(b)

Figure 5.3 Zhang Qinqiu, Bell and Drum Tower Plaza, Xi'an

undertook an urban design project for Shanghai's North Bund.

During the second half of the 1990s, significant progress was also made in compiling and publishing urban design standards. In 1997, China's Ministry of Construction promulgated its building technology policy (1996–2010), which clearly defined the relationship between architectural design and city planning in the respective roles they play in urban design. The policy stated: "To enhance the concept of urban design, when designing individual buildings, be sensitive to dialogue with the surrounding environment ..." Designers were advised to "cooperate with city planners and explore the system of China's urban design in order to enhance the quality of the city's built environment and its quality of life." Article 3.0.3 of the *Basic Technical Terms of City Planning* (GB/T50280-98) defines urban design as the holistic arrangement of the city's spatial environment, which pervades the process of city planning. This regulation was implemented in February 1999. In 2000, the Ministry of Construction and the China Institute of City and Country Planning began to compile the fifth volume of *City Planning Data Collection — Urban Design* (similar to the time-saver series in the US).

In addition, provincial and municipal governments promulgated a number of local technical guides for urban design. For example, the *Shenzhen Urban Design Bylaw* (July 1998) is the first law that includes urban design as part of local planning bylaws. In the following year, Hebei Province began to implement the *Urban Design Technical Guides of Hebei Province*.

In general, from the mid-1990s, because of the continuing growth of the national economy and the extensive construction taking place in Chinese cities, coupled with the increased attention that it was receiving, urban design in China could boast of a number of distinctive achievements, both in quality and quantity.

CHARACTERISTICS OF CONTEMPORARY URBAN DESIGN THEORY AND PRACTICE IN CHINA

The rapid development of urban design is the result of fast-paced urbanization. After the open-door policy was adopted, China's cities entered a period of drastic expansion: numerous old rural towns were upgraded to cities or a district of nearby big cities. According to the 1997 statistics, there were 668 cities, 18,316 rural towns, 30,324 bazaar towns, and 3,659,335 villages (Zou 1999), forming a whole system of human settlements in China.

The functions of the city tend to become more sophisticated. The 1980s was the decade in which China began to learn and understand urban design, the next ten years from 1990 to 2000 witnessing the widespread application and practice of urban design in China. During these ten years of implementation, urban design professionals gradually shifted their focus from merely copying Western theories to looking at the particular problems of China itself, including traditional beliefs, geographical and weather conditions, and the ways in

which indigenous housing was understood and experienced.

Among his numerous publications, Professor Wu Liangyong wrote an article, "Reflections on City Planning Inspired by the Design Concepts of Traditional Chinese Human Settlements," in which he presented the idea that China's traditional habitation integrated building, city, and landscape, instead of treating the building separately. This holistic approach to the built environment has a particularly dynamic significance for current practice.

Professor Wu's books *Generalized Architecture* (1990), *Introduction to Built Environment Science* (1992), *The Future of Architecture* (1995), and *Architecture, City and Human Environment* (1997) have profoundly influenced China's professionals and students. His design for Beijing's Ju'er Hutong neighborhood (see also Chapter Six), the urban renewal of the White Pagoda Area, and the campus of the Central Academy of Fine Arts likewise utilized his ideas. In 1996, Qian Xuesheng, the father of China's nuclear and missile programs, also proposed the concept of a "city of mountain and water," which was enthusiastically received by professionals.

Scholars at Southeast University, for example, Dong Wei and Wang Jianguo, also researched sustainable development modes for China's major cities. Other scholars, designers, and people in planning and management have conducted in-depth research into the urban design process, including management, implementation, and user participation. Their findings can be found in numerous academic journals published in China.

Furthermore, as a result of foreign influences from abroad, urban design in China is now more diversified. The earlier two-dimensional approach (plan only) to urban design has been superseded by a dynamic three-dimensional or spatial approach. In addition, various specialties that come under the rubric of urban design have developed, including urban design as a branch of the arts, urban design as applied to public spaces, urban design that deals with a city's functional organization, urban design that focuses on human behavior, urban design that studies the development process, and urban design viewed in its widest and most universal sense.

No matter how scholars categorize this new discipline, the practice of urban design has to run along its own track shaped by the particular situation of the country. Urban design as it is practiced in contemporary China takes place on the following levels.

Urban Design at the District and Municipal Levels

This type of urban design attempts to set the planning and design of the city against the larger background of the geographical district in which it is situated; for example, Guangzhou in the Pearl River Delta and Shanghai in east China possess their own unique set of considerations. The municipal level, in contrast, deals with the districts within the city; for example, Shanghai has nineteen districts;[2] Hong Kong has eighteen districts. This urban planning focuses primarily on the built area of the city. It studies the city's morphological form, cityscape, scenery, and public domains and their organization. Its contents include land use, spatial structure, road grids, artistic characteristics, scenery, skyline, and landmarks, basing decisions on the city's ecology, culture, and history. At this level in China, the following two types of urban design are employed.

One is in the level of master planning. An excellent example of urban design is the Shenzhen Urban Design Study, created by the Shenzhen Institute of Urban Design and Research. Another is the master plan and spatial

(a)

(b)

Figure 5.4 Urban planning of Shenzhen, (a) City center of Shenzhen, (b) Master plan of 1998

organization of Guangzhou. Yet another is Wuhan's "image design," which made this industrial city more beautiful and attractive.

The design of Shenzhen, jointly developed by the Shenzhen Institute of Urban Design and Research and the English firm Llewelyn-Davies Planning & Design Company, embodies and extends the principles of the city's 1985 master plan. The study includes macroscopic strategic policies, specific urban design guidelines, and landscape and environmental recommendations. It focuses on the Futian Center area, the Luohu Commercial Center, and the urban renewal of run-down areas (Figure 5.4).

These urban master plans laid a solid foundation and established clear directions for future works. Based on these directions, *Urban Design of Futian Central City* was published in 1994. The design of the Civic Center, the subway line and station, and the public spaces in the central axis were completed in 1997. The documentation for the central district and two city blocks was completed in 1998. The following year, an international design competition was held to solicit schemes for the plaza design, central city design, and the use of underground space. After fifteen years of rapid development, Shenzhen's new city structure was finally complete, as was its division of functions. However, the city area grew more rapidly than was originally expected; therefore, a new round of urban planning had to be carried out in 2000. For its prominent achievements, Shenzhen won the Sir Abercrombie Award at the Twentieth UIA Congress in Beijing in 1999.

The second aspect is in the cityscape. Beginning in the late 1980s, some small- and middle-sized cities, such as Liaocheng and Weihai in Shandong Province, began to explore their urban characteristics, landscapes, cityscapes, and key urban areas. Their areas of concern included identifying the city's character and the direction of its development; preserving the city's historic and cultural heritage; and identifying indigenous civic traditions, zoning, height zoning, and the visual corridor; environmental concerns; the city's building style, including color control and detailed planning for "key" areas. Such initiatives have proven effective in enhancing the overall image and reputation of the cities concerned. Learning from Shandong, other provinces, such as Liaoning, inaugurated similar urban planning efforts in the 1990s. They concluded that the cityscape was an essential part of a comprehensive planning process, which complemented and deepened urban planning. Cityscape planning can be realized through various proposals, principles, and technical indexes (Figure 5.5).

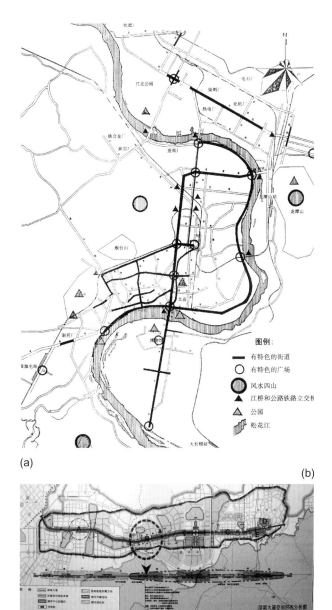

(a)

(b)

Figure 5.5 Cityscape design in search of an identity, (a) Planning of city's characteristics, Jilin City (b) Spatial morphology of Shennan Road, Shenzhen

Urban Design at the District Level Within the City

At this level, the typical research concerns of urban design are those areas that have relatively independent functions. The design should try to conform to the environmental principles of the upper-level urban design plan and the natural and social environment and cultural ecology of the urban renewal plan. These independently functioning areas include civic centers, historic communities, commercial centers, and large public buildings.

A lot of development focuses on this level of urban design. Beginning in the early 1990s, Shanghai's Lujiazui CBD, Dalian's Xinhai Bay, and Shenzhen's Futian Center held international competitions to solicit urban design schemes. Later, urban designs for Beijing's Zhong Guan Cun (China's "Silicon Valley"); the Guangzhou Train Station to the Tianhe Sports Center; Guangzhou's Pearl River waterfront; the image design of Shanghai's North Bund; Shanghai's pedestrian Nanjing Road; Ningbo City's central waterfront; and the waterfronts of Fuzhou, Xiamen, Haikou, and Sanya were implemented. Beijing's Olympic Park and CBD are quite attractive. Some of these examples are discussed in more detail below (Figure 5.6).

(1) Lujiazui Central Business District, Shanghai. The planning of Shanghai's Lujiazui district was an early example of international competition in China. The area of 1.7 sq km is the point at which three rivers and more than ten streets physically and visually converge. It is on the east side of the Huangpu River, opposite Shanghai's historic Bund. The area was zoned as a CBD in Shanghai's master plan of 1986. Fueled by the development of Pudong on the east bank of the Huangpu River, the municipal government organized an international urban design competition for Lujiazui in 1992, inviting firms from China, France, Italy, Japan, and Britain to participate. Richard Rogers & Partners won first prize. The design was a circular composition with an east-west axis and featuring carefully organized traffic flow.

At the time of the international competition, several skyscrapers were already under construction in the Lujiazui area, and the ground plans could not be altered. Rogers' entry and those of the other firms were considered too dense and difficult to implement and had to be modified so that development could follow existing conditions.

Figure 5.6 Huaqiao Cheng, Shenzhen, Urban design at the district level

Several of the landmark super high-rise buildings are surrounded by waterfront greenery and central greenery; others soar upwards in independent isolation. The urban space has not been organically organized to blend with the buildings (Figure 5.7).

(2) Futian District, Shenzhen. An international competition was held in 1996, and John M. Y. Lee/Michael Timchula Architects was awarded first prize. In 1997, Kisho Kurukawa expanded the plan and suggested that Lianhua Hill be part of the central area. Lee's firm designed a 250 m wide park oriented in a south-north direction, Lianhua Hill at the back, and down to the seashore. The main traffic thoroughfare of Shennan Road cuts across the park by means of an underground tunnel, in order not to disturb the continuity of this green space. Not merely a square and a green area but a sophisticated pedestrian walkway, subway station, retail, and leisure system link the entire civic plaza. The north part is largely composed of a civic center, library, and concert hall; the south part is a high-rise business-office park and exhibition-convention center. Three parks with different themes connect to streets with hotels and retail outlets. The densely arranged commercial facilities provide a human touch and the necessary funding for constructing this civic plaza. The entire area is imbued with a feeling of both majesty and light-heartedness (Figure 5.8). The urban design of Shenzhen's new central area is a continuous dynamic process. It is a valuable case study for observing China's urban change. The construction of the civic plaza is carried out in stages, as moving local residents is logistically difficult.

(3) Northern Bund, Shanghai. The Northern Bund developed naturally along the west bank of the Huangpu River, with an area of 237.8 ha and building floor area of 2,880,000 sq m. It was originally a manufacturing and wharf district. Financial, commercial, entertainment, residential areas, and a wharf merge in this sleepless center of activity. The pedestrian level was elevated and vehicular traffic confined to the lower level. A monorail tram is also used for transportation. Various innovative strategies were utilized; financial models that allocated investment benefits, sophisticated infrastructure, plot ratio incentives, and bonuses for investment were explored (Figure 5.9).

(4) Olympic Park, Beijing. Olympic Park is located at the north end of Beijing's "imperial" central north-south axis. The plans for Olympic Park that were drawn up in the year 2000 impressed people with their dramatic twin towers feature. In the 2002 planning competition, fifty-four design schemes by international practitioners were submitted. The organizing committee hoped that the winning plan would satisfy the requirements of the Olympic Games in the short term, and focus on sustainable

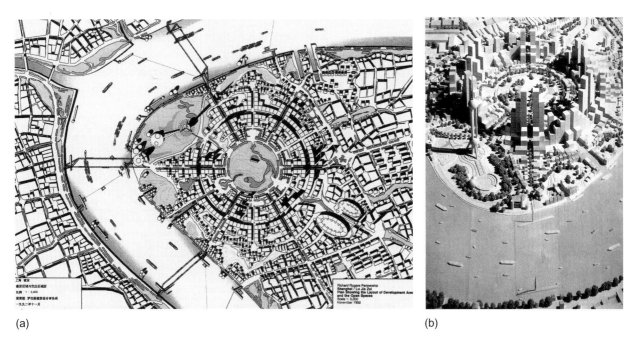

(a)   (b)

Figure 5.7 Lujiazui plan, Pudong, Shanghai, 1992, (a) Richard Rogers' scheme, plan, (b) Model

(a)

(b)

(c)

Figure 5.8 Futian Center, implementation plan, Shenzhen, (a) and (b) model of the plan, (c) Children's Palace is part of the plan

and environmental concerns in the long term. The traffic system had to be able to accommodate the heavier traffic of the Games and be suitable in general. Olympic Park also had to express the identity of Beijing and emphasize the significance of the central axis. The plan could be divided into different phases and had to be easily financed. Singapore planner Liu Taige, chairman of the jury, felt that Beijing's central axis was so critical to the city's character that it should remain free of buildings.

Figure 5.9 Scheme of North Bund, Shanghai

The Sasaki Company of Boston and Huahui Architectural Design Ltd. of Tianjin won the competition. This design scheme does not put any buildings on the central axis. The hills, forest, lake, river, and meadow are treated as sculpted landforms in the park. Various functions are carefully calculated and connected; for example, the volume of traffic and the parking. The plan allows for the individual buildings to have room to be displayed, fostering creativity. The plan is most respectful of the significance of the central axis to the city and is deliberate in choosing to place new buildings at the edge rather than on-axis. The enduring power, boldness, and simplicity of the Cultural Axis extend beyond the relatively temporal nature of buildings. Along the axis, the plan seeks to commemorate the achievements and contributions of the various Chinese dynasties, from the Zhou Dynasty (1100 BCE–221CE) to the Tang (618–907), Song (960–1279), Yuan (1271–1368), Ming (1368–1644) and Qing (1644–1911) Dynasties. The Olympic Axis, which has an angle with the Cultural Axis, begins within the existing Asian Games stadium, extending northwest through the proposed National Stadium, continuing onward to a Sports Heroes Garden, intersecting with the Cultural Axis and park. Thus, the Olympic ideals of sports, culture, and environment are equally represented within the Olympic green plan (Figure 5.10).

Building Complexes and Streets

Urban design at this level primarily includes the architectural design of a particular building and vicinity;

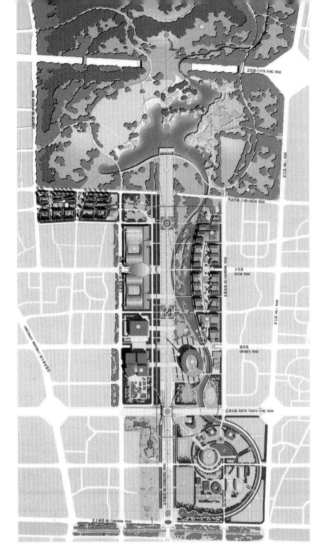

Figure 5.10 Sasaki and Huahui, Olympic Park, Beijing, 2002

significant urban form has become extremely limited" (Frampton 1999, 2004). In China, there might be more "possibility of creating significant urban form" because of the government's determination and fast pace of demolishing the old city area. But Professor Frampton's views best illustrate the functions of such a megaform: "urban designers, architects and planners have tried to evolve alternative piecemeal strategies for development and/or modification of urban form". "A megaform may be defined as being: (i) a large form extending horizontally rather than vertically, (ii) a complex form which does not necessarily express its structural and mechanical elements, and (iii) as a device that is capable of inflecting the existing urban context because of its strong topographical character" (Frampton 1999).

Consider Shanghai's Jing'an Temple Square, for example. The square is located beside a traffic intersection adjacent to the Jing'an Temple and the exit of a subway station. The square is sunken, has an underground commercial mall, a pedestrian subway for crossing the

(a)

(b)

Figure 5.11 Lu Jiwei, Street-level design; sunken square of Jing'an Temple, Shanghai

for example, streetscapes, squares, traffic centers, large buildings and their surroundings. This dimension of urban design is micro-scale and detailed, mainly associated with engineering challenges and considerations. However, these buildings greatly influence the city and its design. Some "key areas" within the city and residential districts can be included in this level. To name a few examples: Beijing's Oriental Plaza at the junction of Chang'an Street and Wangfujing, Shanghai's Jing'an Temple area, Xi'an's Bell and Drum Tower Square, Chongqing's People's Square, Nanjing's Xinjiekou area, Harbin's Sofia Church Square, Beijing's Xidan Civic Square, and Shenzhen's Old Street Subway Station (Figure 5.11).

Urban design at this level of building complex may be categorized as what Professor Frampton proposed, "megaform as urban acupuncture." As he observed: "the contemporary environment is now so conditioned by maximized technology that the possibility of creating

road and a fresh air to service the subway. The 2,800 sq m square is composed of an amphitheater and colonnade. Its intimacy with the street and community means it is accepted by local citizens and passers-by. Looking at the other major building projects mentioned above, for example, in Beijing's street junctions of Xidan and Wangfujing, and Shanghai's Xujiahui, the megaform shopping mall or office complex by and large fulfills the three functions proposed by Professor Frampton.

Historic Neighborhoods and Preservation

The modern theory of urban design takes preservation as an essential component of any urban design strategy. China has a splendid history, but the preservation of its heritage started much later than that of Europe. The preservation movement in China began in the twentieth century, with archeological research. In 1929, Zhu Qizhen and his colleagues at the Department of Education in Nanjing launched the China Institute of Architectural Research. Professor Liang Si-cheng and Liu Dunzhen used modern methodology to investigate ancient buildings (see also Chapter Two). The work of these two pioneers laid a solid foundation for the preservation of China's heritage.

In 1982, the State Council announced the designation of a group of national heritage buildings. The *Law of Heritage* was also promulgated in the same year. In 1986, a group of twenty-four historic towns at the national level were announced. Historic neighborhoods, streets, blocks, building complexes, and villages were given protected heritage status. The establishment of this preservation system can be seen as a major achievement of city planning in China in the 1980s. In 1994, China announced another group of famous historic towns, increasing the number to ninety-nine.

Pingyao of Shanxi Province, Lijiang of Yunnan Province, and Zhouzhuang of Jiangsu Province are several successful examples of historic towns that have high cultural, historical, and tourist value. Some ancient streets, such as Tunqi Street in Huang Shan City, Ziyang Street in Linhai, Wuzhen Street in Tongxiang City, Dongguan Street in Yangzhou, Zhongshan Road in Quanzhou, and Dajinfan district in Hangzhou City are just a few examples of excellent street-level preservation (Figure 5.12).

While traditional neighborhoods decayed in the early twentieth century, colonial architecture was flourishing in the coastal cities. These are also valuable cultural heritages of China; for example, the Bund of Shanghai, and Badaguan of Qingdao. However, as a result of the

inappropriate use of these colonial buildings by the communist regime before 1980, the existing situation of Bund and other similar areas is unsatisfactory. Tongji University Professor Chang Qing and his team carefully investigated the Bund of Shanghai and participated in several restoration projects of old colonial buildings. Professor Chang proposed the concept of "source of the Bund" and confirmed the waterfront area close to the junction of Huangpu River and Suzhou Creek the very source of this glorious historic Bund. The team presented a scheme of renewal, which included the original British Consulate and several old banks and clubhouses. The scheme has been implemented and will greatly revitalize the Bund, which is actively applying for status as a world cultural heritage site (Figure 5.13).

Questions will always be asked about how best to preserve a city's traditional character, how to maintain the relationship between preservation and development, and about authenticity and the scope and range of preservation. However, at present, most historic buildings and blocks in the center of China's cities are threatened by the rapid development of real estate properties, before they are gazetted as historic heritages. Even in the capital city of Beijing, traditional courtyard houses and alleys have been periodically destroyed by bulldozers. As mentioned in Chapter Four, the developers and short-sighted local governments will conjure up every reason to grab the valuable land in the city center. Profit invariably takes precedent (Figure 5.14).

SOME PROBLEMS OF URBAN DESIGN IN CHINA

Although urban design has developed significantly since the 1980s, its status in contemporary China is still far from satisfactory. The problems associated with urban design need to command wide attention and serious study in order that better solutions can be found. Some of these problems are as follows.

Most of China's numerous large cities have undergone considerable development in recent years, and their central areas bristle with new construction; yet these new urban areas still lack any strong or unique sense of identity. A steel and concrete jungle soars into the sky, but the majority of these high-rise buildings wear the same anonymous face. These new developments usually lack any coherent sense of aim and order, the result being that the urban space loses its meaning and atmosphere. According to

(a)

(b)

(c)

Figure 5.12 Preservation of a historic city, (a) and (b) Zhou Zhuang, 80 km from Shanghai, was revitalized as a tourist attraction, (c) City Temple, Shanghai, built in the 19th century and renovated in the 1990s

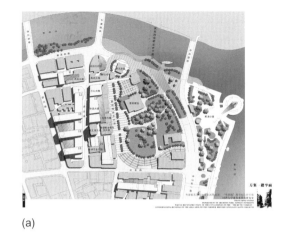

(a)

(b)

Figure 5.13 Chang Qing and his team's restoration and renewal design of the Bund, Shanghai, (a) Master plan, (b) Street scene

traditional Chinese energy systems, the harmonious balance of *feng shui* has been severely disrupted.

The *feng shui* is worsened by the motor vehicle traffic, as an increasing number of cars clog city streets; the crowding, noise, and pollution generated compromise the original pedestrian purpose of the street. Traditional street space is inexorably disappearing, as redevelopment nearly always favors the imperatives of the automobile. The contradiction between development and preservation in such cases is obvious. A number of traditional communities have even witnessed the demolition of entire city blocks, and wholesale destruction of their social and cultural fabric. The input and advice of preservation consultants is urgently required before civic governments approve such projects.

(a)

(b)

(c)

Figure 5.14 Endangered alleyway and courtyard houses, (a) Courtyard house in demolition, Beijing, (b) Terraced lane house (*lilong*) at a dangerous stage with growing population and little interest from developers, (c) Old neighborhood in Shanghai

Urban design is usually a long-term project originating with a feasibility analysis and ending with the completion of construction. A critical question in urban design is "what should be managed and what should not?" Appropriate revisions and changes should be allowed in some long-term design projects, but the requirements of the design should generally be loose and flexible. This makes urban design an open and dynamic process. Public participation and interaction between designers and end users should always be encouraged. In China today, urban design remains a "roller coaster" process, the public and end users being excluded. It goes without saying that this state of affairs needs to be changed.

Public participation has not been fully realized, only the input of the officials. In China, large public building projects are important, so that local government officials can keep their positions and get promoted. The construction of squares and plazas is seen as landmark projects for a town and city and as an achievement for the mayor and his administration. On one hand, these projects stimulate urban design; on the other, these plazas in the center of the city are usually too large for the area. Many such projects have been abandoned because of financial problems.

For example, Anji County in Zhejiang Province forcefully merged sixteen villages, five communes, and half of an agricultural county into an "economic district." The county's financial income was less than 190 million yuan, but it invested more than half of its income to build a government building of 300,000 sq m and an "ecological" plaza similar in size to Tiananmen Square. Such grandiose human-made "urbanization" ignored the normal rate of growth of the economy and the needs of ordinary citizens. As a result of this decorative indulgence, thousands of acres of high-yield agricultural land were deserted and hundreds of thousands of dollars were used up years in advance, depleting future resources and squandering the birthright of the next generation (Li 2002) (Figure 5.15). In the economic boom of the 1970s–80s, Japan built extravagant town halls in various prefectures. The twenty-first century is China's turn to construct big civic plazas.

The management and approval system is also important. Design competitions, bidding, and the selection of tenders should be based on systematic grounds. In 2001, Nanjing held an international design competition for its new Olympic Center. Before the selection was made, the planned land was rezoned, thereby wasting the energy and resources of the designers. Similar situations have occurred elsewhere. For example, in the process of implementation, a number of projects have not been built according to the design. Design competitions of urban projects hide many secret and informal deals (Xue and Shi 2003). This is a common phenomenon in China today.

Education in urban design lags behind practice, too. Research institutes in universities and colleges in China usually pay excessive attention to the physical aspects of urban design. These institutions develop programs for physical planning, but feasibility assessments and financial and social effects have been less studied. The results of design competitions are too often influenced by persuasive or seductive presentations, and the content of worthy design schemes are often neglected or overlooked. In contrast, the majority of urban design projects are undertaken by architects, who generally focus on the spatial effects of a building complex rather than on human elements. These projects usually stress the technical or engineering aspects of a design and often lack a comprehensive vision of what is ideally possible in the circumstances.

Today in China, city development projects designated "urban design" have been so popular they may even outnumber "city planning" projects. If a building or building complex design involves several streets, the project will of course be connected to "urban design," both by the developers and designers. The expanding appetite of urban design is exposing the limitations of and supplementing the existing architecture and urban planning paradigms.

No doubt, this bodes well for the future of urban design as the concept has been widely accepted by research institutes, design companies, developers, management sectors, contractors and the general public. However, its success and acceptance should be carefully monitored because, among the proliferation of urban design projects, inferior works will inevitably be built. Some projects may also be merely "window dressing" without any future commitment. This will affect the healthy development of urban design in China.

Over a period of twenty years, the national economy's super high-speed growth and the earlier stagnation of urban development from the 1950s to 1970s provided a strong impetus for urban design in China. The performance of

Figure 5.15 Out-of-scale urban plaza, in a town of 30,000 people.

Figure 5.16 New building emerging from the old town, Shunde, Guangdong Province

the national economy and the pace of construction remain important factors for predicting the future of urban design. In the twenty-first century, the development of China's economy will inevitably slow, following the explosive growth of the past twenty years, as will urbanization. Urban design and construction will conform to this trend.

Therefore, in urban design practice, the market will be more demanding in its requirements and seek more elegant and decent designs rather than being satisfied with mere quantity. At the same time, urban design theory will become more integrated with traditional culture and contemporary realities in China. In the theoretical realm, more research into urban design and its functions will be carried out. This will include studies of design goals, open design processes, plural assessments, and the adaptability of design outcomes.

NOTES

1. Voluminous literature exists on the definition, scope, and works of urban design since the 1980s. Examples are Cliff Moughtin's books, *Urban Design, Street and Square* (Architectural Press, Oxford, 1992); *Urban Design, Method & Techniques* (Architectural Press, Oxford, 1999); *Urban Design: Green Dimension*, 1996; Cliff Moughtin, Taner Oc, and Steven Tiesdell, *Urban Design: Ornament and Decoration*, (Architectural Press, Oxford and Boston, 1995); Jon T. Lang, *Urban Design, the American Experience* (Van Nostrand Reinhold, New York, 1994); and two international journals mainly based in the UK: *Urban Design* and *Urban Design International*.

2. Shanghai had ten districts in the city and ten rural counties, a system that lasted almost forty years. In the wave of urbanization of the 1990s, rural counties were gradually renamed "districts," to show the pace of modernization, as in the collective consciousness of Chinese people, "urban" is always superior to "rural." By 2000, the nine counties had been changed to districts; only Chongming, the third largest island of China and formed by the sand from Changjiang (Yangtze) River, kept the title "county." Also see Chapter Four.

6

Housing is a common concern of society. It includes not only the problems of building design but of social policy as well. How to house over a billion citizens is a perpetual and challenging question facing China's government. Since 1990, urban housing policies have changed dramatically. Private developers and the commercialization of housing have resulted in an opulent residential landscape. The recent change in China's housing provides a vivid example of form following social policy. After 1999, the unleashing of private sector housing served as the catalyst for the rich diversity of housing design that flourishes in and around China's big cities. China's housing epitomizes the building revolution in this period.

This chapter is written jointly by Charlie Xue and Chen Xi.

CHAPTER SIX

FORM FOLLOWS POLICY:
THE EVOLUTION OF CHINA'S HOUSING

The previous five chapters extend the discussions in various architectural discourses of macro problems (Chapters One, Two, and Three) and macro-scale (Chapters Four and Five). This chapter concerns a building type: housing. Housing is a problem not only of building design but also of social and economic significance. From 1980 up to today, Chinese city-dwellers have seen their living and housing standards dramatically upgraded, and housing prices skyrocket. China's housing is, no doubt, the epitome of the building revolution in this period.

In a country with a "socialist" dictatorship, a planned economy, and a large population, the physical planning of housing property development is closely linked with the policies of the State. This chapter gives an overview of the evolution of housing planning and design in China since 1978, examining the relationship between physical planning and government policies, which, though intangible, have an enormous effect on housing. The first part primarily describes the planning of housing estates from 1978 to 1990. After the commercialization of housing in China, housing design gained momentum in both the public and private sectors. This situation is discussed in the second part of the chapter. The third part interprets the new phenomenon after 1998, when the state-sponsored system of allocating housing was essentially eliminated. The final part of the chapter is a predictive look at the future and suggests what might lie ahead for China's housing industry. The purpose of this chapter is to give some perspective on the physical planning and design of China's housing since 1978 and to show how housing has evolved in a socialist country.

HOUSING FOR WORKERS: 1978 TO 1990

After the Communist Party came to power in 1949, all land became the property of the State. A variety of State enterprises were given the right to use portions of land for specific purposes, and these rights were not transferable.

Compared with broader issues of land policy, the physical development of residential areas had a more direct effect on people's daily lives. The development of residential areas was mainly influenced by land-use policies, the economy, and China's social structure during the decades under consideration.

The year 1978 represents a dividing line in China's political and economic history. After the "leftist" conservative force was removed, the country opened its doors to the outside world, and the elements of a market economy were gradually introduced. During the period from 1949 to 1978, housing estates of around 500 million sq. m. GFA were completed throughout the country, a figure that is modest in scale when weighed against a population of 900 million (Zhao and Kai 1999). The country was dominated by the planned economy and welfare policy. Residents in towns were ensured of having a bed and a roof over their heads, although living standards were low.

The year 1978 started to see the operation of a market economy along with the planned economy. The construction work carried out in the following years seemed to merely fill the enormous gap that had been left in the previous decades. Investments from the government and from several large employers increased rapidly, as did the volume of construction and living space per capita in towns.

Evolution of Planning of Residential Areas

As the amount of construction increased, the design and regulations of housing estates underwent tremendous changes. Several residential design guidelines reflected this evolution in housing design; for example, *The Economic Index Guidelines for Housing Design* and *The Housing Regulations for Housing Design* (GBJ986). Various provinces and cities also created their own regulations.

Before 1978, the development of residential areas was influenced by the national planned economy, the housing allocation system, and even political ideology. During this period, housing development and the physical form of housing was identical across the country. Planning and building standards were continuously modified, along with the policies.

In the early 1950s, residential areas (usually called "workers' new villages") adopted the "neighborhood" theory. Primary schools and retail outlets were arranged inside the estate. Buildings were usually two to three stories high, similar to courtyard houses, and were organized in groups (Figure 6.1). In the mid-1950s, as projects made possible by the support of the Soviet Union were implemented, the Soviet mode of planning was introduced to housing estates: residential areas and street blocks were combined. Such street blocks were usually 5 to 6 ha, enclosed on four sides, and included a few public buildings (Figure 6.2). The internal courtyards of the estates were usually spacious, had ample greenery, and were free from external disturbances. However, the symmetrical and formal composition plan was achieved at the expense of sunshine and ventilation for some housing units.

For example, in the 1950s, the Bai Wan Zhuang Residential Area of Beijing adopted a planned mode of double peripheral blocks. The central public green area of 19 ha was surrounded by six groups of double peripheral blocks. The housing buildings were three stories high. The enclosed courtyard was divided into streets. It was a quiet environment, but the double layers of building blocks created dead corners and shadows. The internal zigzag arrangement of building groups made it difficult for residents to find their way. The low density was also unsuitable for Chinese cities, whose large populations put continual pressure on the already overstretched supply of land.

Figure 6.1 Early houses in Shanghai, (a) Caoyang Residential Area, Shanghai, 1953, (b) Worker's house of 1960s, photographed in 2004

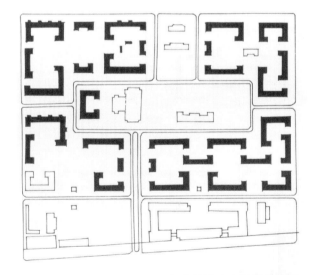

北京棉纺厂生活区总平面

Figure 6.2 Master plan of living quarters, Beijing Cotton Textile Plant, 1950s

In the late 1950s, residential areas were built; these were typically 10 ha in area and comprised two structures, a residential area and an internal cluster. The latter included a kindergarten and a residents' committee (a kind of autonomous semi-government, semi-citizen organization). The Hepingli Residential Area of Beijing is an example (Figure 6.3). In the 1960s, the street was usually formed first, followed by the next stage, the block. A main street appeared in the middle of the residential area, with shops, restaurants, hotels, and theaters on both sides, which created a lively scene. After 1962, based on lessons learned from such successful residential areas, planning was adjusted to accommodate various types of grouping, open space design, new relationships between high-density and low-density, the inclusion of green space, phased construction, and full utilization of the land (Chen and Zhao 1999).

After 1978, increasing numbers of residential areas were built. The open-door policy called for higher living standards; hence, a more systematic method of planning, design, construction, and management was adopted, using a tripartite structure of district, residential area, and block group. The projects featured central green space, a hierarchy of roads, and clearly defined zoning. This practice lasted until the 1990s. These estates, ranging from 10 to 35 ha in area, had good support facilities, such as schools, shops, and entertainment. Examples such as the Jinsong district of Beijing (Figure 6.4) and the Quyang district in Shanghai represent the achievements of residential development in this period. The blocks typically face north-south and are adequately spaced to allow for sunshine, but because of their dreary uniformity are more like military barracks than places to live. In the 1980s, criticism of their dullness mounted throughout the country, as evidenced by the newspaper reports and professional journals from those years.

During this period, the government shifted its attention to the national economy and people's standard of living, issuing a series of new policies for the construction of residential areas. Attention was given to several facets. One was the more methodical planning of infrastructure and support facilities such as schools, retail outlets, and other conveniences, in order to improve functionality. The second was a greater concern for spatial diversity and the richness of the residential areas. The third was the enhancement of the living environment, whether this meant increasing the floor area per person per unit or implementing improvements at a macroscopic level.

(b)

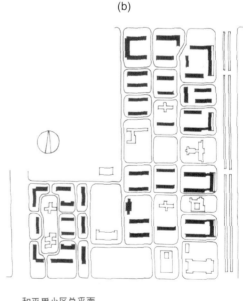

和平里小区总平面

Figure 6.3 He-ping-li Residential Area, Beijing, late 1950s to early 1960s, (a), (c) House building, (b) Block plan

(a)

(c)

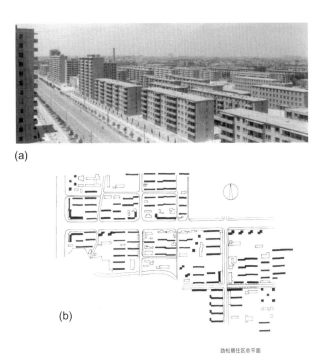

(a)

(b)

Figure 6.4 Jinsong district, Beijing, 1978, (a) Bird's eye view, (b) Block plan

(a)

住宅建筑
保留建筑
公共建筑
绿　地

(b)

(c)

Figure 6.5 Examples of early 1980s housing, (a) Master layout plan of Yanzhishan Residential Area, Jinan, Shandong Province, (b) Yanzhishan housing, (c) Housing of 1980s in Hangzhou, Zhejinag Province, photographed in 2001. After twenty years, most residential areas suffer from poor maintenance.

Beginning in the mid-1980s, various provinces started to promote "sample residential areas" as showcases for the rest of the development. These areas usually stood out in their environmental friendliness, superior spatial organization, safety and security, the quality and reliability of their essential services, and their location within a pleasant landscape. Representative works include Qing Yuan Xinchun in Wuxi, the Yanzhishan Residential Area of Jinan (Figure 6.5), and Chuanfu Xinchun in Tianjin. These projects were cited by the Ministry of Construction as showcase examples of housing in south, north, and central China. New housing developments were urged to learn from these successful models.

During the development of these residential areas, the facilities and services that have come to form an essential element of today's housing estates made their debut. In the transitional process from the old planned economy to the new market economy, the service industry adopted the functions and procedures of the market economy. A variety of commercial services were increasingly seen in the housing property sector. In addition, more attention was paid to the value of land and its potential to generate revenue. The original courtyard wall that formerly defined the periphery of residential areas was replaced by two-story high retail buildings, which served the community and generated commercial profits.

The Evolution of Housing Types

Compared with the planning of residential areas, the physical construction of housing has been more restricted by national policies. The earlier system that provided housing for the employees of state-owned companies or civil servants placed strict controls on housing standards, including floor areas, materials used, layout, view, and environment. Building design for housing during this period was almost identical throughout the country and had little relationship to local, traditional, or vernacular characteristics.

Beginning in the early 1950s, residential building design itself underwent a series of evolutionary changes; most housing blocks in that era were three-story-high wood and brick load-bearing structures with pitched roofs and little use of reinforced concrete (see Figure 6.1). In the mid-1950s, the Soviet Union was used as the model in housing design. The living room was replaced by an internal corridor, resulting in more rooms and improved kitchen and washroom facilities. The typical plan usually included a staircase, three units, and five bays (structural spans) in the front (Figure 6.6). To conserve land, larger depth and smaller bay width was encouraged. But these kinds of unit were usually shared by two or more households, which increased inconvenience.

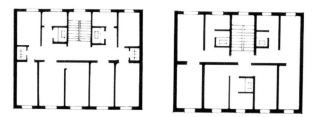

Figure 6.6 Typical house plan in the 1950s and 1960s

In the 1960s, when the Chinese government's "design revolution" movement prevailed (the purpose of which was to use fewer materials, because of the weak economy), the size of housing units, kitchens, and washrooms were reduced, and the technology of the shallow foundation and thin wall was adopted. (In 1957, in the same spirit, China had initiated a national movement against waste.) The national planning committee promulgated *Several Regulations Concerning the Housing Economic Index*, which specified that the usable area of each household must not exceed 18 sq m. Narrow and small, these units had low ceilings and thin walls. In 1965, extolling the virtues of "industrial production first and comfort of living

second" (Zou 2001), housing blocks were built that had a GFA of 32 to 34 sq m per home, only simple doors and windows, no screens on the windows, and no heating or private bathrooms. Because of their excessively shabby character, the housing blocks of this period were soon demolished.

After 1978, housing types were diversified, and several design competitions were held throughout the country. At the same time, issues of local identity, plan and layout, building materials and aesthetics were thoroughly studied. On October 20, 1978, China's patriarch, Deng Xiaoping, visited several housing estates in Qiansanmen in Beijing and declared: "housing design should pursue a rational layout, add usable floor area and pay more attention to the convenience of the residents. If possible, showers and other facilities should be installed, internal decor should be pleasant, and more new light-weight materials should be used in order to lower building costs." Deng's visit and his words were publicized on the front page of the *Beijing Daily* the following day. Beijing's municipal government and construction committee immediately issued an official memorandum to implement Deng's instructions and improve housing design standards. The Beijing Institute of Architectural Design subsequently published technical standards for the city, "Beijing Housing 1980–1981" (Figure 6.7).

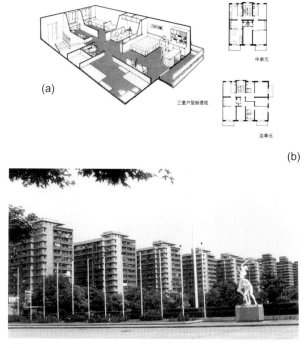

Figure 6.7 Housing in early 1980s, (a) House plan featuring a square hall, 1980, (b) Slab housing in Shanghai, 1980

After 1979, the Ministry of Construction held several national housing design competitions that reflected the living styles and technical standards of the time. In the urban housing design competition held in 1979, a compact design of one staircase for each two housing units appeared. Within each housing unit, the narrow corridor gradually evolved into a square hall, and then a hall with natural lighting (Figure 6.8). Standardization and diversity were embodied in a number of different structural systems, modules, and parameters in implementing industrialization.

(a)

(b)

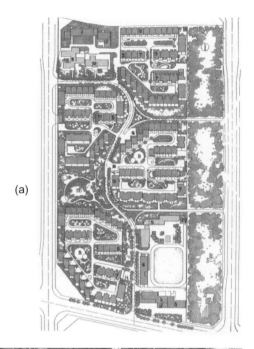

(a)

Figure 6.8　Housing in late 1980s, (a) Housing plan featuring a large hall and small bedrooms, (b) Staff quarters, Tsinghua University, 1987

Bricks and blocks were the main building and load-bearing materials used in China at this time. In 1984, a housing design competition for this category was held by the Ministry of Construction. Interior decoration, kitchen and washroom facilities, partitions, and furniture were standardized to accommodate the increasing industrialization and to speed up the pace of construction. Bay width was used as the basic module for creating different housing forms: garden, cascading, courtyard, and blocks. Using bricks and blocks as the main materials, mostly low-rise, high-density housing blocks were built.

In the 1987 housing design competition, big halls and small bedrooms became the prevailing form. There was also more emphasis on kitchen and washroom design (Figure 6.9).

(b)

(c)

Figure 6.9　Enjili Residential Area, Beijing, 1993, (a) Plan, (b) and (c) Housing buildings

ALONG TWIN TRACKS: 1990 TO 1998

In 1987, in the Shenzhen Special Economic Zone, the Chinese government auctioned off its very first piece of land. And in 1988, the Seventh National People's Congress passed a highly significant amendment to the Constitution of the People's Republic of China, permitting the leasing of government land (Xue 1999).

Each province or city has its own National Land Bureau and leases out land according to a quota. A city will propose the class, usage, duration, and other conditions for leased land. For example, urban land in Shanghai is divided into ten classes according to location. The different types of building determine the different land prices. The highest land price is for land destined for commercial developments or hotels, the second highest is for private housing, and the third highest is for land designated for cultural and entertainment purposes (Xue 1999).

The reforms to China's housing system began in the mid-1980s in a number of cities across the country. Before this time, Chinese citizens had been dependent upon the State through their employer to provide them with housing. Salaries were very low; in turn, employees received a housing unit. Because of the advent of a free market economy, this system of the employer providing housing to employees was abandoned. Once this arrangement was broken, an individual could buy a house in the open market, and was no longer bound to the State-sponsored housing allocation system. The percentage of salary held by the employer was now credited directly to the employee and could be used for borrowing money from a bank to purchase a house. The new system released the government from the responsibility and burden of supplying housing to China's citizens and of building millions of square meters of housing every year. Despite the new system, the majority of residents could not afford housing. The ratio between the price of housing and annual average income hovered at 20:1 in the mid-1990s (Xue and Xin 1992; Xue 1999).

After the 1990s, urban housing construction in China boomed (see Table 6.1). In the late 1980s, the annual figure for completed construction was around 200 million sq m GFA. This figure reached 500 million in 1999 and 540 million in 2001. The living space per capita in cities and towns was around 9.3 sq m (National Statistics Bureau 1998).

The decade from 1990 to 2000 marks a transitional period in China's urban housing revolution. The changes that took place were reflected in a number of ways.

Improved Standards

The increased number of housing developments being built improved the living standard of China's citizens. In Shanghai, for example, the living space of 3 to 4 sq m per person in 1980 was increased to 10 sq m in 1990; as a result, the original *Housing Design Regulations* became outdated in the 1990s. Beginning in 1994, cities like Beijing, Tianjin, Shanghai, and Guangzhou began to publish their own local regulations. In 1996, eleven institutions, led by the China Research Institute of Building Technology, enacted a set of new *Housing Design Regulations*, based on a series of investigations into the housing industry in China.

Compared with the old regulations, the new regulations made more sensible and detailed suggestions concerning the floor area of standard units, kitchen and washroom facilities, elevators, location of meters, and the appropriate use of pitched roofs. For example, the living room (hall) is suggested in the new housing design; the floor areas of various rooms increase one third to double of their original size (Li 1999, 11).

Implementing Housing at the "Affluent" Level

Since 1990, research studies such as "Affluent Housing in Chinese Cities" and "Housing Science and Engineering in the year 2000" have greatly improved the planning and design standards of urban housing (Ministry of Construction, *Planning and Design Guidelines for a Sample Residential Area in 2000 for Affluent Housing Engineering*). Quality of living, behavior, and habits of end users were the main concerns of housing design in this period. Living conditions, housing types, and property management received emphasis. The principles of the new guidelines are summarized as follows:

(1) *Community*: Before 1990, the concept of community was not well developed in China, but it now became a concept used to nurture a new kind of culture and sense of belonging; new social and human relationships were consciously created.

(2) *Diversity*: The earlier planning structure of district, residential area, building group, and housing block was diversified in order to create new types of function that would enhance standards of living.

(3) *Sustainability*: The value and importance of this principle at all levels and areas of application was reaffirmed, special attention being paid to conservation

(a)

(b)

Figure 6.10 Wangjing Residential Area, Beijing, 1997

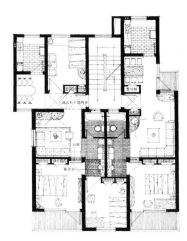

Figure 6.11 Plan of an entry scheme in a housing design competition, 1991

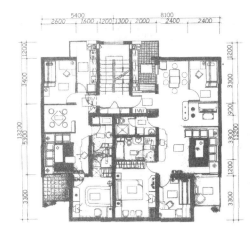

Figure 6.12 Entry design for "China's Housing in the Twenty-first Century," 1998

and recycling. Flexibility and adaptability were encouraged.

(4) *Property Management*: Housing planning took into account property service and management, including surveillance, waste removal, and other essential services, so that convenience and efficiency would become a design feature of every housing property.

Twenty-two pilot projects conforming to the new planning guidelines were built in Chinese cities, including the Enjili Area of Beijing (Figure 6.10), the Kangle Area of Shanghai, the Sanyuan Area of Suzhou, the Hongmei Area of Changzhou, the Xihuili Area of Wuxi, and the Mijiaqiao Area of Xi'an.

In 1997, several built residential areas were recognized with "Design Across the Centuries" awards, including Zhonghuang Square and the Wanli Area of Shanghai, Taihu Lake Garden in Wuxi, the Wangjin Area of Beijing, and the Jinxiu Area of Dalian (Figure 6.11).

Design Competitions and Design Guidelines

The 1991 housing design competition reflected a change in emphasis from quantity to quality. The use of new building materials, the more complete utilization of land

and space, and comfort and safety concerns were addressed in the competition entries, as were headroom variations combing high and low ceilings, duplex space, and pitched roof designs (Figure 6.12).

A design competition with the theme "China's Housing in the Twenty-first Century" was held in 1998. The submissions addressed various design issues popular at the time; for example, improving basic living comfort (plan dimensions, views, lighting, ventilation, sunshine); sustainability (open plan, flexible partitions, alternative interiors in the same plan); kitchen and washroom design; conservation of natural resources; deep building and reduced bay width; duplex units; the use of high-efficiency thermal insulation in external walls; new technology and "intelligent" homes (access Internet, video tele-communications, electronic monitoring, automatically controlled air-conditioning systems, automatic metering); and ecology (recycled water systems, garbage sorting and disposal, solar heating, recycling of rain water, green space).

THE MARKET DOMINATES AND DESIGN DIVERSIFIES: 1998 TO THE PRESENT

In May 1998, the government promulgated an inspection index for residential areas, which gave a quantitative standard of measurement. Also in 1998, the government completely stopped the earlier practice of allocating housing units as a kind of welfare, a practice in China for forty-eight years. Employers combined housing allowances with salaries; as a result, end users now possessed purchasing power and had more types of housing to choose from in the burgeoning housing market. The housing reform that started in the mid-1980s now saw its fruits.

The commercialization of housing raised new issues for China. To a great extent, large-scale development solved China's housing problems, but the rapid increase in the population and expanding urbanization put even more pressure on housing quantity. For example, as a result of the new changes, living space per capita was increased from 4 sq m to 15 to 30 sq m. China had to build more housing to satisfy this demand. Also, when end users purchase flats with money out of their own pockets, they inevitably have higher expectations. The keen market competition has encouraged developers to be more resourceful and creative in attracting buyers.

The Southern Enclave

Because of the shift to a market economy, the Chinese government's role has changed from that of supreme arbiter to responsive facilitator and supervisor in matters of housing — commands have been replaced by guiding principles. Some provinces and areas have fully grasped the opportunities presented by this new situation and have nurtured a prosperous property market; the Pearl River Delta in southern China is one excellent example.

Even before 1998, when Shanghai, Beijing, Guangzhou, and other cities might have been required to follow the instructions of the central government through the Ministry of Construction, a number of high-quality garden housing projects sprouted up in the Pearl River Delta. Retired Hong Kong people were the market. These garden housing estates proliferated throughout second-tier cities such as Dongguan, Zhongshan, Panyu, and others. Low-rise (two to three stories) and mid-rise (five to six stories) buildings are the norm; the estates are surrounded by exuberant gardens, luxurious clubhouses, and delicate artificial botanic environments, and are usually situated in 60 or more hectares. Most Hong Kong people suffer from the stress caused by high density and the hectic pace and high-priced environment of their small city. Such retreats, usually available at one-tenth of Hong Kong's housing prices, hold a great attraction for Hong Kong people.

These estates were financed by Hong Kong capitalists or joint ventures between Hong Kong and China, designed by Hong Kong or international architects, and managed according to the Hong Kong model, often labeled "star-hotel-style management." As the investment is from outside mainland China, the estates are exempted from certain procedures and regulations. These kinds of garden estate represent a unique southern Chinese housing style and have really set an example for the whole country. After the success of their sales, the developers usually go on to other fields, such as golf courses, property management, nurseries, international schools, entertainment, restaurants, building materials, or even zoos and theme parks. Renowned examples are Pit Gui Yuan in Panyu (Figure 6.13), Agile Garden in Zhongshan, Horizon Cove in Zhuhai, Le Parc in Shenzhen, and New World Garden and New Babylon Garden in Dongguan.

Pit Gui Yuan is one of the earliest large-scale housing estates in the Pearl River Delta, developed by a consortium from Guangzhou and designed by various design institutes in China. The first estate is located about 50 km from Guangzhou, and the several phases of development have expanded the estate from four to five ha. to more than ten ha. The estate includes low-rise single-family houses, townhouses, multi-story (five to six stories) flats and middle-rise and high-rise housing (twelve stories). There are bus terminals as well as several all-inclusive clubhouses, each of which is 2,000 to 3,000 sq m in area, with parks, fountains, hotels, restaurants, library, swimming pools, bowling alleys, and golf course. After ten years of expansion since 1992, Pit Gui Yuan has developed more than ten large estates in Shunde and Guangzhou, with more than 100,000 residential units, all villa and low-rise types. The consortium built kindergartens, schools, colleges, hospitals, and high-class

(a)

(b)

(c)

Figure 6.13 Pit Gui Yuan in Panyu, Guangdong Province, 1992–2000, (a) Phase III of the planning, (b) Single family housing, (c) Apartment housing

hotels in its own estates and tried to attract people from various age groups. It hired more than 30,000 employees, including in-house architects and planners, and its permanent exhibition room opens at busy Nathan Road in Hong Kong.

As a competitor of Pit Gui Yuan, Agile Garden originated in Zhongshan. It started to extend its influence to the central city of Guangzhou in 1998. Ten large estates of more than 70 ha were developed, from Guangzhou to Zhongshan, which house 300,000 people, mostly from Hong Kong. The developer tried to position the estates at an international level and with good taste. Single-family houses, row houses, apartments, clubhouse, and golf courses are located in scenic areas, on the west side of the Pearl River (Figure 6.14).

Further south, Zhuhai is another town that is enhancing its tranquil living environment to attract people from its crowded neighbor, Macau. Zhuai's 40-km -long

Figure 6.14 Agile Garden, advertisement in Hong Kong newspaper, (*Singtao Daily*, August 7, 2004)

waterfront promenade guarantees an open view for the high-rises and low houses facing the sea. Horizon Cove in Zhuhai is situated near the sea, its main façade extending along Jing Tang Road. The clubhouse, swimming pool, and artificial stream are arranged in the center, and low-rise and high-rise housing blocks surround the public area

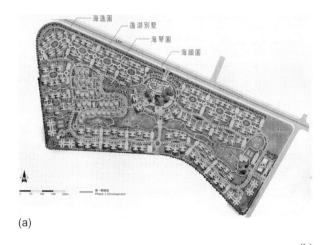

(a)

(b)

Figure 6.15 Horizon Cove, Zhuhai, 2002, (a) Master layout plan, (b) Typical house plan

on four sides. A commercial center, primary schools, and tennis courts have been built on the periphery. Units in Horizon Cove were being sold by the Hong Kong developer Hutchison Whampoa in 2003 while other phases were still under construction (Figure 6.15).

Because of its proximity to Hong Kong, Shenzhen was once a magnet that attracted capital and talented people from all over China, especially in the 1980s before Shanghai's rise. Shenzhen's housing design was influenced both by Hong Kong and the Mainland. The housing estates, with parking underneath and gardens above, first appeared in the city and were soon copied in other cities. The housing estates in Huaqiao Cheng enjoy the breeze and natural scenes of the mangrove forest in Hong Kong. The greenery and sculptures are interspersed among the buildings. Le

Parc in Shenzhen is also the work of Hong Kong's Hutchison Whampoa. Within the city, it primarily consists of twenty-two-story high-rise buildings. The existing roads divide the estate into four parts, representing four phases in construction. In addition to the pleasant lawns and fountains in the four parts is a central park and sports-club facility (Figure 6.16).

Facing fierce competition, the developers and designers have to come up with some unique features. New Babylon Garden, designed by Charlie Xue, Li Lin, and Chen Xi, has an innovative design that permits vehicles to reach the door of each home in the six-story high, 336-unit housing complex (Figure 6.17).

As the target market for most of these estates is wealthy people in Hong Kong, Taiwan, and the Mainland, the estates are located near expressways, railways, or harbors. In general, a one-way trip from Hong Kong, Shenzhen, or Guangzhou to these estates takes one-and-a-half to two hours, making daily commuting almost impossible. Consequently, these large and luxurious housing estates remain empty on most working days and are even sparsely populated on weekends. They are only crowded during long holidays, such as Chinese New Year, Easter, and Christmas. Suburban living seems to be unable to ease the housing shortage in cities.

As a result of the rise of Shanghai, the glamour of the Pearl River Delta faded. Shanghai and other cities showcased the new ideas of housing design after the "southern enclave." In Pudong, Shanghai, several estates have introduced the concept of a large artificial lake within the project. Housing blocks are surrounded by water. The developers have tried to create a more idyllic atmosphere, but this kind of design may bring problems and higher maintenance costs. In the original west suburb of Shanghai, villas of single-family houses are everywhere, several properties even asking for several million US dollars for a house (Figures 6.18 & 6.19).

Steven Holl's design of Liusha Peninsula Development in Nanning, Guangxi Province, created a new lifestyle in a muddy flat plateau. The low-scale housing is covered with grass, aiming for a maximum porosity with natural ventilation and shading. Precast concrete sections with 50 percent wall and 50 percent window are the basic structural elements forming porous architecture. Hybrid buildings of several stories (with a defined cubic envelop of 60 by 60 by 60 m) yield rich urban experiences with multiple functions and views over the garden city. The master plan allows for the eventual construction of seven mountain buildings (Figure 6.20).

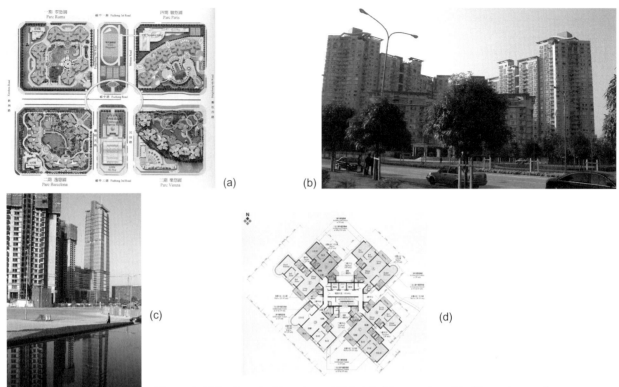

Figure 6.16 Le Parc in Shenzhen, 2003, (a) Master plan, (b) Phase I seen from cross the street, (c) Phase II in construction, (d) Typical floor plan

Figure 6.17 Creative design in the Pearl River Delta, (a) and (b) Charlie Xue and Li Lin, New Babylon Garden in Dongguan, Guangdong, 2002, (c) and (d) Fei Xiaohua, Hillside Sea Cabana, Shenzhen, 2004

Figure 6.18 Housing estates in the south, 2003, (a) Housing blocks overlooking Century Park, Pudong, (b) Apartment downtown, Shanghai, (c) Interior of an apartment, Shanghai, (d) Housing estate in Hangzhou

Figure 6.19 Xiang Bingren, Jiangning Residential Area, Nanjing, 2004

The foregoing examples are only a few of the thousands of such estates built recently in southern and northern China. They epitomize the rapid increase in the standard of living in China and the housing demands that have been created as a result. Newspapers in China are full of eye-catching advertisements that provide new concepts and definitions of housing.

Management, Construction Quality, and Use of New Materials and Technology

Before the 1980s, housing estates were managed by residents' committees, a semi-government, semi-civil organization. The Hong Kong-style management company and owners' association were first imported to Shenzhen and Guangzhou, gradually spreading to the rest of the country. Security technologies, centralized control, automatic metering, and home telecommunications were gradually adopted.

In China, the quality of construction work is inspected and assessed by government supervisory organizations in accordance with various national, provincial, and municipal assessment standards; for example, GBJ301-88. For projects undertaken by the central government and its various ministries, authorized inspection stations assess the quality, whereas non-government projects are examined and assessed by local inspection stations. By means of a variety of evaluation methods, worthy projects are awarded a status of "excellent." This award system exists at the municipal, provincial, and national levels, and its highly touted "selection of excellent projects." Since the 1980s, an inspection system for construction work has also been implemented, because the lifespan of a building is related to the quality of its construction. In 1997, the passing rate for housing construction projects was around 92 percent. However, the number of projects deemed "excellent" remained low.

Figure 6.20 Steven Holl, Liusha Peninsula Development, Nanning, 2002

Advances in science and technology have improved the quality of housing in China. The effects of industrialization can be observed in the changes that have been made to existing standards, the greater use of prefabricated products, fewer on-site operations and "wet work," reduced labor-intensive building methods and increased productivity, and thus significantly shortened building completion times.

In building structure, a common approach is to use big space for the open design, later adding flexible partitions, shear wall structures, new types of block structure, big spans, pre-stressed forms, and new wall materials. A research group at Shanghai's Tongji University designed a number of experimental, twenty-story buildings using lightweight steel and new wall materials. Several of these designs were successfully built in Shanghai.

China is a vast country stretching almost 4200 km north to south and 5000 km east to west. Because of its varied climatic and geographical features, each province and city wrestles with its own problems and challenges. Whether to keep the heat in or out depends on where one lives in China. In northern China, the outer insulating wall is of critical importance. External and internal insulation systems, door and window strips and insulation, heating and temperature controls, central heating and central hot water systems, cooling-heating-hot water systems, local heating, and passive solar technology have all been researched in China's various provinces.

Kitchens and washrooms have also stimulated the interest of researchers, who have explored "whole box" prefabricated technology and novel ways of eliminating fumes and smoke. Methods for optimizing the use of elevators have also been studied; for example, installing simple elevators in old multistory (6-7 stories) housing.

In 2000, the Chinese government banned the use of clay bricks, to conserve agricultural land, thus eliminating this traditional building material that has been a staple of Chinese building for the past 3000 years.

PROBLEMS AND PROSPECTS

The above sections briefly review the evolution of China's housing design and planning design in the last quarter of the twentieth century. It is obvious that changes in the physical form of housing in China followed changes in national policy.

However, the close relationship between national policies and housing changed with the new circumstances created by the market economy. China's national policies no longer affect the physical planning as powerfully as before. Market conditions now lead and inspire new designs. Since 1997, housing development and planning have remained vigorous, although many challenges exist. These are summarized in the following section.

The Government's Role as Facilitator

In a hard-driving market economy, the government may lack the expertise or will to be an effective supervisor or facilitator in formulating and implementing policies and guidelines for development. Stimulated by the huge profits to be reaped, developers in China have gone overboard in building luxurious housing properties, glutting the market. At the same time, low-income residents have suffered from a lack of proper housing, an imbalance that can cause instability within a society (Fang 2000).

A number of surveys have determined that most units that remain unsold within these sumptuous compounds are the larger-sized and higher-priced ones. These "garden mansions" and "palaces" are ubiquitous in China, glamorously trumpeted in full-page advertisements in newspapers and glossy magazines and conspicuously sprinkled along major thoroughfares or nestled idyllically in remote suburbs. At the same time, the supply of low-cost and more modest housing is far from adequate. In 2001, the sale of housing units across China was sluggish and the vacancy rate climbed; there was a vacancy increase of 11 million sq m in GFA (representing more than 1 million flats) as the result of a building surplus and declining sales (National Statistic Bureau, *December Index of Housing in the Country* 2001). In Beijing, tens of thousands of people lined up for low-cost housing, but large numbers of luxurious housing units stood empty. Many people demanded to know if these expensive housing properties could be converted to low-cost homes (http://www.realestate.gov.cn/default.asp, July 2002). The government needs to better regulate and control investment from the private sector. A more balanced and mature property market is desperately needed.

The government should have foreseen the problem and taken action sooner. In the autumn of 2002, it sponsored a national low-cost housing design competition. Clearly, the ratio between low-, middle- and high-cost housing needs to be adjusted.

Low-income groups receive subsidies from the government and constitute the majority of people in society with housing needs. The policies of the government can include giving raw land to developers so that they can build low-cost housing for low-income people, reducing developers' taxes and controlling housing prices and profits. The challenge for developers is to construct cost-effective low-income housing that will generate sufficient profit for them, so that they will no longer be reluctant partners in the process.

Chapter Four mentions the land acquisition problem and the grabbing of inner city land. The city centers are occupied by the high-profit property of glamorous housing or office blocks, whereas the underprivileged class who originally lived in the old city area is forced to move to the remote periphery where the infrastructure and service fabric are inadequate. Most cases related to the land disputes reveal the developers are in collusion with the local government. In this regard, the government no longer acts as supervisor or facilitator but is part of a commercially criminal group.

Short-sighted Development

Despite the problems previously noted, most housing estates in China are quite beautiful and of exceptional quality, although sometimes too majestic for housing estates. Housing design should also be visionary, so that what is built can accommodate changes that may take place 50 or 100 years in the future. This is quite a rigorous requirement for housing design but serves the interests of end users. As expected, most estate and housing designs are lacking in this regard.

The rampant proliferation of luxurious housing has swallowed up large amounts of high-yield agricultural land surrounding China's cities. In the 1990s, Guangdong,

Jiangsu, and other coastal provinces lost 10,000–20,000 ha annually of agricultural land (Zheng 2002; Xue 1999). Is 100–200 sq m of floor space per household suitable for a country with such an enormous population and a severe shortage of agricultural land? In the course of China's development, environmental and ecological issues have also been ruthlessly ignored; natural topographical contours and coastal lines have been devastated by the recent construction of high-priced "ocean view" housing estates, examples of which can be seen in the cities of Yantai, Qingdao, and numerous other coastal areas.

Another problem brought by the housing revolution in China is that housing estates were originally occupied by people who worked for the same company or institution, but they now comprise people from the same social class or income bracket. Different districts and housing estates reflect the country's social disparities, which are more extreme in contemporary China. Therefore, residential estates composed of a number of social classes are more desirable, as they provide a better community mix. Experiments of this nature have been carried out in the United States and Hong Kong, but the residents of these projects often resist the ideal social model, especially high-income earners who worry that their community might become "contaminated" and their property devalued. Improving the quality of the living environment in low-income residential areas remains an imperative.

China's transition from a planned economy to a market economy has resulted in unprecedented changes in housing, including planning, design, construction, and standards. However, the country still has an enormous amount of work to do, to effectively house its growing population of urban residents.

Part III

Architects and Creations

Portraits of Chinese Architects

Experimental Architecture: The Rising of the Younger Generation

Behind the Building Revolution: Private Practice Unleashed

China is proud of its splendid history and ancient buildings, yet who designed these venerable relics remains unknown. Architecture as a profession only emerged in the twentieth century when foreign firms practiced in China's coastal cities and the first batch of Chinese students graduated from Western universities, becoming the first generation of architects in China. However, for a period, Chinese architects failed to enjoy the status they deserved. After 1978, when people became free to think for themselves, the creativity of designers was stimulated, "creation" replacing the term "design" in many instances. As a group, architects flourished in such fertile times. Although materials and investments were scarce by Western standards, China's architects used their talents to create high-quality work within strict physical limitations. They enjoyed the respect of society and the admiration of their students and peers. "Chinese," indigenous, *genius loci*, poetic, and appropriate technology were the goals they pursued. However, when they were eventually recognized, most were in their sixties or seventies.

CHAPTER SEVEN

PORTRAITS OF CHINESE ARCHITECTS

The colorful and diversified performance of Chinese architecture, described in the previous chapters, is propelled by the numerous hands of building professionals, known and unknown. This chapter highlights a group of architects who exerted their influence mainly in the last two decades of the twentieth century.

Because of its long feudal history, China has always been considered a country with a rich architectural heritage, though it had few well-known designers. Architecture as a profession began in China around 1920, when a group of young people returned to the country after studying architecture in the United States, the United Kingdom, Germany, and Japan. Private practices sprung up in the major coastal cities. Zhuang Jun, Yang Tingpao, Zhao Shen, Tong Jun, Tung Dayou, Zhu Bing, Fan Wenzhao and H.S. Luke — the first generation of Chinese architects — were either directors or design chiefs of firms in Shanghai or Nanjing. Some of them later immigrated to Hong Kong.

After the Communist takeover in 1949, private practices were gradually replaced by "public and private joint ventures." The first state-owned design institute was established by the Ministry of Building Engineering in the 1950s, and Zhuang Jun, who graduated from the University of Illinois at Urbana-Champaign in 1914, was appointed the first engineer-in-chief (Xue 1999).

All architects at that time belonged to a particular design institute. Faithful to the principles of Marxism, "From everyone according to his capacities; to everyone according to his needs," they were cogs in a national machine and contributed to the construction of the socialist edifice.

In the 1950s and 1960s, the pursuit of individualized architectural form was considered a "crime" in architectural design in a country that was enduring economic hardship and whose leaders repeatedly criticized "capitalist ideology." Those who had graduated from overseas institutions or from the few architectural schools that existed in China before 1949 felt extremely uncomfortable having to work in such a dogmatic and repressive political atmosphere.

As noted in Chapter One, an ill-conceived "design revolution" was launched in 1964, based on the principle of frugality. Starting in 1966, numerous design institutes throughout China were dismantled and engineers and architects sent to rural areas for "re-education." Design activities fell drastically during this period. In general, little construction work was completed before 1980, compared with China's enormous population; dismissed and ignored, the architect's role was a far from satisfactory one.

CELEBRATED CHINESE ARCHITECTS AND THEIR WORKS

After the open-door policy was implemented, the volume of construction in China increased significantly. People's minds were unshackled and they became free to think in new and imaginative ways. In a society that was taking the first steps toward a market economy, people began to be aware that architecture could not only create pleasing and memorable designs but also construct buildings that function reasonably well within a limited budget.

In the 1980s, **Yang Tingbao** (1900–83) and **Dai Nianchi** (1920–91) still played a leading role in China's architectural design. But the torch was gradually passed to the generation that graduated after 1949. These new designers came to occupy center stage, following the reforms to the old political system.

Among them, **Qi Kang** (b. 1931) is a notable and outstanding example. He graduated from Nanjing Institute of Technology (now Southeast University) in 1952, where he was a student and assistant to Professor Yang Tingbao. Qi drew inspiration from his prolific drawings and extensive travels. His main design work started in the 1970s; by 2000, Qi had become one of the most influential architects in China, designing more than thirty museums, art galleries, and memorial halls, and writing more than twenty books and hundreds of articles. His writings have been published in France, Germany, Italy, and Japan, countries that have also held exhibitions of his work. Qi's studio, in the Department of Architecture at Southeast University, has attracted a group of energetic and talented young architects and doctoral and master's degree students. In the 1990s, he was elected a Fellow of the China Academy of Science, the highest honor that can be accorded a Chinese architect.

Professor Qi's design for the Memorial Hall of the Japanese Massacre featured an unusual design approach with its use of an asymmetrical layout for the structure, rarely seen in a memorial building.

In a six-week period in December to January 1937–38 in Nanjing in Jiangsu Province, 300,000 Chinese citizens were slaughtered by invading Japanese troops in one of the most barbaric massacres in human history. To commemorate this event, the municipal government of Nanjing decided to build a memorial hall. The excavated bleached bones of the victims inspired Qi Kang to use the entire site rather than a single building to memorialize this atrocity. "Place" and "wall" became vocabularies of this design. The white pebbles covering the major portion of the site symbolize "death"; the grass at the periphery and steps expresses the desire for "life." The subterranean exhibition room of bones is half below ground level, its sunken aspect and low windows creating a coffin-like feeling. The 2-m-high walls at the entrance to the square give visitors the impression of entering a tomb. The irregular 50-m-long "crying" wall with its carved reliefs of the victims leads to the exhibition room that depicts scenes of the massacre. "Wall" in this design has a dual function; it both oppressively encloses the visitor and provides temporary relief when the emotional impact becomes overwhelming. The use of "wall" creates the memorial atmosphere. "Bridge" is also an element that Qi likes to use in memorial buildings. To Qi, it is a kind of transition across zones, the changing of place and meaning. Tangible and intangible "bridges" were designed into this site. While entering the memorial, visitors can see only the sky, but when they arrive at the summit of the entrance, the entire site is in view (Figure 7.1).

Wuyi Mountain Village was a project started in the late 1970s under Professor Yang Tingbao's direction. The village is located in the Wuyi Mountain resort area. The design is based on the principles of low-rise instead of high-rise, scattered instead of gathered, indigenous instead of international.

There are three functional zones in the complex: public, private, and transitional. Connection, separation, high and low, long eaves and tiles on the roof, interior materials and decoration; various vocabularies are fused to form a building complex with a strong southern rural taste. Over the years, the complex has been expanded, and these new additions have been built underground to reduce the aboveground density. The interlocking courtyards are enclosed by colonnades and have streams running through them, creating an intricate maze-like effect reminiscent of traditional Chinese gardens (Figure 7.2).

In 1998, Qi's design for Henan Museum was completed. Located in the heart of China, Henan is the cradle of Chinese civilization. The museum has collected 120,000 artifacts and will expand to 300,000 pieces in another twenty years. Twenty-three exhibition zones are planned. Designers have tried to grasp the essence of the *genius loci* of central China and express it in the plan. The 310 m by 270 m site is at the end of a straight street, which made a symmetrical layout possible. The four functional zones are the main exhibition halls, the storage area for artifacts, the community outreach area, and the building's internal operating facilities, which together have a total GFA of 78,840 sq m. Equipped with central air-conditioning, a security system, automatic fire alarms, a sophisticated power system, and "intelligent" offices, Henan Museum is one of the three largest museums built in China in the last decade of the twentieth century.

The main hall is a pyramid-shaped, 46-m-high all-purpose exhibition room surrounded by auxiliary exhibition buildings that form four small courts. The north part of the main building is connected to the storage area

(a)

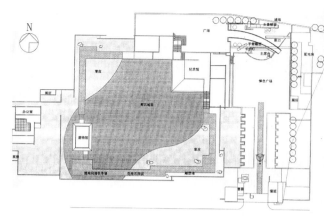

(b)

(c)

(d)

Figure 7.1 Qi Kang, Memorial Hall of Japanese Massacre in Nanjing, (a) Entrance, (b) Site plan, (c) Ground with pebbles, (d) "Crying wall"

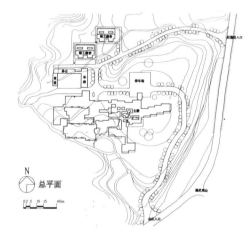

(a)

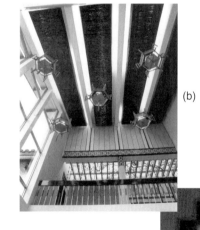

(b)

(c)

(d)

Figure 7.2 Qi Kang, Lai Juqui etc., Wuyi Mountain Village. (a) Site plan, (b) Dining hall, (c) The hotel, (d) Window with a scene

for antiques. The ancient astral relics in the museum inspired the pyramid shape of the square plan. A reverse trapezoid, hollowed out by a circular skylight, is placed on top of the pyramid. The white heads of the nails in the façade symbolize the nails in traditional wooden gates and the constellations in the universe. The spatial truss inside the entrance, and the grand interior space of the lobby convey a contemporary feeling. The main sculpture in the hall is of a gigantic person pushing two elephants, a metaphor for Henan Province and the civilization that originated in central China (Figure 7.3).

In his long practice of architectural design, Qi came to the conclusion that the elements of design should include harmony, picturesque scenery, and creative thinking. To Qi Kang, architects should be educated in culture, technique, and ethics. An architect lacking knowledge of the city will be an imperfect designer; Qi therefore pays attention to urban planning as well as design. Professor Qi is undoubtedly one of China's masters in designing important buildings (Figure 7.4).[1]

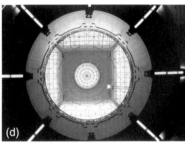

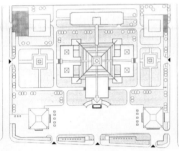

Figure 7.3 Qi Kang, Provincial Museum, Henan, 1999, (a) Professor Qi Kang, (b) Site plan, (c) Museum building, (d) Atrium, looking up, (e) Prelude hall

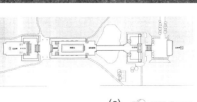

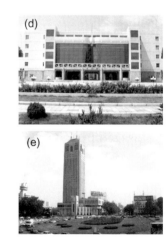

Figure 7.4 Other design works of Professor Qi Kang and his team, (a) Yuhuatai Memorial of Revolutionary Martyrs, (b) Memorial Hall, (c) Site plan of Yuhuatai, (d) Science Building, Nanjing Institute of Aeronautical Engineering, (e) Post office headquarters, Nanjing

Cheng Taining (b. 1935) is another outstanding architect. He has not published as many books and papers as Qi Kang has, but he speaks through his works, which are adored by his colleagues as well as by young architects and students who usually prefer overseas design masters.

In the 1980s, Chinese architecture was strongly influenced by its Western counterparts and by the Chinese classical revival. Where to stand between tradition and the future is the question every architect must face and answer. Cheng Taining has proposed that we "start from where we are and stand on our own two feet."

Cheng Taining is opposed to the use of "national form" and indigenous or local styles in contemporary Chinese architecture, because he believes that reliance on such forms stifles variety in architectural design. To him, traditional and stereotypical Chinese architecture is not worth inheriting. Assimilating the essence of "national form" and using the style of local structures are means to an end rather than ends in themselves. Some elements of traditional buildings, such as details, figures, roofs, and so on, are visible and can be duplicated, transformed, and applied to modern buildings; the use of these elements, if properly incorporated, can result in success. What architects can bring to contemporary architecture is largely something invisible, like philosophy, mood, and concepts of space. Cheng stresses that technology is only a tool of creation and that fine works can be produced in different ways in different periods and places.

What does "standing on our own two feet" imply? The implicit directive here is that architects must consciously train themselves to maximize their strengths and minimize their weaknesses and to speak in their own voice after conducting a rigorous self-examination.

Cheng's design talents were showcased when he completed several projects in Hangzhou, the exquisite capital of Zhejiang Province. As the result of China's generous support of Third World countries, Cheng and his colleagues were given an opportunity to design projects in Africa and to experience and interpret an exotic culture characterized by exuberant forms of social and artistic expression, tribal rituals and fierce primitive energies — a world that was utterly different from the formalism of Chinese society. However, additional promising projects in Africa had to be abandoned because of insufficient investment and the whims of decision-makers in China.

In 1988, Cheng designed the Ghana National Theatre, which includes a 1500-seat audience hall, exhibition center, rehearsal hall and an open theater, with a GFA of 11,000 sq m. The details of both the building and its surroundings were critical factors in the design. Cheng wanted to make the theater a remarkable and unforgettable structure. During the process, the designers felt excited and inspired by the extravagant, exaggerated emotions and mysterious style of Ghanaian dancing, sculpture, and murals. To express the spirit of African art and to highlight the theater's unique characteristics became Cheng's primary goal.

Influenced by the local cultural background, Cheng's design created a dynamic synthesis of boldly powerful and romantically exquisite interior and exterior spaces through the use of three deformed cubes. After its completion in 1992, the theater was enthusiastically received by the Ghanaian people and became a successful contemporary theater equipped with the most advanced technology. In 1994, this design won the Creation Award of the Architectural Society of China and the National Perfect Design Award of the Ministry of Construction in China (Figure 7.5).

In the 1980s, Cheng designed Dragon Hotel, a project that established his reputation throughout China. Dragon Hotel is a 40,000 sq m four-star hotel located in the idyllic West Lake district of China. The relationship between the building and its scenic location was undoubtedly an important aspect of the design. The functional requirements of such a hotel can also be complex. The consideration of these two aspects shaped the initial design.

The design eschews the usual style of typical large and mid-sized hotels, adopting instead a unique compositional style similar to the technique of leaving empty spaces in traditional Chinese paintings. About 500 guest rooms are divided into three groups of two building blocks each, leaving spaces between the blocks, so that the built space and natural environment blend perfectly into each other. The creation of concept and atmosphere is more important than the pure design of the visible form of the building. When guests enter the lobby in the evening and see the brilliantly illuminated restaurant located in the partially concealed courtyard with its artificial lake, they may feel as if a scene from "Night Banquet" (a famous traditional Chinese painting) has been miraculously brought to life. Mountain scenes viewed from the hotel windows look like vivid Chinese ink wash paintings. The skilful use of empty space in the complex heightens the artistic charms of the hotel and makes staying there a memorable experience. This design won the National Perfect Design Prize in 1991 and the Creation Award of the Architectural Society of China in 1992 (Figure 7.6).

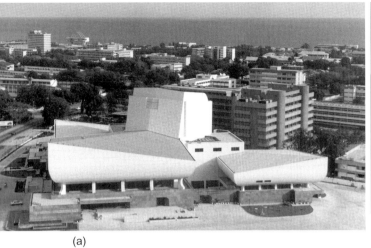

(a)

(b)

Figure 7.5 Cheng Taining, Ye Xianghan etc., Ghana National Theater in Accra, 1990. (a) The theater, (b) A corner, (c) Plan

(c)

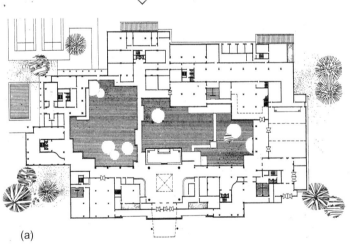

(a)

(b)

(c)

Figure 7.6 Cheng Taining, Ye Xianghan etc., Dragon Hotel, 1986, (a) Plan, (b) From the window, (c) Dragon Hotel close to the Lake Xihu

Following the success of the Ghana National Theatre, Cheng and his colleagues designed the Convention Center of Mali, using a similar style (Figure 7.7).

In 1990, Cheng presented a design scheme to the competition for He-mu-du Relics Museum. Wooden structural remains had been excavated in Yuyao and proved to be traces of the He-mu-du civilization that flourished 5000 years ago. The design concept was rejected by the authorities for being "not like a building" and having "no sloping roof" and "no railing style." However, who can say what a design, especially one like He-mu-du Relics Museum, should express?

For Cheng Taining, to create a certain kind of atmosphere and concept is more important than to merely adopt a certain style. He wished to capture the mysterious and historic atmosphere of the ancient He-mu-du culture by evoking the original feeling of the excavated field and unearthed artifacts. He could never have been content to merely copy an ancient building, slavishly following "national form." This is the worst method of all, according to Cheng.

The design concept began with a photograph of the excavation site. The excavation pit has three setback levels connected with each other by descending pathways. Tools, barns, and the remains of wooden houses from different periods were found at different levels. Cheng had the idea of inverting the invisible negative volume of the pit to create its visible counterpart, a series of "solid" steps; placed upon these steps is a series of exposed posts and beams, which create the skeletal impression of the vanished buildings, reinforcing for the visitor the feeling of actually being at the ruins as they were excavated. In this design, the "ruins" rather than the museum is what is most important in the design.

The structure itself contains a network of interconnected passages that provide access to the various rooms, which hang suspended in the air at different levels. The style of the structure is derived from the mortise-and-tenon work of the site's wooden building remains. Cheng feels that the appropriate scale and simple shape of the structure are representative of the Yaojiang area (Figure 7.8).

(a)

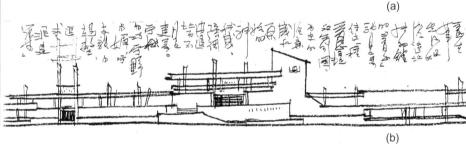

(a)

(b)

(b)

Cheng
Taining

Figure 7.7 Cheng Taining, Convention Center of Mali, 1992, (a) Convention center, (b) Entrance plaza

Figure 7.8 He-mu-du Relics Museum, (a) Cheng's sketch, (b) Perspective

In his design for the Hangzhou Train Station, Cheng skillfully handled this large-scale project of 140,000 sq m GFA that included waiting lounges, retail stores, and hotels in different functional zones. The general concept of the design was to treat the station house and the plaza in front as a whole, while separately organizing the circulation of vehicles and pedestrians on three levels: underground, ground level, and elevated. People leaving the station can take a taxi at the underground level or can go by escalator up to the ground level to take a bus. Those entering the station on the ground level can go by escalator up to the elevated level. When entering or leaving the station, passengers can take the shortest route to their destination. The sharply pitched roof on the top and in the middle of the station shows Cheng's intention of speaking the local dialect (Figure 7.9).

Figure 7.9 Cheng Taining, Hangzhou Train Station, 1999

After he stepped down from the directorship of his large, well-established firm, the Hangzhou Design Institute of Architecture, Cheng organized his own design team. He concentrated on design, theory, and creation; the production and profit-making were handed to younger and more energetic colleagues. His team designed the civic plaza of Shaoxin, a town 100 km northwest of Hangzhou. A plaza between the buildings and a plaza with a glass pavilion were combined to form a single entity. Cheng's design of Grand Hangzhou Theater and an office in Shanghai (2000) are also notable. Cheng is talented in painting, calligraphy, and literature, because of his early training in high school and at the Nanjing Institute of Technology (now Southeast University). In architectural design, Cheng deliberately pursues elegance consistent with the intellectual and the spiritual status of traditional Chinese arts. His designs are distinguished by their brilliance and wisdom (Figure 7.10).[2]

(a)

(b)

Figure 7.10 Other works of Cheng Taining, (a) Hangzhou Grand Theater, (b) Shaoxin Cultural Plaza

As the first architect in China to advocate "environmental design," **Bu Zhengwei** (b. 1939) strives to express the identity of the particular city for which his projects have been commissioned. Graduating from Tianjin University in 1962, Bu worked in Hubei Province for more than ten years until 1980, when he started to design projects throughout China: Chongqing, Tianjin, Beidaihe, Yantai, Xuzhou, Zhuhai, Dongyin, Shenyang, and Dalian. Aesthetic experiences of natural surroundings, human circumstances, historic context, and future scenes — *genius loci* — of a particular city are vital to him. He embraced these cities, experienced life there, and absorbed their subtle tastes. These experiences take place either before or while he is conceiving the design scheme. What

(a)

preoccupies him is how to link the materials collected from experiencing these cities to the new architectural image.

During his tenure as chief architect of the Design Institute of Civil Aviation, Bu had an opportunity to design several airports. In the design of Chongqing Airport, Yantai Airport, and Laishan Airport, as well as the civic plaza of Dongying, Bu grasps the *genius loci* and tries to express it intuitionally. In his works, we can see sign, symbol, and metaphor at work as well (Figure 7.11).[3]

Peng Yigang (b. 1932) gained a reputation in China and Taiwan through his popular textbooks on architectural rendering, design principles (space organization), Chinese gardens, and rural town construction. He seems to be the Francis D. K. Ching (author of a series of hand-drawn undergraduate textbooks published by Van Nostrand Reinhold and John Wiley) of China. His pictorial approach to architecture gives his designs elegance, coherence, and clarity. Unlike commercial designers and firms, Peng has done some small-scale designs for several campuses and some design work during his travels, in addition to his teaching, research, writing, and drawing.

The particular constraints of certain projects may not be impediments but may enlighten the designer and creatively inspire him or her to find a unique solution or discover a novel form. From macro-environment to the articulation of details, Peng treats his designs carefully and tries to create buildings that conform to their era, locality, and nationality. His books and designs represent the characteristic pursuits of the second generation of Chinese architects.

Tianjin University has taught architectural studies for more than half a century. In the early 1980s, the Department of Architecture prepared to build its new home. Peng's design plans were abandoned one after another, primarily because of budget, until one was finally approved and built. The site is at the end of the 1200-m-long central axis of the campus. A U-shaped plan fits the triangular site. A courtyard with a pond is placed in the center of the main building. Several aphorisms of Lao Tzu, a philosopher of the Spring and Autumn Period (770–476 BCE) and their English translations are inscribed on the two sides of the front wall. (Lao Tzu, it should be noted, was greatly admired by Frank Lloyd Wright, who was especially fond of the quote: "The reality of the cup is not the cup itself, but the space within the cup.") On the Chinese side is a sculpture of a Dougong (a unique bracket in traditional Chinese architecture); on the English, an Ionic Order capital. More symbolic decorations are included in the design of the courtyard. Peng strives to

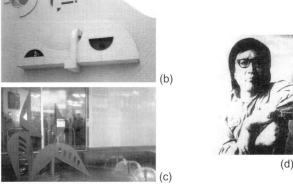

(b)

(c)

(d)

(e)

(g)

(f)

(h)

Figure 7.11 Design work of Bu Zhengwei, (a) Chongqing Airport Terminal, 1990, (b) "Mask," window decoration on the external wall, (c) Red Bird, sculpture designed by Bu, (d) Professor Bu Zhengwei, (e) Yantai Airport, domestic terminal, (f) Entrance of the international terminal, (g) Interior design of the domestic terminal, (h) Rending Lake Park, cultural pavilion, Beijing

achieve clarity, order, and function within a limited budget (Figure 7.12).

In 1894, the Chinese Navy was defeated in the Yellow Sea in a war with Japan. The JiaWu naval battle is commemorated as a lesson in patriotism. Liu Gong Island was the headquarters of the Northern Ocean Navy in the Qing Dynasty (1644–1911). The Memorial Hall was first proposed for the central hill of the island, but after having a look at the site, Peng suggested moving the memorial to a projecting peninsula on the southern seashore, where the future building would have its back to the mountain and be facing the sea. The location can be clearly seen from Weihai, a city affiliated with Liu Gong Island.

Peng abandoned a conventional symmetrical design from the beginning. A long path leads visitors from the wharf to the exhibition hall. Layered podiums are stacked on top of each other, the ground one extending the maximum distance to the sea. A transitional section on the bottom level is defined by the second-floor ceiling. Some artillery and iron anchors are exhibited here. The exhibition hall was designed in the shape of a boat. An inverted and broken boat shape is incorporated into it, and Chinese and English titles and reliefs are inscribed on the entrance wall. In the entrance, a sculpture of a sea captain emerges from the wall of the building, and a broken mast rises from an adjacent column. Both dramatically symbolize the museum's motifs. When taking the ferry from Weihai to the island, visitors are attracted by the distinctive profile of the exhibition hall as it comes gradually into view (Figure 7.13).[4]

Figure 7.12 Architecture School at Tianjin University

(b)

(c)

Figure 7.13 Peng Yigang's works, (a) Memorial Hall of Jiawu Naval Battle, 1994, Site plan, (b) The memorial, (c) Peng Yigang, (d) Memorial Pavilion of Beiyang -Tianjin University

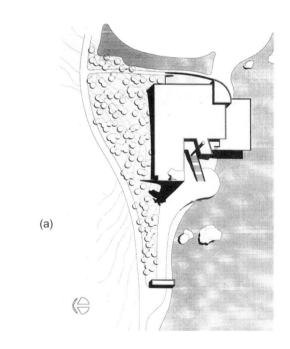

(a)

(d)

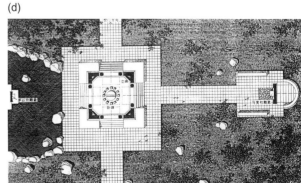

As academics, two professors, **Dai Fudong** (b. 1928) and **Wu Lusheng** (b. 1930), have established their niche in medium- and small-sized buildings. Offices, hotels, academic buildings, science buildings, and public buildings — these two architects have tackled most of the building types one can think of in the past fifty years.

New ideas continuously spring from Dai's fertile mind: how to grasp the *genius loci*, how to use local materials, how to achieve the maximum benefit from limited resources. The two regard architects as organizers of space-activity, and as artists. Architects should be sympathetic toward human beings and nature as well as being passionate about life and art. The pair is particularly keen on integrating the products of other artistic disciplines with the environments created by their buildings. In their designs, various art forms are included: sculpture, wall installations, relief and abstract murals. These art works also symbolize the meaning of the place.

In the design for the architecture school at Tongji University, the two parts of the building divide the students from the faculty, each part having its own atrium. The lobby and the balconies above are used for exhibitions. Greenery is planted in the central courtyard, the atrium, and the planters. The second phase of construction enhanced the students' section of the building, adding a glass roof to the top of the atrium. The student reading room was placed in the center of the atrium. On top of the reading room, several large steps were added to accommodate the computer room inside and the lecture theater outside, which is a multi-use public venue, the wall of the theater being used as a screen as well as for major social events. A bell inscribed with the names of faculty from 1952 to 1997 hangs in the corner of the atrium. Both the interior and exterior of the building are clad in dark red tiles. The building was designed with function foremost in mind. It is simple and powerful in appearance.

The construction costs of the building, 9767 sq. m. GFA, was 4.92 million yuan (US$570,000). In 1997 in Hong Kong, the same amount of money would have bought only a 50 sq m GFA flat! Institutions of higher education in China faced an embarrassing financial situation at the time. Professor Dai and his colleagues created a wonderful space for the Tongji faculty and students, working within a very stringent budget (Figure 7.14), not only in this architecture school but in their subsequent designs of the Run Run Shaw Building (Figure 7.15) and the Graduate School at Tongji University.

In the late 1950s, Dai and Wu designed a resort in Wuhan for Mao Zhedong, China's patriarch from 1949 to

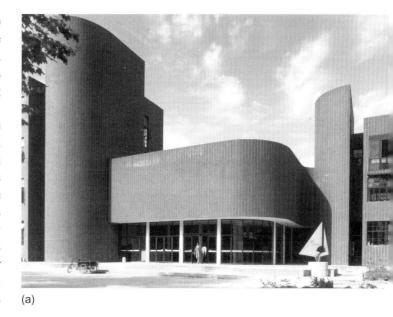

(a)

(c)

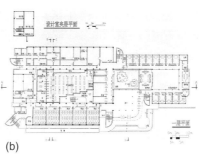

(b)

Figure 7.14 Dai Fudong and Huang Ren, Architecture School at Tongji University, 1988, (a) Entrance, (b) Plan, (c) Above the library is an open lecture theater under the skylight

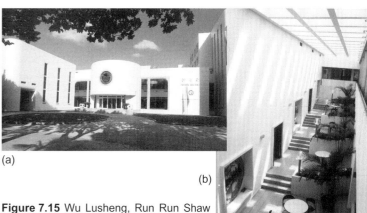

(a)

(b)

Figure 7.15 Wu Lusheng, Run Run Shaw Building at Tongji University, (a) Exterior, (b) Interior

the 1976 (Figure 7.16). Their love of local materials and use of other artistic works has also been evident in several recent works; for example, the International Hotel in Zun Hua and Big Dipper Mountain Village in Shandong Province, 1992–93.

Big Dipper Mountain Village is located on the Jiaodong Peninsula facing Bo Hai. The local peasants usually build the walls of their houses with stone and use seaweed that has been carried ashore by the tides to cover their roofs. Dai was inspired by these indigenous methods and persuaded the local authorities to use these rustic materials in the design of a small hotel, primarily used by guests of the government.

Seven buildings were scattered along the contours of the hill facing the sea. The plan looks like the seven stars of the Big Dipper, after which it is named. Local masonry and local seaweed were used to fashion the exteriors, but the interiors are completely modern and quite cozy. The attic of the pitched roof is used as a bedroom. The local peasants had never thought that the circular pebbles on the beach were of any value, but the designer used them as paving stones, planting grass between them. The result cost less than cement paving and looks much nicer.

Professor Dai firmly believes that space and form are generated only for functional and technological reasons. In his design of Noble Center, Shanghai (2002), for people with disabilities, Dai created the shape of swimming hall through a series of cuts based on the square shape of swimming pool. To find a suitable steel material for the roof truss, Dai visited several steel plants before finding Wuhan Steel Plant, which produced the materials that can withstand both heat and humidity. In the hotel part, Dai found that a group of hearing-impaired people could easily lose their way in the long straight corridor; therefore, he designed an "8" double-ring shape for the hotel plan, so the hearing-impaired people could easily find their companions in the circular corridor. These ideas generated from practical use also gave clues for differences in building appearances (Figures 7.17 & 7.18).[5]

(a)

(b)

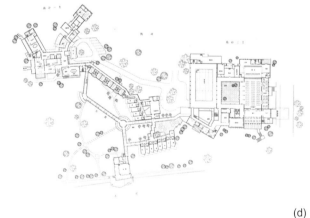

(d)

(c)

Figure 7.16 Dai Fudong and Wu Lusheng, Mao Zedong's retreat in Wuhan, 1958, (a) Mao's retreat, (b) Indoor swimming pool, (c) Close to the lake, (d) Site plan

(a)

(b)

Figure 7.17 Dai Fudong, Big Dipper Mountain Village, 1993,
(a) Entrance to the village, (b) Interior

(a)

(b)

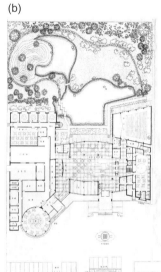

Figure 7.18 Other works of Professor Dai Fudong, (a) Zunhua International Hotel, (b) Hotel site plan, (c) Professors Dai Fudong and Wu Lusheng, (d) Swimming pool, Nobel Center, Shanghai, (e) Model, Noble Center, (f) Plan of hotel part, Nobel Center, (g) Hotel part, (h) Graduate School building, Tongji University, 2000, (i) Nationality Park, Beijing

(c)

(f)

(d)

(e)

(g)

(h)

(i)

Another professor of Tongji University, **Lu Jiwei** (b. 1936) extended his plain and functional style in a series design of sanitaria and educational buildings. His design of Ma Shan Sanitarium in Lake Taihu was published in the twentieth edition of Sir Banister Fletcher's *A History of Architecture*. In the 1990s, Lu's interests were mainly in the renovation of the old Shanghai lanes and terraced house (*lilong*) and urban design. Professor Lu typically represents the architects of his age and generation (Figure 7.19).[6]

The first architect to introduce the "image of the city" criteria of MIT professor Kevin Lynch to mainland China as well as to use architectural semiotics, **Xiang Bingren** (b. 1944) switched from academia to private practice. In

(a)

(b)

(c)

(d)

(f)

(e)

Figure 7.19 Work of Lu Jiwei, (a) Oil Workers' sanitarium, Taihu Lake, 1984, (b) Site plan of the sanitarium, (c) Elders' House, Yangpu District, Shanghai, 1986, (d) Training center of Communication Bank, Taihu Lake, 1996, (e) Professor Lu Jiwei, (f) Urban design of Jinan District, Shanghai, 1998

his eyes, there are only a few masters, even fewer so-called "signature" architects. The unique style of their design is so recognizable that it has become their trademark. To Xiang, the designs of these master architects transcend the profession and enter the domain of art and culture.

However, most "unknown" architects are engaged in providing professional services. In general, the architect's task is to find solutions to the client's problems. It is by no means an easy job but one that requires talent and wisdom, as well as knowledge, experience, and a continuous commitment to excellence. In most cases, architectural design is a matter of searching for the right balance of function, cost, and aesthetics. Being creative does not mean blindly fashioning something new but discovering unique solutions to problems. However, for Xiang, the process itself is more important and fascinating than the end product.

Xiang was one of the first practitioners to use architectural semiotics as an approach to exploring local culture and its symbols. After moving to Hong Kong in 1993 from four years' working in the US and then back to Shanghai in 2000, he designed several "commercial works" which reflect his belief in quality, process, and the importance of cooperation among the various design and construction parties. Of these works, a bank building in Changsha, a communications building in Nanjing, and some public buildings in Shanghai are notable. He designed the gate of Fuxing Park in Shanghai, a French-style park formed in the 1920s. After studying the historic pictures, Xiang captured the image of that era by using bold timber materials and decorated pattern. His design of Fuchun Mountain Village in Hangzhou, and Jiangning Residential Area in Nanjing shows his understanding of southern vernacular style and modern taste. Xiang is a bridge between the architects of this chapter and those of Chapter Eight, not only because of his frequent involvement of activities in these two parties but his changing ideas in keeping up with the world pace and his background of overseas study (Figure 7.20).[7]

Xing Tonghe (b. 1939) has consistently received the commissions that other architects covet. Since the 1980s, his name has been associated with many new projects in Shanghai. For the past forty years, he has worked in one of Shanghai's major design firms, rising from technician to architect-in-chief of a design-construction consortium with over 2000 staff. He boldly seized the opportunities of the early 1990s and designed several landmark buildings in Shanghai, including the renovation of the famous Bund, Shanghai Museum, People's Square, Shanghai Martyrs'

Mausoleum, Children's Museum, Children's Palace in Huangpu (Figure 7.21), the renovation of Shanghai Fine Arts Museum (Figure 7.22), Lu Xun Memorial Hall (Figure 7.23), and International Shopping Center in Huaihai Road, to name a few. He has explored the relationship of these buildings with their surroundings and attempted to express the essence of Shanghai — a city bursting with vitality — through them.

Located in the heart of Shanghai, Shanghai Museum occupies a 2.2-ha site with a GFA of 38,000 sq m and is renowned for its collection of ancient bronze vessels. The inspiration of the design came from these sculptured bronze works and the old Chinese concept of a "round heaven and square earth." The external wall is adorned with the decorations of ancient China, but these are set against the contemporary abstract style of the building itself. In the interior layout, Xing broke through traditional concepts of exhibition design and presented the exhibits in innovative ways (Figure 7.24). Following his success in Shanghai, Xing participated in the restoration of Deng Xiaoping's hometown in Sichuan Province (2003) and played a pivotal role in the planning of the Shanghai International Exposition 2010. In his mid-sixties, Xing frequently appears in planning and design activities, lectures, seminars, publications, and other activities.[8]

In the years following 1980, when the Chinese government was implementing its policies and regulations throughout the country, Guangzhou and southern China seemed more like an enclave than part of China proper. Geographically and traditionally, southern China is far from the administrative center of power and has been less involved in the political turbulence that has periodically embroiled the rest of the country (see the section on Guangzhou in Chapter Four). **Mo Bozhi** (1914–2003) and **He Jingtang** (b. 1938) are no doubt the most outstanding architectural representatives of this area. They are dedicated to creating a southern China architectural style based on local weather, culture, and heritage.

Mo's early designs for Nanguo Restaurant (Figure 7.25) and Baiyun Shan Village Hotel (Figure 7.26) were imbued with the soul of the vernacular buildings and gardens characteristic of southern China. He created an atmosphere of natural freshness by adroitly blending indoor and outdoor spaces and by using lush and exuberant greenery throughout. These designs were executed during the period when "national form" was the predominant style in Beijing and other cities.

In the design of Baiyun Hotel (1977) and the subsequent White Swan Hotel (1984) (Figure 7.27) in

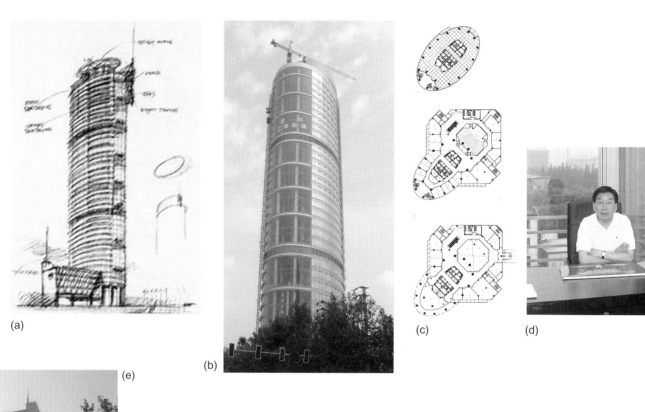

(a)

(b)

(c)

(d)

(e)

(f)

(g)

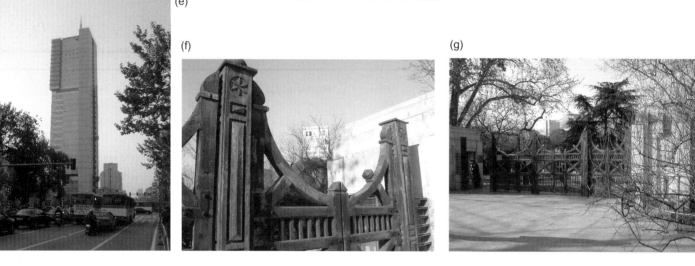

(h)

(i)

(j)

Figure 7.20 Works of Xiang Bingren, (a) Sketch of Communication Building, (b) Plans, (c) Communication Building, Nanjing, 2001, (d) Professor Xiang Bingren, (e) Mobile Communication Building, Nanjing, (f, g) Gate of Fuxin Park, Shanghai, 2000, (h-j) Fuchun Hill Village, Hangzhou, 2003

Figure 7.21 X i n g Tonghe, Children's Palace in Huangpu District, Shanghai

(a)

(a)

(b)

(b)

Figure 7.22 Xing Tonghe, Renovation of Shanghai. Fine Arts Museum, 1997, (a) The interior, (b) The old 1930s' façade of jockey club was retained 1989

(c)

Figure 7.23 Xing Tonghe, Lu Xun's Museum, 2000, (a) The old façade of 1960 was retained, (b) New extension, (c) Interior

(a)

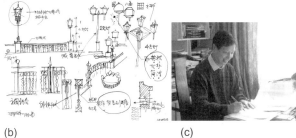

(b)　　　　　　　　　　(c)

(d)

(e)

(f)

Figure 7.24 Shanghai Museum and other works of Xing Tonghe, (a) The Bund, Shanghai, 1992, (b) Sketch of the Bund, Shanghai, (c) Professor Xing Tonghe, (d) Shanghai museum, 1993, (e) Façade in street, Shanghai Museum, (f) Children's Museum, Shanghai, 1995

(a)

(b)

Figure 7.25 Early works of Mo Bozhi, (a) A restaurant in Guangzhou, (b) A resort

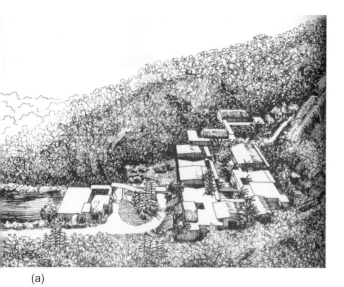
(a)

(b)

Figure 7.26 Baiyun Shan Village, (a) Mo's sketch, (b) Garden and guesthouse

Guangzhou, Mo began to pursue a contemporary architecture that took into account local weather and environment. His buildings in Guangzhou showed that alternatives existed to the officially sanctioned "national form" of monumentality and the pitched roof. Mo also designed several important buildings in cooperation with He Jingtang. Mo and He designed the Museum of Nanyue King (Han Dynasty, 206 BCE–24 CE) (Figure 7.28) and the Memorial Exhibition Hall of the Lingnan Painting School (1992) (Figure 7.29), for which they received numerous prizes. In Mo's later designs, such as the Memorial Theater of Hong Xiannu (a famous Cantonese opera singer) (1999) (Figure 7.30), the Memorial Hall of Liang Qichao (2002), and Guangzgou Fine Arts Museum, (Figure 7.31) the forms were freer — Mo called them "expressionism" (*Architectural Journal*, May 2000). His career path and designs epitomize the evolution of architecture in southern China since 1950.[9]

(a)

(b)

Figure 7.27 Mo Bozhi, She Junnan etc., White Swan Hotel, 1984, (a) Seen from the Pearl River, (b) Atrium

(a)

(b)

(c)

Figure 7.28 Mo Bozhi, He Jingtang etc., Museum of Nanyue King, 1990, (a) Stairs, (b) Upper part, (c) Front elevation

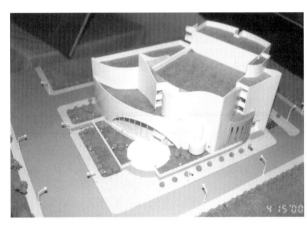

Figure 7.29 Mo Bozhi, He Jingtang etc., Museum of Lingnan Painting, 1992

Figure 7.30 Mo & Associates, Memorial Theater of Hong Xiannu

(a)

(b)

(c)

(d)

Figure 7.31 Other works of Mo's office, (a) Mo Bozhi, 88, (second left) in his office, 2000, (b) Court of Arts Museum, Guangzhou, 2000, (c) Interior of Arts Museum, (d) Subway control center, Guangzhou, 1998

He Jingtang, professor, design master, Fellow of the China Academy of Engineering and director at the Design Institute of South China University of Technology is a leading exponent of the southern style as well. His designs for the Opium War Memorial Hall in Humen (Figure 7.32), the civic plaza and complex of Dongguan (Figure 7.33), and the academic building of the Wuhan Water Resource and Hydropower University show his sensitivity toward the natural environment and his often delicate and flexible design gestures. In his winning plan in 2001 for the new campus of Zhejiang University, He increased the size of the original river that ran through the site and created a green belt on each side with an artificial lake, placing a group of academic buildings in the main area and dormitories on opposite sides of the river. As Professor He and his team won so many design competitions of campus planning around 2000, he and his design institute were considered the authority in designing tertiary education campus and buildings (Figures 7.34 & 7.35).[10]

Figure 7.32 He Jingtang, Opium War Memorial Hall, 1998

Figure 7.33 He Jingtang, Civic plaza and complex of Dongguan, Guangdong, 2000

Guan Zhaoye and **Hu Shaoxue** are professors at Tsinghua University, where their major projects are also situated. Guan designed a group of academic buildings at this famous campus and at Peking University that reflect the flavor of the 1900s. These two institutions of higher education were established at the turn of the twentieth century, primarily by Americans and by American religious groups. Libraries, teachers' offices, dormitories, and sports complexes built from the 1900s to the 1940s are a nostalgic reminder of the past. In the design for the expansion of Tsinghua Library, Guan succeeded in handling the subtle relationship between the new library extension and the old library, creating both a pleasant space and an academic atmosphere. The outer walls are clad in dark red tiles, just like the old library, and the shapes of the buildings are delicately organized, with just the right sense of proportion (Figure 7.36). His other designs, such as the Sciences Building, the Life Sciences Building at Tsinghua, and the New Library at Peking University (Figure 7.37) are also faithful to the original design of the campus.[11]

Hu Shaoxue also designed the architecture schools and several other academic buildings at Tsinghua University in its new campus area. In his design for the Wu Weiquan Building, Hu tried to create an energy-saving building (Figure 7.38). His buildings use contemporary vocabulary and are usually clad in white tiles.

Architects such as Qi Kang, Cheng Taining, Peng Yigang, Dai Fudong, and their peers are the first generation of architects that graduated from Chinese universities whose education was modeled on the Beaux-Arts tradition and the academic system of Soviet Russia. At the same time, they retained and honored the tradition of old Chinese artists, who act as painters, calligraphers, and poets. Most of these architects excel at drawing and composition, viewing architecture as art. They were isolated and exiled during the Cultural Revolution (1966–76). When opportunities arose for them to practice again, they wished to be creative but found themselves in an extremely awkward position, constrained by various ideological restrictions. Although young architects and students today are more likely to emulate overseas design masters instead of looking for inspiration in the works of their compatriots, this generation of Chinese architects are to be admired because they passionately dedicated themselves to designing works that could not bring them profit or reputation — at least not until much later in their careers. Nonetheless, they created quite a number of good buildings in spite of very restrictive conditions.

(a)

(b)

(e)

(c)

(d)

(f)

(g)

Figure 7.34 New Campus Plan of various universities, designed and directed by Professor He Jingtang, (a) Nanhai College, South China Normal University, 2001, (b) Master plan, new campus of Zhejiang University, (c) Professor He Jingtang, (d, e) Academic Building, Zhejiang University, (f) Street in Jiangnan University, (g) Master plan, Jiangnan University

Figure 7.35 He Jingtang, 9/18 Memorial Hall, Shenyang (On September 18, 1937, Japanese invaders triggered a war in northern China.)

(a)

(c)

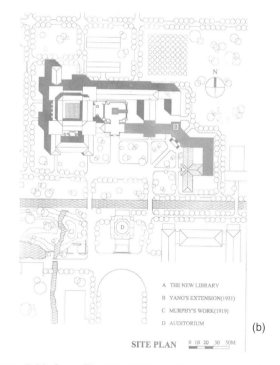

A THE NEW LIBRARY

B YANG'S EXTENSION(1931)

C MURPHY'S WORK(1919)

D AUDITORIUM

(b)

SITE PLAN 0 10 20 30 50M

Figure 7.36 Guan Zhaoye, Library Extension at Tsinghua University, (a) The right-hand side is the old library, the left-hand side the new wing, (b) Site plan, (c) Internal court

(a)

(b)

Figure 7.37 Guan Zhaoye, Sciences Building at Tsinghua University , (a) Elevation, (b) Court

(a)

(b)

(c)

Figure 7.38 Design works of Hu Shaoxue at Tsinghua University campus, (a) Seen from the design institute, (b) Interior of Design institute, (c) Academic building in the new district of Tsinghua campus

IN SEARCH OF LOCAL IDENTITIES

Beginning in 1990, China started to confer the honorary title of "Master of Design and Engineering" on planners, architects, and structural and civil engineers. About forty architects have now been awarded this title. Higher still is the Fellow of the China Academy of Engineering or the China Academy of Science, the most prestigious title an architect or scientist in China can hold.

The standards and process by which a Fellow is elected may be arguable, but those who have been so honored generally represent the outstanding practitioners in their particular area of expertise. For example, Wu Liangyong, a professor at Tsinghua University, has made an important contribution to the field with his theory of "Organic Renewal," eloquently articulated in his book *Rehabilitating the Old City of Beijing*, and by his renovation of the old Beijing courtyard house (see Chapter Two). His theory of regional planning was applied to Shanghai and the region of eastern China as well as the Pearl River Delta of southern China. Guan Zhaoye's designs for the Library Extension at Tsinghua University, the Library at Peking University and the Science Building at Tsinghua University carefully followed and extended the context of old traditions. Mo Bozhi and He Jingtang, as mentioned, are the chief exponents of the "southern style" and designed a series of buildings that reflect sensitivity to the region's climate as well as to its cultural context. Professors Qi Kang and Dai Fudong, two Fellows of the China Academy of Engineering, try to express the "spirit of Jiangnan" (south of the Yangtze River) with local materials.

In addition to the individuals mentioned in this chapter, architects from southern and northern China have all tried to explore local indigenous identities in public, cultural, or government buildings. For example, Rao Weichun and his colleagues in Yunnan are attempting to establish a series of "Yunnan style" designs in the southwest. Wang Xiaodong and his colleagues based in Urumqi have created a style belonging to Xinjiang, a region of the Silk Road that contains several minority nationalities.

In conclusion, the architects mentioned in this chapter can loosely be categorized as the second or third generation of modern architects in China. They have contributed greatly to new China's architecture and building industry in the last twenty or thirty years of the twentieth century. Although most urban architecture is far from satisfactory in function and aesthetics, the buildings and their designers described in this chapter stand out from the large quantity of mediocre works and represent the glittering apex of this giant pyramid. Their achievements were acknowledged by the government, a series of official awards, and honorary titles. Inevitably, they were also limited in understanding the new environment and methodology at the turn of the century. The task of breakthrough in invention naturally falls on the shoulders of the next generation.

NOTES

1. Professor Qi Kang's views are mainly adapted from the materials Qi sent to the author in October 1998.
2. Cheng Taining's views are mainly adapted from *Cheng Taining: Contemporary Chinese Architect*, Vol.1, 1997, Vol.2, 2002, both published by China Architecture and Building Press; and also from the author's interview on July 22, 2001.
3. Bu Zhengwei's views are mainly adapted from the materials Bu sent to the author in September 1998 and his book, *Form Freely: Beyond the Style and School*, Heilongjiang Press of Science and Technology, 1999.
4. Peng Yigang's views are mainly adapted from the materials Peng sent to the author in March 1999 and his book, *Creation and Rendering*, Heilongjiang Press of Science and Technology, 1994.
5. Dai Fudong's views are mainly adapted from the materials Dai sent to the author in January 1999, his book, *Dai Fudong and Wu Lusheng: Contemporary Chinese Architects*, China Architecture and Building Press, 1999; and from the author's interviews on January 14, 1999 and July 20, 2004.
6. Lu Jiwei's views are mainly adapted from the materials Lu sent to the author in October 1998, and from Lu Jiwei, *Intention and conception of architectural design*, China Architecture and Building Press, 2002
7. Xiang Bingren's views are mainly adapted from the materials Xiang sent to the author in September 2004, his book, *Xiang Bingren: Selected and Current Works*, China Architecture and Building Press, 2002; and from the author's interviews on June 28, 2001 and July 8, 2003.
8. Xing Tonghe's views are mainly adapted from the materials Xing sent to the author in July 1998, his book, *Xing Tonghe: Contemporary Chinese Architects*, China Architecture and Building Press, 1999; and from the author's interviews on July 15, 1998 and April 8, 1999.
9. Mo Bozhi's views are mainly adapted from the materials Mo sent to the author in April 2000, Zeng Zhaofeng (ed.), *Works of Mo Bozhi*, South China University of Technology Press, 1994; and from the author's interviews on April 8-9, 2000, March 21, 2001 and January 12, 2003.
10. He Jingtang's views are mainly adapted from the materials He sent to the author in November 1998 and October 2002, and from the author's interviews on August 27, 2002.
11. Guan Zhaoye's views are mainly adapted from the materials Guan sent to the author in March 1999.

W hereas the older generation of architects can essentially be categorized by style, ideas, and method, the generation originating in the 1980s has emulated recent international trends, elaborating upon certain forms, vocabularies, and new technologies. Speaking a different language with different tones and a different text, they mostly mimicked the Western tongue. Only a few have explored deeper layers of expression that are inherently Chinese. Their projects may be small in scale, but they have gradually won the praise of an increasing number of admirers. Thanks to the strong catalyst of the open-door policy, they have grasped the opportunities of realizing their "paper architecture," having the advantages of youth and open-mindedness. The ideas and vital presence of this rising young generation of architects are a breath of fresh air sweeping across the country. Their works fulfill China's long-held dream of being connected to the international architectural community.

CHAPTER EIGHT

EXPERIMENTAL ARCHITECTURE: THE RISING OF THE YOUNGER GENERATION

THE OPEN DOOR AND THE OPEN MIND

Chapter Seven describes the prominent architects in China, most of the people who shone in the 1980s and graduated before 1967. The Cultural Revolution (1966–76) interrupted the continuous training and supply system of professionals. During those ten years, China's universities stopped taking new students and suspended entrance examinations. In 1978, on the initiative of Deng Xiaoping, China restored its system of higher education, especially its rigorous entrance examinations, and education once again became a national priority. In addition to the usual higher education, China sent scholars and students overseas. Since the 1980s, about 500,000 Chinese students and scholars have studied and worked abroad, many of them in the United States; since 1995, more mainland Chinese students have studied in the US than in any other country. Students who returned to China after working or being educated overseas brought new ideas and knowledge with them, injecting life and vigor into China's building industry.

Architects in China have always been burdened by a sense of cultural mission. This sense of mission is driven by a wide range of theoretical discourses and is often fueled by single-minded and extremist viewpoints, such as anti-Westernization, Westernization, doctrines of "contemporary architecture with Chinese characteristics," or those that stridently oppose the restoration of ancient forms. Such rigidly held positions can only lead to a dead end, as shown by some of the inferior and awkward buildings that have resulted from the adherence to such dogmatic ideologies. As one scholar has observed, "China's academic thinking has always been mired in the swamps of classicism or anti-classicism, Westernization or anti-Westernization, a situation which makes it impossible to see the horizon or to have a new vision of culture" (Lin 1988).

This misnamed "culture" prevents China's architects from grasping the spirit and principles of modern architecture. The pursuit of Chinese identity results in a kind of bottleneck, stifling creative expression. The new generation of Chinese architects described in this chapter has found freedom by returning to the roots and basic conceptual principles of modern architecture.

Most of China's cities acquired their present form during the planned economy of the 1950s to 1980s, many of the buildings designed by State-owned design institutes, as described in previous chapters. After only a few decades, most of these structures had become functionally useless, and the country's once-proud urban landmarks and former government buildings were left derelict and empty, mournful symbols of the failure of China's building industry.

In the early 1980s, China's rising new generation of architects expressed their dissatisfaction with existing conditions and started to experiment with and explore alternate architectural methodologies. In many cases, they were artists in other media — painters and sculptors who exhibited their work in galleries or did avant-garde installations or performing arts. As a revolution in the arts swept across China, these architects who had formerly occupied the periphery began to play an increasingly important role in determining the future of the country's architecture.

During this period, the experimental arts flourished in China. New styles emerged in poetry, novels, fine arts, drama, and music, as people celebrated their liberation from the predictable and sterile orthodoxy of the socialist state. This revolution in the arts influenced all aspects of Chinese society. A number of outstanding Chinese artists showed their work in important international art exhibitions, such as the Biennale di Venezia, or moved to Europe or the US (Figure 8.1).

In the country's vast building industry, China's new generation of architects gradually became recognized and respected; voices crying in the wilderness now sounded throughout the vast realms of China, confirmation of the adage, "Nothing is more powerful than an idea whose time has come." There followed an unprecedented explosion in architecture, a proliferation of rich and complex works such as China had never before witnessed.

Those young architects who were already sophisticated designers and experienced at running architectural practices also came armed with knowledge of the contemporary world, having visited and absorbed the latest architectural ideas from the leading designers and countries. Several major events marked the emergence of this group; for example, the "5/18 Symposium of Young Architects and Artists" in Guangzhou (1998) and the "Chinese House" exhibition of the work of five experimental architects in Shanghai (2001). At the Twentieth UIA Congress in Beijing, art critic Wang Mingxian organized an exhibition of experimental architecture that provided a platform for a group of ambitious young designers. In September 2001, Aedes Gallery in Berlin held an exhibition of "New China Architecture," showcasing China's experimental architecture through the works of Ai Weiwei, Chang Yung Ho, Liu Jiakun, Ma Qinqyun, Wan Shu, Zhang Lei, Wang Qun, Zhu Jinxiang, and Ding Wowo. To celebrate the "Sino-France year" of 2003, an exhibition of "Alors, la Chine" was staged in the Pompidou Center of Paris from June to October 2003. Eight young architects and firms showcased their design works on behalf of China, including Chang Yung Ho, Wang Shu, Liu Jiakun, Zhang Lei, Qi Xin, Ma Qingyun, Cui Kai, and Dashe Studio (Figure 8.2). Moreover, Shanghai and Beijing frequently launched such events as a "biannual arts festival" in the new millennium, showing their aspirations to become global cultural leaders.

Figure 8.1 Active street arts, (a) Sculpture in Shanghai street, (b) Sculpture garden, Guangzhou, (c) Street scene in Beijing

Figure 8.2 Diversity in architectural culture, (a) Plaza of public art, Shenzhen, 2001, (b) Old shipyard transformed into a park, Zhongshan, Guangdong, 2000

This chapter delineates and analyzes this emerging generation, and categorizes the people into several different types, although architects of different types may share some characteristics. This category may be helpful in predicting China's further development.

LEARNING FROM THE WEST

If the Western system of design and theory is regarded as mainstream, there is an obvious gap between China and the world. Many people have sensed this and strived to fill this gap by learning from the West. They were regarded by observers as being bold and unusual, expressing the audacious new spirit of contemporary architecture; although these designs were inspired by Western influences, they expressed the brilliance of their creators.

Wang Tianxi (b. 1943), a graduate of Tsinghua University, worked in I. M. Pei's office in New York in the early 1980s. He was among the first group of architects sent by the Chinese government to study abroad, after the implementation of the open-door policy. Wang researched the geometric relationships of Pei's designs and tried to apply the concept of grid/axis distortion in a series of his own designs. He was one of the first architects in China to make an analytical study of form. In some of his works, for example, the Beidaihe Sanitarium (1990) and the Vanuatu Convention Center (1988), he partially realizes the intentions of his own grid distortion experiments

(a)

(b)

Figure 8.3   Works of Wang Tianxi, (a) Training center in Nan Daihe seashore, Hebei Province, 1985, (b) Sanitarium at Beidaihe, Hebei Province, 1988

(Figure 8.3). His semi-state, semi-private firm was incorporated early in 1986, helping him to design according to his ideas.

If Wang Tianxi can also be included in Chapter Seven, considering his graduation year before the Cultural Revolution, **Chang Yung Ho** (b. 1956) possesses all the conditions of the next generation. Son of a renowned architect, Chang entered Nanjing Institute of Technology (now Southeast University) by the strict entry examination in 1978, and then went to the United States in 1981 and got his bachelor's degree from Ball State University and master's from the University of California at Berkeley. He produced dozens of experimental designs during the 1980s and received many international awards. He won the *Japan Architects* design competition several times during the 1980s. In 1996, he was honored with the *Progressive Architecture* Citation Award. In 1993, he gave up his faculty position at Rice University in Houston and returned to Beijing to be the principal architect in his own Atelier FCJZ or Fei Chang Jianzhu Atelier. Fei Chang Jianzhu literally means "very architectural" or "very special architecture" (Figure 8.4).

Chang's early works in Beijing include the Xishu Bookstore, Villa Shan Yu Jian, several office renovations, and the Morningside Center for Mathematics, all of which show his concern for the details of construction and the role they play in creating fresh and exciting visual effects.

In his design for an office in the International Trade Center in Beijing, Chang planned an innovative type of office environment. Traditional cubicle offices enclose workers, shutting out natural light and creating a sense of imprisonment. Open office plans provide natural light and a view, but at the expense of the worker's individual privacy. One design is too enclosed, the other too open. Chang designed an office environment in which the workstations are partitioned with glass walls that are transparent on the lower half and translucent on the upper. The worker has privacy sitting in the glass cubicle and when standing up to take a break, go for coffee, etc. In effect, the office acts as two architectures on a single floor, the glass cubicle approach utilizing the best of both cubicle and open office space plans.

Chang has often asked: Where does a building end and a city begin? How are their structures and organization similar? How small can a city be, and how large can a building be? Can a building have streets and neighborhoods just like a city?[1] These are interesting theoretical questions that Chang has tried to apply in some of his building designs.

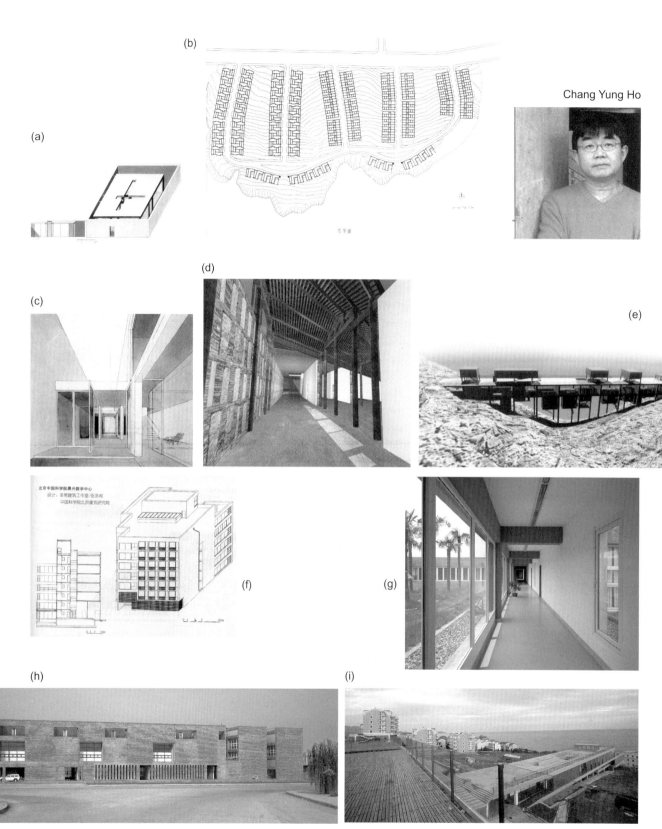

Figure 8.4 Works of Chang Yung Ho, (a) Isometrics of a house, (b) Public housing, Qingqidi, *Progressive Architecture* citation, (c) Interior of public housing, (d) Small Fine Arts Gallery, Quanzhou, 1996, (e) Seashore house in Shenzhen, (f) Morningside Center for Mathematics, Beijing, 1994, (g, h) R & D center of Beijing University, Chongqing, Sichuan Province, (i) Beijing University Conference Center, Qingdao, Shandong Province

In Chang's design for the Morningside Center for Mathematics in Beijing, the idea of the little city is applied directly to the design of this research complex situated on a very small urban site. The design brief asked for a single structure to accommodate all of the daily activities of the mathematicians except for dining, because they eat in nearby restaurants and food courts. In order to bring to the research center's residents a subtle sense of the experience and excitement of living in a city, an urban architecture was created within the building. The structure is "dissolved" into a group of internal building elements or "micro-buildings." These reinforced concrete shear wall structures are connected by hallways and receive natural light through various light wells and skylights. The spaces between the buildings function like traditional Chinese courtyards, though here they are squeezed into a contemporary Asian city milieu. Several small bridges cross the courtyards. The window units of the building are divided into two parts: the fixed glass area and the aluminum panels that can be opened for ventilation.

In his article "Ordinary architecture" (1998), Chang expressed the idea that construction should be the starting point of design, which must focus on materials and how best to display them. He gradually formulated his idea of design as material-construction, utilizing tectonic forms and spatial logic. In this design approach, questions of style and social culture are not addressed, technical considerations being paramount. When he was in his twenties, Chang was an excellent water colorist, doing numerous renderings while studying in the United States, including many for his mentor Lars Lerup at the University of California at Berkeley. A mature craftsman, Chang creates beauty, but it is a beauty generated from the materials and the details of their use in the structure.

Chang Yung Ho's work has been extensively exhibited, displayed, and published, including at the Architectural Association in London and the Architectural League of New York, as well as in countries such as Germany, Italy, and Denmark. There have been around sixty such events since 1990. Chang has also launched several design competitions for young architects and students in China. These have usually explored conceptual matters; for example, space without an "up or down" orientation.

In 1999, Chang founded an architectural research center at Peking University. Taking graduate students only, he turned the center into an experimental arena for architecture based on constructible details rather than the fine arts. In an article about architectural education, Chang vigorously rejected traditional "fine arts architecture" and the Beaux-Arts tradition, which has dominated Chinese architectural thinking for a century (Chang 2001). His center has only two directions: one year is in architectonic, defined by Professor Kenneth Frampton (1995), and another year is in city study, similar to the studio of Harvard Graduate School of Design Professor Rem Koolhaas's course. Chang himself was appointed Kenzo Tange Chair by Harvard University, to run the studio as a guest in 2002. As a result of his increasing fame, design commissions have poured into Chang's office, staffed by about a dozen individuals.

Chang's recent works use cladding of gray concrete blocks as well as specially made laminated board and double-layered glass. Chang plays with the essence of these materials and their construction potential, using a sophisticated dialectic. His design approach is evident in his renovation of the loft of the Ocean Arts Center (2000) in Beijing and the Qingdao Academic Center at Peking University (2001). Chang's architectural language is often intentionally ambiguous, driven by his strong design rationale for using certain materials in certain ways and his mimicry of Western forms, particularly modernist and minimalist vocabularies. In 2000, as a representative of the new generation of Chinese architects, Chang's work was exhibited at the Biennale di Venezia. In 2003, his English monograph was published in Hong Kong and New York.[2] In 2004, an exhibition of ten years of his work at Atelier FCJZ was held in Beijing, to which *The Architect* devoted a special issue. Chang concluded his methodology of taking architectural design as part of urban concern, taking building as human-made topography, and his way of pursuing special Chinese problems in three directions: space, construction, and urban (Chang 2004).

Chang Yung Ho's close follower Dong Yugan has experimented in the same direction but more on "paper architecture." He has used the famous Rubik's Cube for inspiration, along with various other abstract vocabularies, to construct experimental new structures. Dong's design of "furniture" architecture — in this case, the home of a writer, which was several stories high and looked like a high-rise "pencil building"— explored the duality of structure, both as "furniture" and as domestic structure. Dong has joined Chang Yung Ho's faculty team at Peking University and contributed his energy and imagination to its experiments (Figure 8.5).

In 2000, at the same time as Chang Yung Ho set up the architectural research center at Peking University, a graduate school of architecture was also set up at Nanjing

(a)   (b)

(c)

Figure 8.5 Works of Dong Yugan, (a) Writer's house, furniture house, (b) A waterfront house, (c) Rubik's cube, students' work

University. The city was once the capital of the Republic of China before 1949 and is now staffed by university personnel, including architects who have received their doctorates from overseas. The institute is experimenting with new architectural methodologies as well as new and less formal teaching methods. Some electives, for example, the study of tectonic culture, and the human body and architecture, may reveal some of their tendencies.

Zhang Lei (b. 1964) is a group member in Nanjing. A graduate of Southeast University and of ETH Zurich, Zhang is a professor at Nanjing University and plays a major role in the research institute. He experimented with geometric forms in a series of designs in Jiangsu Province, including a hotel, middle school, government office, and a graduate student hall at Nanjing University. In the design of the student hall, Zhang deliberately experimented with the building's envelope and the interesting results to be obtained by juxtaposing various local building materials of different composition. Like several other young Chinese architects, he has been inspired by Jacques Herzog and Pierre de Meuron, the 2001 Pritzker Architectural Prize Laureates, to concentrate on the surface or skin of a building. Zhang Lei's pursuits in rational structure and homogeneous materials/texture are shared by his colleagues at Nanjing University, who have a similar continental European background of education (Figure 8.6).

When Chang Yung Ho and Zhang Lei returned to practice architecture, a young man was leaving for the town to construct real buildings. This young man is **Ma Qingyun** (b. 1965). Ma received his bachelor's degree from Tsinghua University (1988) and master's from the University of Pennsylvania (1990). After four years of working with Kohn Pedersen Fox, he returned to teach in Shenzhen for a couple of years and went to the American east coast again, lecturing and being the guest critic at the University of Pennsylvania and at the Graduate School of Design of Harvard University. He coordinated the city research project of Rem Koolhaas in the Pearl River Delta. That led to his consultant's appointment for Koolhaas's CCTV and Beijing CBD project some years later.

In 1999, he started his own practice, MADA s.p.a.m., in Beijing and later in Shanghai. He has designed several influential building complexes in Ningbo, Zhejiang Province, for example, the shopping mall in the city center and new campus of Zhejing University in Ningbo. Using the methods learned from KPF, Ma treated the design with unified languages and good proportion. He tries to be authentic to the available materials and technology; this is obvious in his father's house in Xi'an, Shaanxi Province, an interesting small work of only 150 sq m. The site is on half of a plateau parallel to the mountain. It is a transitional strip from the stony mountain and the infinitely flat field. The river not only forms the valley but also brings stones of various sizes, colors, and shapes. The stones have been fully applied to his father's house, and thus minimize the non-local construction technique. However, this house is no more than a monster in the eyes of the villagers (Figure 8.7).

The people mentioned above are mostly from private firms or have a university background. In fact, a group of people in the traditional state-owned design institute are also moving forward. **Meng Jianmin**, Director of Shenzhen Architectural Design Institute, is one of them. After working in Nanjing for some years, Meng went to Shenzhen in the early 1990s. He soon seized the opportunities Shenzhen afforded during the urban development boom. As the major designer of the largest design institute in Shenzhen, Meng created several successful buildings, such as the city library, commercial complex, and church. The scale of these buildings is larger than that of other examples discussed in this chapter (Figure 8.8).

Young Chinese architects like Chang Yung Ho, Ma Qingyun, and Zhang Lei are very much in touch with international architectural trends. Highly sought after, they frequently publish articles and have exhibitions or are interviewed by magazines, because they understand how to use the media to spread their ideas. As in the West, the shrewd use of the media in China today can quickly catapult a young architect into the spotlight. Their designs

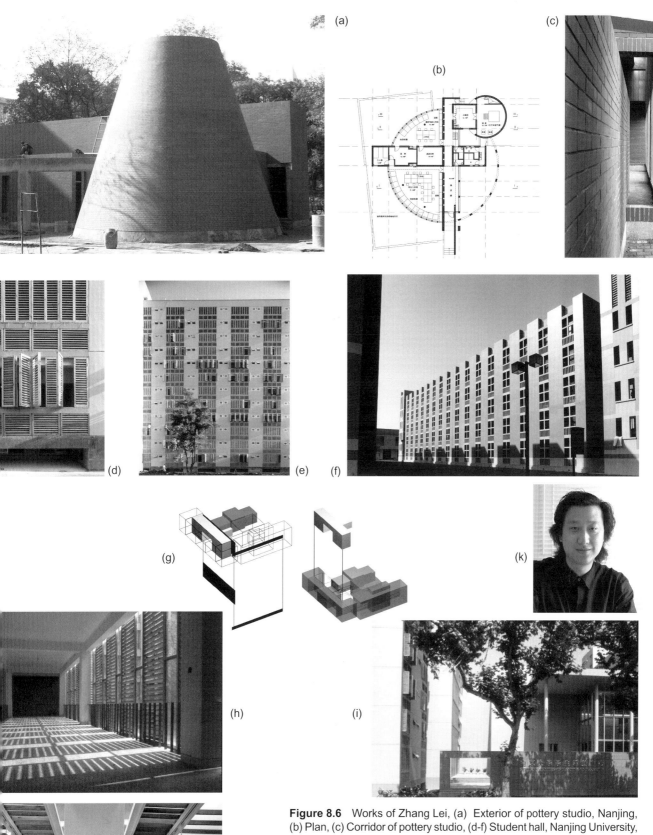

Figure 8.6 Works of Zhang Lei, (a) Exterior of pottery studio, Nanjing, (b) Plan, (c) Corridor of pottery studio, (d-f) Student hall, Nanjing University, (g, h) Renovation of Nanjing University library, (i, j) Students' center, Nanjing University, (k) Zhang Lei

Figure 8.7 Works of Ma Qingyun, (a, b) Father's house, Lantian, Shaanxi, (c) Food Crossing Nanjing (d) Composite building, Nanjing and (e) CBD, Wuxi

Figure 8.8 Works of Meng Jianmin (a) Noah's Ark Church, Shenzhen, (b, c) City Library of Hefei

and explanations are easily understood by Western curators, juries, commentators, and journals. In a country that unquestioningly accepts Western values, this group of architects soon became the new "stars" on China's stage.

CHINESE TASTE: ANOTHER WAY OUT

Although mimicking Western concepts is popular in China, especially for the younger generation, a few architects did not follow the main (Western) stream or the early way of Chinese "national form" (see Chapter Two). They tried to find another way out, relying on rich sources in Chinese culture and traditions.

Miao Pu (b. 1950), a professor at the University of Hawaii, received his undergraduate education at Tongji University, Shanghai, and his master's and Ph.D. degrees at the University of California, Berkeley. Since 1993, he has practiced architecture in his native Shanghai and in other provinces in China. Unlike a typical scholar or architect, Miao has simultaneously pursued design, theory and criticism, and teaching.

Miao's designs focus on fundamental issues in contemporary Chinese architecture and urban design, and have benefited from his research into urban patterns in high-density Asian cities and the structural characteristics of Chinese traditional space. Welcoming the globalization of modernist architecture, Miao learned from the duality of the Western version of modernism and its universally valid fundamentals of form, function, and technology, as well as from other incidental elements, such as its isolation from landscape and its obsession with high-tech construction. He believes that a truly authentic Chinese architecture can only be created by localizing and enriching the fundamental ideas expressed by the unique cultural, economic, and technological realities of contemporary China.

Miao's design explorations have contributed to Chinese architecture in two noteworthy areas. First, he developed new concepts of space and form in response to the unique behavioral and cultural patterns of contemporary Chinese society. In the Reception Center of Minhang Ecological Garden in Shanghai (2004), Shenzhen Institute of Sculpture (1996), Hillside Villa in Suzhou (2001), and Chapel in Zhuzhou (1999) he paired every major indoor space with an outdoor space to serve each function in the building, an idea derived from China's much admired courtyard house but reused in these projects in an innovative way. Miao has also experimented with

the gentle, spontaneous curvatures (without clear separation from the orthogonal geometry), local color schemes, and construction methods that he feels are unique to the Chinese temperament and material context.

Inspired by the principle of the Chinese garden, the "stepped space" in his teahouse at Xiaolangdi Dam Park, Luoyang (2002) connects a hilltop and a lake below. Each window frames selected scenes in the landscape so visitors and diners can enjoy the view to the greatest extent. The building has also become an integral part of the tourist route, in contrast to the European tradition of mainly viewing buildings from their outside as sculpture. In his design of Reception Center of Minhang Ecological Garden (2004), the outside of the complex displays a mysterious presence with long walls punctured by slits and a double-layered façade. A canal and several visual corridors leading to these openings crisscross the site, simultaneously maintaining privacy within a public park while creating space flows with the surroundings. All main halls and rooms are coupled with an outside garden or balcony. The inside and outside spaces are controlled in different sets of modules.

The second noteworthy area of Miao's design consists of typological solutions to the challenges brought by the high-density of Chinese megacities. The planning for the No. 1 Neighborhood, Middle Block of Jingqiao Estate (1999) in Shanghai uses "self-defensible" building groups to replace the standard model of the gated community and promotes the use of the sidewalk as social space, much needed in congested Chinese cities. The entry structure and restaurant of Sanquan Park, Shanghai (1998) has a vine-covered framework that envelopes the building, which not only compensates for the loss of precious green space at the building site but also provides a pleasant roof terrace under the framework to increase the usable outdoor area in this small urban park. In Miao's scheme for the renovation of Jingan Park (1998), an oasis in a busy Shanghai retail center, about 60 percent of the site is paved but is interspersed with tree pits and green trellises, so that the grounds can accommodate an enormous number of users while maintaining much green space (Figure 8.9).

Miao Pu has immersed himself in Western culture. He makes a living by teaching architectural theory at Hawaii University, mainly contemporary Western theories. But his pursuit of design is deliberately inner Chinese. Along this line, we can find several other architects. Unlike Miao, all grew up in China.

The first is **Zhao Bing** (b. 1963). He received his Ph.D. from Tongji University, Shanghai, in 1988 at the

Miao Pu

Figure 8.9 Works of Miao Pu, (a-d) Restaurant at Xiaolangdi Park, Henan, 2003, (e) Entrance to the restaurant of Sanquan Park, Shanghai, (f, g) Reception, Ecological Garden of Minhang, Shanghai

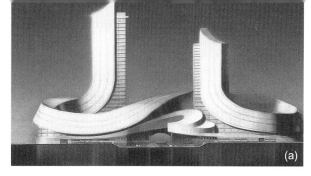

age of twenty-five. He now teaches architecture at Wuhan University. A lonely deep thinker, Zhao shapes his beliefs with Western theology, Chinese Buddhism, Yi, and Daoism.[3] He integrates traditional Chinese thinking with Western civilization and is capable of positioning the Chinese culture in a world scenario. He also practices *qi gong* and meditation, and has gradually reached a state of communicating with heaven and earth.

In recent years, he has explored iconic symbolization in architectural design; for example, in his "book" series, the buildings resemble open books. One of them is, appropriately, a bookstore. He has also designed a number of temples that use the shape of the lotus. In addition, he has used dragon shapes and images from Chinese calligraphy, modeling buildings on symbols for particular Chinese words. His drawings and buildings attempt to tap into deeply felt Chinese archetypal patterns; whether such forms can be directly used and "written out" remains problematic, as some of the buildings seem somewhat awkward and strange (Figure 8.10).

As a result of the development of his "writing" methodology, Zhao felt breezes in his heart, using his words, "the wind blowing the field (site) of building, the buildings are formed after the air movement by the wind. Because of the differences of site, the feel of wind could be gentle or fierce. You can find this wind feel in my design works." In addition to the feeling of wind, he felt water in recent years. "When the single buildings are integrated to blocks, when blocks formed part of the city, a feel of water ripples in my mind — it flows freely on the earth" (Cui 2003). "Wind" and "water" are the literal translations and two factors of Chinese *feng shui*, originating in landscaped southern China thousands of years ago. Zhao's methods of design seem difficult for other people to experience. They are quite personal and idealistic.

Zhao's methodology of using Chinese calligraphy to "write" building form has been gradually accepted by his clients, who are mainly located in China's interior. Zhao's use of low technology and conventional concrete construction may restrict him from more extravagant visual displays. His symbolism greatly relies on the building form itself, which may be contrary to the authentic expression of the building functions. Wuhan, where Zhao lives, is located in the middle of the Changjiang (Yangtze) River

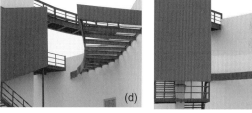

Figure 8.10 Works of Zhao Bing, (a) Scheme of a bookstore, (b) China Center of Jade Culture, (c) Exhibition Hall of Learning from Lei Feng, (d, e) Details of exhibition hall, (f) A traffic building in Hubei

and at the mid-point of the Beijing-Kowloon (Hong Kong) railway. The city is a historically important area of Chinese culture. Zhao serves as Dean of the College of Architecture and Planning at Wuhan University and tries to unite architectural thinking in central China.

The second architect is **Liu Jiakun** (b. 1956), based in Chengdu, Sichuan Province. Also known as a novelist, Liu understands that his hometown is destined to be different from costal cities. It is definitely not Beijing, Shanghai, or Guangzhou (see Chapter Four). Nurtured by a long agricultural civilization, the city, which he defines as a "typical Chinese city," is passively dragged along the path of modernization. He has to deal with the limited resources, but the rural environment and context let him display more on the light, material, space and *genius loci* — all in the scope of conventional architectural design (Liu 2002). These ideas are reflected in several of his designed artists' studios, youth camp, vernacular museum, and design competitions in suburban Sichuan. He experiments with low-technology construction methods found in China's rural areas and the use of materials like clay brick and stucco; such low-cost buildings can be assembled without a crane or machinery and can be an interesting alternative to the usual "high-tech" solutions so popular in contemporary architecture. When clay brick was banned by the government for its waste of soil, Liu turned to the concrete block and other products that dominate China's building industry. In his hostel design of Nanjing, he tried to assemble a contemporary Chinese settlement by using black, white, and gray concrete products.

In addition to the rural context, Liu is concerned with building design in the city. In cities, the conventional methods of architectural design, using Liu's words, are pale and weak when facing sophisticated financial momentum. He has to go to the the basics of the projects and discuss strategies which his clients; then his esthetic pursuits can be based on a more solid rationale (Liu 2002). But in the eyes of some people, Liu's design show traces of some international architects' works, for example, Luis Barragan, Ricardo Legorreta, and Alvaro Siza. Rural buildings are usually located in a natural environment; the primitive materials and techniques arouse a strong feeling of the countryside (Figure 8.11).

The third example may be some of Wang Shu's designs. Based in Zhejiang and Shanghai, **Wang Shu** (b. 1964) has done experimental interior designs for avant-garde artists and patrons. He learned from carpenters how to pay careful attention to details and joints. In his interior design for two residential flats in Zhejiang, Wang achieved near perfection in his use of brick, wood, steel, and glass, beautifully displaying their properties to the utmost. The different materials meet directly, without transition. The leftover corners in this design are filled with white pebbles. Wang's completed interiors have an evocative unfinished quality in which everything seems to remain in the "draft" stage; as in Chinese calligraphy, one can trace each stroke of the brush. Wang has also applied the special design methods of Chinese gardens to his interior designs, creating a kind of "crystallized" tension. He also uses fiction and narration in his approach; his interiors seem to tell a story, conjuring up subtle suggestions of traditional Chinese literature.

In 1998, Wang had the opportunity to apply his ideas to a bigger project, the Library of Wenzheng College at Suzhou University. A building is never just an artifact to be viewed, he believes, but is a container for people to enter and use. In this building, the functions are interchangeable. For example, the building has several standard divisions that can be used as lecture halls, reading rooms, or offices. In the interior, as in his other designs, Wang attempts to create a world of illusion in a variety of subtle and skillful ways. In his design of the new campus for the China Academy of Fine Arts (in a mountainous area), Wang lowered the headroom of the interior, trying to create a horizontal picture through the window frame. The dimness of the interior, according to Wang, can make the old collections shine. Some of the spatial designs are derived from scenes of ancient landscape paintings of southern China and from his very personal experiences. He has researched Heidegger, Witggenstein, Roland Barters, made friends with avant-garde and foreign artists, and influenced his students with the reverted process of building and fictional concepts. Only artistic, not "sweet" commercial, eyes can understand and support his design. He lives in his own secluded world of contemplation (Figure 8.12).

In this section of four architects, Miao Pu and Zhao Bing try to arouse the inner complex feels of Chinese tastes, whereas Liu Jiakun and Wang Shu use traditional techniques based on their own locales and context. Miao and Zhao walk a solitary road of independent contemplation, but Liu and Wang are already in the ranks of Chang Yung Ho and Zhang Lei, who have enjoyed much exposure nationally and internationally.

Liu Jiakun

Figure 8.11 Works of Liu Jiakun, (a-e) Luyeyuan Museum of stone sculpture, (f, g) Fine Arts Institute, Chengdu

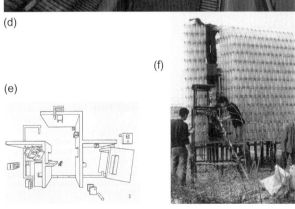

(c)

(d)

(e)

(f)

Figure 8.12 Works of Wang Shu, (a, b) Wenzheng College library, (c, d) Xiangshan Campus building, China Academy of Fine Arts, (e) Wang's home, (f) Assignment of students' design

OTHER TRENDSETTERS

The other "trendsetters" may not have a very clearcut design ideology, but they work hard in creating something fresh, different, and interesting, and exert some influence at various levels. There is quite a long list from north to south China. We have chosen some examples.

Wang Lifang, a professor at Tsinghua University, is a proponent of modern architecture. In her design of the Primary School at Tsinghua University, Grades One and Two, Three and Four, and Five and Six are separated into three differently designed and shaped two-to-three story buildings. She employs narrative by using different building forms to define or differentiate growing periods in the lives of children. The children who go to school here will experience different indoor and outdoor architectural spaces — enclosed, semi-open and open — during their growing years. The memories of these buildings will be imprinted upon them long after they have grown up and moved on (Figure 8.13).

Wu Yaodong, another Tsinghua University professor, designed a three-story market for the university staff residential area. The market was originally housed in a one-story shed that provided the local populace with daily food and groceries. The new three-story market locates all of the hawkers and shops in a single enclosed building. Wu deliberately designed a straight stairway leading to the upper floors, to retain the airy and open feeling of the street in the naturally lit atrium. The beams and columns are clad with red tiles and interconnect. Small square windows are punched in the sidewalls to remind people of the original temporary shed. The market has a casual and joyful atmosphere.

In his design for the Ministry of Education, Wu and his colleagues discarded the stuffy official face of solemn tradition and designed a building that was more lively and approachable. The louvers in the outer wall become defining features somewhat reminiscent of the human eye, and help to create a more stylish and lighthearted public edifice (Figure 8.14).

In this category, we can find Doreen Heng Liu, who superimposed different spaces in her design of the Science Museum in Nansha in the Pearl River Delta; Li Xinggang's mimicry of Zaha Hadid in his award-winning design of a model home in a real estate property in Beijing; Dashe Studio of Shanghai, which designed the Sino-German College Building of Tongji University and other housing buildings. Their smooth use of the fashionable architectural vocabularies garnered applause from young students and

(a)

(b)

(c)

(d)

(e)

Figure 8.13 Works of Wang Lifang, (a-c) Primary School at Tsinghua University, (d, e) Campus amenity space

(a)

(b)

Figure 8.14 Wu Yaodong, convenience market in Tsinghua University staff quarters (a) Interior, (b) Exterior

society. They are followers of "learning from the West" but obviously not in the first-tier (Figure 8.15).

BORROWING FROM OTHER ARTS

As remarked at the beginning of this chapter, a twentieth-century revolution in the arts inspired and shaped the architecture that we experience today. The bold and imaginative experiments of artists throughout the world remain a stimulus and catalyst for Chinese architects, who are increasingly including installations and sculptures as stand-alone features in their designs. The joining of the artists and artist-architect make experimental architecture extremely colorful and give a new angle to the designers. Many concepts are first publicized through sculpture, installation, video, or other performing arts. The enthusiasm to experiment is further fueled by the design work and discussions from the overseas Chinese scholars who frequently do design consultancy and submit papers in China; for example, Zhu Tao from Columbia University and Wang Weijun from the University of Hong Kong.

As China's leading architect with an international reputation, Chang Yung Ho is often invited to various exhibitions. Chang is more relaxed with his works for exhibitions than with real building projects, and tries to realize some bold concepts with exhibition installations. Some installations become part of building space, some indoor installations are large enough to accommodate people, and some are tiny and only have visual effects. In the Paris Exhibition of 2003, Chang was given a linear space along the façade of the Pompidou Center. He designed a series of screens, mixing various materials of metal, bamboo, plastic tubes, and Chinese ink paper (a translucent, thin sticky-rice paper), communicating their current use in China. When given a circulation space in the Graduate School of Design at Harvard University, Chang found that it was impossible to install any "space" there. He brought in six crates containing six of his design models; therefore, the exhibition was named "Six crates

(a)

(b)

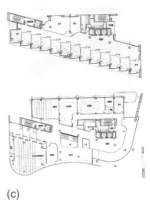

(c)

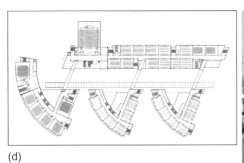

(d)

(e)

Figure 8.15 Works of young architects, Shanghai, (a) Balcony, Sino-German College at Tongji University, (b) The block, (c) Plan, (d, e) Li Linxue, academic building, Sichuan University

of architecture." They stood in the building corridor of Harvard. Interestingly, the six crates open up in different ways, according to the characters of the building they contain (Figure 8.16).

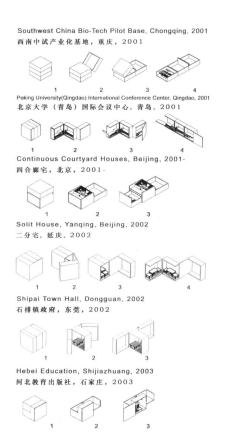

Southwest China Bio-Tech Pilot Base, Chongqing, 2001
西南中试产业化基地，重庆，2001

1   2   3   4

Peking University(Qingdao) International Conference Center, Qingdao, 2001
北京大学（青岛）国际会议中心，青岛，2001

1   2   3   4

Continuous Courtyard Houses, Beijing, 2001-
四合廊宅，北京，2001-

1   2   3

Solit House, Yanqing, Beijing, 2002
二分宅，延庆，2002

1   2   3   4

Shipai Town Hall, Dongguan, 2002
石排镇政府，东莞，2002

1   2   3

Hebei Education, Shijiazhuang, 2003
河北教育出版社，石家庄，2003

1   2   3

Figure 8.16 Chang Yong He, Six Crates of Architecture, 2003

Notable works that incorporate sculpture include the environment and sculpture designs of Ying Jia from Shanghai; and Ai Weiwei, Wang Jiahao, and Cai Guoliang from Beijing. Ying Jia and his partner Liu Keming are professors of fine arts in the Department of Architecture, Tongji University. Since 1980, they have used mosaics, wood, porcelain, concrete, stainless steel, and bronze extensively to form murals and sculptures. Their works blend in well with the buildings, the interior, and the environment (Figure 8.17).

Not having received formal architectural education, Ai Weiwei and Wang Jiahao are freelance artists and initiators for various exhibitions and visual arts/ architecture activities. Son of a famous Chinese poet, Ai Weiwei (b. 1957) was a consultant on and initiated several building projects such as the Commune by the Great Wall

Figure 8.17 Liu Kemin/Yin Jia's works, (a-c) Murals in various stations of Shanghai's subway, 1996, (d) Wood relief carving in Science Hall, Shanghai, (e) "Power of Knowledge", Run Run Shaw Building, Tongji University

and a comprehensive development in Jinhua, Zhejiang Province, designed by Herzog & de Meuron. Ai's design of his studio house and art archives and warehouse are loft buildings, renovated from deserted factories or warehouses. The "de-architecture" methods plus artistic installation make these buildings cynical and full of black humor (Figure 8.18). As youths destroyed by the "Cultural Revolution," Ai and the artists of his generation have a general cynical attitude towards society.

Whereas Ai is more architectural in designing his installations and buildings, Cai Guoliang uses non-architectural media, for example, fire. Zaha Hadid invited Cai to cooperate in an installation in Rovaniemi, Finland, for the snow festival of February 2004. Hadid designed an ice and snow building like layered sails, three parts enclosing a "snow bar." Cai designed a stream of fire flowing through the building, fueled by vodka. The blue flames shone with splendid color and gently stroked the cold and firmly frozen ice. The ratio of water and alcohol was carefully calculated, so that the flame would burn, and the ice slowly melted in fifty days. The snow water flew zigzag through the icey object and converged at the bottom pool, creating a surrealistic world (www.abbs.com.cn, February 16, 2004). Cai is really very special among his contemporaries.

The more active involvement of the arts in the built environment is driven by the wave of urban design and the beautification movement in various cities and districts. In this regard, the city of Shenzhen has done a lot of work in its old and new districts. A semi-government-owned Sculpture Institute, a group of three-dimensional visual artists and their works, can be seen in the city; for example, life-sized sculptures in Huaqiao Cheng, the civic center under construction, as well as a remarkable sculpture garden, "A Day in Shenzhen."

(a)

(b)

(c)

(d)

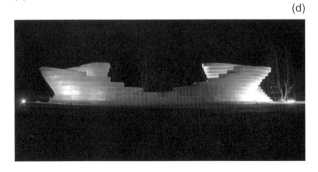

(e)

Figure 8.18 Works of Ai and Cai, (a-c) Ai Weiwei, Arts Archive Store was converted from old building, (d) "Ice and fire," Cai's design in Zaha Hadid's ice sculpture, (e) Dam of Jinhua river, Zhejiang Province

In the latter, eighteen life-sized sculptures of randomly selected people living in Shenzhen with different occupations — doctors, old and young people, a woman, child, job-seeker, waitress, engineer, architect, worker, and so forth — make up the story behind "A Day in Shenzhen." Bronze statues of these characters, with a concise introduction of their background, name, age, job, and hometown, are distributed throughout an outdoor garden. The information relating to the city on November 29, 1999, a randomly selected day — news of the city, China and world, the stock market, weather, prices of daily goods, and life of its citizens — is carved on four black granite walls. The background sound is the recording of programs of Shenzhen Broadcasting Station of that day. All these design elements faithfully record a typical day at the end of the twentieth century in this emerging metropolis adjacent to Hong Kong. This enchanting work is a successful blend of urban planning, landscape design, and sculpture (Figure 8.19).

THE LOFT DESIGNERS

As in Western society, abandoned factories and warehouses in China attracted a group of artists who redeveloped them into studios, and architects who helped to remodel them. As a result of the industrial transformation, the old workshops and warehouses of heavy industry gradually became obsolete. Young artists with infinite imagination took the opportunity to occupy these buildings at low rent. Such loft buildings appear in big cities and soon became the new exciting point of architecture.

A remarkable example is the new 798 Art Area in Beijing. If it were not for the remodeling of former Factory 798, designed by architects from the former East Germany and constructed under the direction of the Soviet Union in the 1950s, this group of buildings with amazing architectural quality would have gone with the memory of a particular era. Since 2002, some artists and companies have transformed it into Dashanzi Art District, an area full of art studios, galleries, design companies, restaurants, and cafés. More or less in a sense of political pop art, all the 1960s red radical slogans on the wall are meticulously kept and juxtaposed with all kinds of contemporary art pieces. Reuse or even creative abuse of not only the cultural and political resources but also the building itself has helped this factory enter the world of culture and fashion. It is an enclave in this monotonous landscape of discarded industries. Workers in adjacent factories stare curiously

(a)

(b)

(c)

Figure 8.19 "A Day in Shenzhen", (a) Ordinary people, (b) An ordinary day, (c) A job hunter

at well-dressed visitors. Although this area may be demolished in two years, all the artists living there and the investors appear quite self-possessed. This might epitomize the situation in China at this time. People seldom seek any permanent values in an era of rapid transformation, and any urban living condition is just provisional (Li 2003b) (Figure 8.20).

Figure 8.20 Factory 798, now the fancy artists' village, Beijing The political slogans can be seen on the wall, e.g., "Long live Chairman Mao"

The trend of transforming old factories soon spread to other cities and provinces. A designer and artist, Teng Kunyen from Taiwan and now living in Shanghai, adapted a 2300 sq m warehouse on the Suzhou riverbank of Shanghai as his studio house. The granary's fastigium frontispiece still has the popular ornamental washing stone from the Art Deco period of 1933. The building was used as a warehouse and a dormitory for workers. The exterior walls are constructed of blue and red bricks; the interior spaces have a structure of pine pillars and flooring imported from the US. After the architect rented this warehouse, 100 truckloads of scrap were removed from the interior, exterior, illegal roof structure, and partitions. A tall internal space appeared to serve this new "design factory." Traditional limewater was used to wash the white ash walls, without a single drop of paint; thus the old brick wall was preserved with its original shine. Traces on the wall of the former habitants over so many years were preserved as part of the design.

To alter the space into use as a contemporary architect's studio, the designer has both demolished and added some floors. A skylight was installed on the roof and windows were enlarged, to improve the internal lighting. Part of the space was divided into a washroom and storage. Others keep the original look. Working tables and furniture were installed, and the space was fused with traditional nostalgia and contemporary meaning. This old rice warehouse is not only the design office and bookstore of Teng and other architects but also the venue of the most fabulous cultural parties in Shanghai. The vertical space serves as the modest setting for temporary installations of weeping willows, bamboo, and local Shanghai vegetables. Because of the architect's residence in the renovated warehouse and his continuous appeals, the government has changed the zoning plan of the riverfront in Shanghai. More than thirty old warehouses from the 1920s to 1930s were partly preserved, leading the trend of preserving and reusing similar old buildings in Shanghai and China (Figure 8.21).

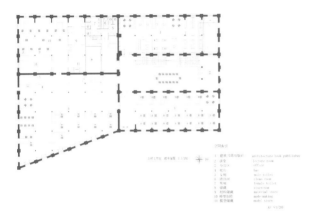

Figure 8.21 Teng Kunyen, Warehouse studio on the bank of Suzhou Creek, Shanghai, a venue for arts design and cultural events.

COMMUNE BY THE GREAT WALL

In 2002, a grand new project captured the imagination of both the public and industry professionals. It could be seen as a collective effort by experimental architects, artists, and developers with an open mind. Twelve influential young architects from Asian countries designed eleven single-family country houses and a clubhouse in an idyllic valley an hour's drive north of Beijing and 10 km from the Badaling section of the Great Wall of China. The community is called Commune by the Great Wall and is developed by Beijing Redstone Industrie Company Limited. The designers include Nobuaki Furuya, Shigeru Ban, and Kengo Kuma from Japan; Seung H-Sang from South Korea; Kay Ngee Tan from Singapore; Chien Hsueh Yi from Taiwan; Kanika R'kul from Thailand; Gary Chang and Rocco Yim from Hong Kong; and Cui Kai, Antonio Ochoa, and Chang Yung Ho from mainland China. Ai Weiwei is the landscape designer and played a key role in the development. He also designed a sculpture for the site (Figure 8.22).

(a)

(b)

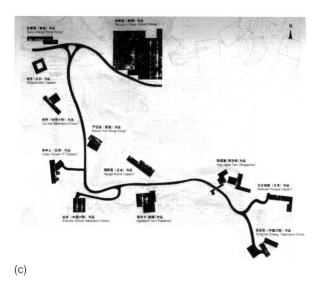
(c)

(d)

Figure 8.22 Commune by the Great Wall: a showcase for Asian architects, (a) Clubhouse, (b) "Terminal" house, (c) Site plan, (d) "Suitcase" house

The project leaves plenty of room for the architects to display their talents, each house representing a statement of their personal philosophy. Taiwan's Chien Hsueh Yi has tried to respect the history and environmental significance of the site. The long stone wall that dominates his design is set into the steep slope of a hill and constructed from stones collected locally. Three protruding rectangular "tongues" that house the living and dining areas of the house poke out from the wall at various angles, to take full advantage of the different vistas.

Gary Chang designed an oblong and timbered Suitcase House, 5 m by 44 m, the bottom stratum of which acts as a container for domestic fittings and equipment, services, and maid's quarters. The sunken compartments are concealed by floor panels, which rise with the assistance of pneumatic lifts. The long, thin internal layout can be subdivided by a series of mobile blinds and screens, giving the users absolute autonomy over the interior configuration.

Cui Kai's house has the theme of "see and be seen." Having two overlapping wings, each part of the house faces a different direction in order to capture the picturesque views of the surrounding countryside. A two-story high lighting chamber located where the foyer and staircases are housed connects the two levels. Cui describes this chamber as a glowing lantern that will light the way home as night falls.

Chang Yung Ho designed two wings that loosely enclose an inner courtyard. The featureless and austere outer walls clearly separate the house from its surroundings, whereas the wood and glass of the courtyard convey a feeling of domestic intimacy. This house is reminiscent of Chang's award-winning design for public housing in Guangdong, drawing on his understanding of Eastern space. It uses rammed earth for the external walls, laminated wood to define the interior space, light-weight steel with studs for the partition walls, glass and wood lath as external cladding, and aluminum-framed windows. The clarity of detail and construction excellence is a rebuke to the inferior craftsmanship that still plagues China. Chang believes that this house is a step beyond his designs for the Qingdao Convention Center and the Chongqing Research and Development Base for Peking University (Ye 2002).

The development of Commune by the Great Wall was driven by the social and cultural aspirations of China's rising economic élite, who are reaching for fame and fortune in the twenty-first century. This social class has a highly sophisticated sense of design and a strong desire to be consumers of these unique houses. People in this upwardly mobile and affluent social class typically own several flats in the city but wish to commute to private weekend villas nestled in green, leafy valleys. This project site has become a paradise for bankers, diplomats, designers, and wealthy entrepreneurs.

The Commune by the Great Wall project is significant for its intention, insight, and organization. Its rapid implementation within two years, the patience of the developers and architects, and the enlightened attitudes of all concerned make this project remarkable in its redefinition of Asian and Chinese architectural identities. Compared with the 1927 Wissenhof Housing Exhibition and the 1987 Berlin Housing Exhibition, however, Commune by the Great Wall suffers from the lack of a clear and unifying theme.

The Commune received a special prize at the Eighth Biennale di Venezia in 2002, and the developer, SOHO China, is preparing to be listed on the Hong Kong and New York Stock Exchanges. Zhang Xin and Pan Shiyi, a couple who own SOHO, successfully entered the niche of serving the burgeoning upper-middle class. They developed Jianwai SOHO, designed by Riken Yamamoto, with a 700,000 sq m apartment space in the eastern part of

Beijing, and the housing estate in Boao, Hainan Province. The former provides a high-density SOHO type flexible office home, and the latter is holiday house next to the Boao Asian Forum. All units were sold even before construction was finished.

Inspired by the Commune, the concept of "group design" was adopted elsewhere; for example, the hotel and artist's house in Nanjing, the science and industrial park in Dongguan of Guangdong Province (2003), museums on the anti-Japanese War, the Cultural Revolution, and folklore in Dayi County of Sichuan Province (2003–04); Software Office Park in Beijing (2004), housing in Pudong of Shanghai (2004), to name just a few.

The Nanjing project is located in a lakeside and involved Isozaki Arata and Kazuyo Sejima of Japan, Steven Holl of the US, David Adjaye of the UK, Odile Deco of France, Gabor Bachman of Hungary, Sean Godsell of Australia, Alberto Kalach of Mexico, Ettore Sottsass of Italy, Mathias Klotz of Chile, Luis M. Mansilla of Spain, Hrvoje Njiric of Croatia, Matti Sanaksenaho of Finland, and Chinese architects Liu Jiakun, Chang Yung Ho, Zhang Lei, Ai Weiwei, Cui Kai, Ma Qingyun, Zhou Kai, Wang Shu, Tang Hua, Doreen Heng Liu (Hong Kong), and Yao Renxi (Taiwan). Launched by Isozaki Arata and Liu Jiakun, these twenty-five architects and artists will design single-family houses and small-scale public buildings sponsored mainly by the private patrons. It will be completed in 2005 (*Time + Architecture*, No. 5, 2003; No. 3, 2004).

FUTURE EXPLORATIONS

When considering the work of the younger generation of Chinese architects described in this chapter, one reaches the following conclusions:

(1) China's experimental architecture is revolutionary in idea and practice, compared with ideology or commerce-ridden architecture. These architects are visionaries who have challenged the establishment and have pursued their vision despite opposition and hardship. They are indeed pioneers, yet their influence is increasing, as projects like Commune by the Great Wall demonstrate. As in experimental architecture everywhere, once the experiment is widely accepted, it ceases to be an experiment and becomes part of a new orthodoxy, which is itself challenged and subverted in a continuing dialectical process. Today's radical style is perhaps tomorrow's

"classic." This process is taking place to some extent in China. By international standards, the "experimental" architecture in China is quite "traditional and conventional." Some controversial topics are actually design norms in the Western world.

(2) China's experimental architecture is a people-centered, typically having greater concern for the end users of a building than does mainstream architecture. It is an architecture that rejects political, ideological, cultural, and historical burdens. It wants to tell the story of ordinary people and do so in a direct and forthright way, though its designs are often dramatic and unique. Rejecting any "great theme" may be a character of today's architecture, as pointed out by Rem Koolhaas: "The fact that this site's archeological aspect is emphasized above its political charge shows that the political innocence is an important part of the contemporary architect's equipment" (2000). However, some designers are too self-indulgent or idiosyncratic in their individualism and rejection of any grand or formal goal. An approach that is too self-centered inevitably limits the domain of the work; one rarely finds experimental buildings in the downtown districts of major Chinese cities. The voice of this group is loud, but the built works are few — it is disproportional to the huge amount of construction in China.

(3) As the buildings described usually originate from the "peripheral," for example rural, instead of "center" and are sponsored by artistic and open-minded patrons, China's experimental architecture uses local and available materials, low technology, and stresses meticulous construction. Liu Jiakun, for example, uses clay brick and easily available concrete to create his building forms. Wang Lifang uses brick veneer, and Chang Yung Ho uses laminated wood and rammed earth. The availability and affordability of these materials mean that these buildings can more easily leave the realm of design concept and actually be built. Their "creative abuse" of the old buildings grants new life and meaning to the otherwise deserted warehouse and factory workshops. This idea of sustainability is most valuable nowadays.

(4) China's experimental architecture uses the pure language of modern architecture, especially minimalism. Compared with the over-design of the commercially oriented buildings produced and later decorated in China, the works of these experimental architects are fresh and unpretentious, as they firmly believe that "architecture has a quintessentially tectonic character whereby part of its intrinsic expressivity is inseparable from the precise manner of its construction" (Frampton 1999). A tectonic quality of building is pursued by a lot of young people in this group. As this kind of "pure" style is identical to the tastes of some exhibition curators and magazine editors (or sometimes, they or their partners are curators and editors), this style of white, clean, minimalist concrete and glass boxes dominates the media and special issues of Chinese architecture in international design magazines (for example, *A + U* of Tokyo, *Architectural Record* of New York, and *Architectural Design* of London). If a Western reader enters China with those "magazine images" in mind, he or she will find that the realities of Chinese cities are so different from what is in the articles.

(5) The discussion on architectural discourses is not limited to architects themselves but includes people from literature, painting, music, and engineering. Some artists directly participate in creating the new built environment, for example, Ai Weiwei and his arts companions.

In the mid-1990s, experiments in architectural design were spontaneous and infrequent, but as this new generation of Chinese architects gradually met each other, either at conferences and seminars or through sharing their ideas in publications and over the Internet, their common aspirations and goals coalesced into a loosely organized but readily discernible movement. After the founding of the architectural research centers at Peking University in 1999 and at Nanjing University in 2000, this generation became more powerful and influential, as the members were now attached to universities and had impeccable academic credentials. Their relatively young age (most are in their thirties or forties) and overseas background also gave their ideas legitimacy. The revolution that they launched gained momentum through their effective use of the media, which have helped to quickly spread their ideas and influence.

A positive influence is that people focus on the construction details instead of empty ideological arguments. Young architects working in China's mainstream design institutes have tried to adopt and adapt these new ideas, but as their officially commissioned works are usually large in scale and come with strict schedules and deadlines, the result is not always significant; even so, the work of the experimental generation is becoming more widely accepted and respected. Whereas "experiment architecture," represented by Chang Yung Ho, gives some philosophical, contemplative, and "reversible" tastes, the young people in the mainstream design institutes present a fluency in dealing with the sophisticated large-scale buildings. The building design of the latter is mature in technology and possesses strong visual effects. The representatives are Meng Jianmin, as discussed above, and Cui Kai, who graduated from Tianjin University in 1982 and is now the chief architect in the Design Institute of Ministry of Construction. As vice-president of the Architectural Society of China and the country's representative to the UIA, Cui appears to be an official figure. The platforms of experimental and mainstream architecture are identical; both are bound by the same economic and physical constraints.

This generation has understood the power of the media and used the media to make broader influences within and outside the architectural circle. They created their own web sites, for example, Free Architectural Forum (www.far2000.com) based in Beijing, ABBS (www.abbs.com.cn) based in Shanghai, and Hyzonet (www.hyzonet.com) based in Shenzhen. These sites explore topical design concerns and provide forums for new ideas, receiving numerous letters and comments from students and young professionals. ABBS has 500,000 registered "abbsers" from China and overseas, and is one of the most popular websites in China. *Time + Architecture*, a bi-monthly magazine with editorial offices at Tongji University in Shanghai and led by theorists Professors Zhi Wenjun and Peng Nu, reports on the latest controversial topics discussed on these sites. The magazine itself is a bastion of the experimental architectural community. MADA s.p.a.m. in Shanghai hired forty employees, some of them assigned to do research and publication, including editing for the Italian design magazine *Domus*. Their books, either "paper architecture" or contemplating similar idiosyncratic overseas designs, are the bibles of young

students. However, these Chinese media international exhibitions and magazines publication, togther with, have offered too much praise and not enough criticism to China's architects.

China's experimental architecture sometimes deliberately keeps its distance from overseas avant-garde trends, such as postmodernism and deconstruction. Some of the young architects do not want to unquestioningly follow Western styles but wish to maintain their own self-respect and creative integrity; they refuse to be replicas of the West. Even so, the methodologies involved in solving design problems and marketing architecture in China are the same as in the West. In the final analysis, China's new generation of architects has its own identity as the voice of China's vigorous new culture.

When one looks at the huge tide of commercially oriented and pragmatic building construction that takes place across China each year, it must be acknowledged that the voice of experimental architecture is only faintly heard. Most designs remain on paper and are never built. If they are, the projects tend to be small in scale and are often funded by wealthy patrons. The language of this architecture is far removed from the daily concerns of ordinary people and can be, in some cases, self-absorbed. Even so, China's generation of experimental architects add color and diversity to a vista that would otherwise be dull and monolithic. These pioneers are an indispensable part of China's architectural scenario and, although they are a lonely vanguard, they are the forerunners of an even greater revolution that will surely follow in the coming decades.

Notes

1. Correspondence with the author.
2. Gutierrez & Portefaix (eds.) *Yung Ho Chang, Chinese Architect*. Hong Kong: Map Book Publishers, 2003.
3. *Yi* and *Daoism* are the traditional Chinese philosophies. *Yi Ching* or *I Ching, The Book of Change*, is a Chinese geomancy book formulated before the Spring and Autumn

Period (770–476 BCE). The description and interpretation of sixty-four (8 times 8) trigrams reveal the universal principles of constant change. *Daoism*, or *Taoism*, is one of the Chinese philosophies originating in the Spring and Autumn Period. It also explains the universal principles of heaven, earth, and humans. It is the theoretical basis for Chinese meditation, medicine, marshal arts, *feng shui*, and other pre-scientific thought.

T he awkward development of Chinese architecture in the 1950s and 1960s was partly due to the absurd political, economic, and social systems. The huge demands of the new era appeal for the reform of the system behind the practice of architecture. Architectural education firmly broke the old Soviet model and created new colors in teaching and learning. At the same time, the design practice experienced a fundamental change from being state-owned enterprises to private corporations. Thousands of old and young firms have to keep themselves afloat in the sea of a market economy. The situation is further fueled by the import of international firms, professionals, and management. These intangible systems thus form part of China's building revolution.

CHAPTER NINE

BEHIND THE BUILDING REVOLUTION: PRIVATE PRACTICE UNLEASHED

The previous chapters have mainly discussed architectural designs, relevant trends, and theories. However, China's architecture had performed awkwardly in a socialist system of a planned economy for decades before 1980; since then it has to first free itself of the shackles of the old system. This chapter discusses the forces behind the building revolution: emerging private practice and how it evolved from the old socialist system.

FROM PRIVATE TO PUBLIC

Before 1949, the architecture practice in China was no different from that in other capitalist societies. The British, American, and European architects dominated the design market at the turn of the twentieth century, until the arrival of the first generation of Chinese architects, who had just finished their studies and training at top American and European institutions. The most active firms are Palmer & Turner, Spence & Robinson of the UK, Henry K Murphy of the US, Udac of Hungary; Kwan, Wu & Yang; Allied Architects (Tong Jun, Zhao Sheng, and Chen Zhi); and Zhuang Jun of China. In 1952, a Shanghai design company was established by the government to absorb the individual designers and engineers, so as to meet the increasing demands of socialist construction. The company was renamed East China Design Institute in 1953 and soon had a staff of over 1000. The key staff members of this company went to Beijing the following year and founded design institutes in the capital city. They were the first state-own design companies in China. In the mid-1950s, private practice was phased out.

China's state-owned design institutes usually belong to a relevant administrative structure; for example, the ministries, bureaus, provinces, cities, towns, districts, and counties can run design institutes to serve their internal demands. Before 1980, design tasks were assigned through the country's economic and development plan; for example, a design institute under the Ministry of Metallurgy would mostly design steel plants and the surrounding residential neighborhoods. As the country was operated according to a strict planned economy in those politically turbulent years, no design fee could be charged and the professionals were paid meager standard government wages. This situation lasted until 1980.

Even after twenty years of the open-door policy, the state-owned companies account for the majority of design companies. According to the statistics of 2001, there were 11,338 building design companies, among which 9599 were owned by the state, accounting for 84.66 percent. There were 4327 design institutes,[1] among which 3488 were owned by the state, accounting for 80.6 percent. Design institutes that were incorporated or privately owned accounted for less than 20 percent (*People's Republic of China Year Book 2002*). The system of ownership, of course, decides the nature and operation mode of design firms.

China's design institutes are stratified into A, B, and C classes, according to the company's professionalism, cash flow, and design portfolio. Class A companies have virtually no limitation in design practice, whereas Class

B and C are limited in the scale and sophistication of building projects. The categorization is administered by the Ministry of Construction and the construction committees in provinces and cities.[2] This system exemplifies the government's care and responsibility towards investments. Before the present registration system of architects existed in China, classification of design institutes ensured the quality control of building designs. Very few other countries have such a strict classification scheme for practitioners, except for Japan. Architects there are classified into either List I or List II, similar to China's new arrangement.

In the mid-1980s, there were about ten Class A design institutes in Shanghai; for example, the East China Design Institute, Shanghai Institute of Civil Architecture, Design Institute of Tongji University, the Ninth Institute, and Shanghai Design Institute of Light Industry. According to the *China Building Industry Yearbook 1994*, there were 158 registered Class A design institutes in Beijing, 46 in Shanghai, and 90 in Guandong, mainly in Guangzhou and Shenzhen. In contrast, there were only three Class A design institutes in Qinghai Province and four in Ningxia Hui Autonomous Region. The disparity between China's east and west could be seen here. In 1996, there were more than 400 Class A design institutes based in Shanghai alone. Some are of local origin, some from other provinces. Some are from overseas, equivalent to Class A level (*China Building Industry Yearbook 1996*).

The major design institutes establish their branches or franchised companies all over China, especially in major cities. For example, the Beijing Institute of Architectural Design has branches in Shanghai, Shenzhen, Zhuhai, Haikou, and other cities. The design institute of Tongji University set up an office in Shenzhen, and the design institute of Shenzhen University does the same in Shanghai.

To maintain both their reputation and business, the design companies have to get more "awards" from various places. This may explain why there are so many design and construction awards in China. The Ministry of Construction, National Education Commission, China Arts Academy, other governmental departments, provinces, and cities each have selection events every one or two years, but these seem random.

Some selections do not have a fixed time span; some others have been phased out quietly. None of these elections has much significance, let alone match prestigious awards like the RIBA gold medal, AIA gold medal, and Pritzker Architectural Prize. However, one or two "celebrity building elections" held in big cities can really promote the architectural culture.[3]

REGISTRATION OF ARCHITECTS

The architect and engineering systems followed the model in the Soviet Union in the 1950s. Professional titles were awarded from the state-owned design institutes and municipal (or provincial) governments. The principles of promotion usually consider the candidates' working performance in the past five years, publications, and foreign language proficiency. The authority sometimes organizes foreign language examination for this promotional purpose. Because of the inflation of senior titles and degrees, recruitment, promotion, and other business activities have increased the demand for a higher education level. That directly led to the scandal of "selling degrees" and corruption in institutions of higher education (*Mingpao Monthly*, March 2003).

But all of these titles produced in the planned economy are being phased out. Instead, the registration of various licenses takes the lead; for example, architect, engineer, attorney-at-law, medical doctor, and accountant.

The Architectural Society of China (ASC) started to contact the Royal Institute of British Architects (RIBA), American Institute of Architects (AIA), and other overseas professional bodies in the 1980s, hoping to establish its own registration system. A tentative examination was held in Liaoning Province in late 1994. The format is the same as the American model — nine subjects. A graduate from a five-year architectural school system should practice at least three years before taking the examination.

At the end of 1995, the first examination of registered architects was held at the national level. In March 1997 was the second examination. The annual examination was held afterwards. Architect registration is divided into Class I and Class II. The principle of this division is the same as that for the classification of design institutes. Registration of structural engineer and other engineers has been increasing since 1996.

In July 1996, the National Management Committee of Registered Architects promulgated a list of Class I architects, totaling 5285 persons in this first batch. Among them, 401 were in Beijing, 256 in Shanghai, and only 11 in Hunan. There were many who worked in various ministries, e.g., 169 in the Ministry of Construction, and 290 in the National Education Commission. In 1998, there were 8260, and up to the year 2003, 12,384 Class I architects were registered (http://www.cin.gov.cn). In a population of 1.3 billion, there is only one architect for more than 100,000 people. In Hong Kong, this ratio is one architect for every 3500 people. In comparison, the United States has around 150,000 licensed architects for a total population of 240 million, or a ratio of roughly one architect for every 1500 people (Yeh 2000).

In China, this small number of architects is distributed very unevenly. Among these 12,000 architects, 2072 are in Beijing and 1007 are in Shanghai. In other words, about one-quarter of the architects are in these two cities. Moreover, there are 984 architects in Guangdong and 837 in Jiangsu. The number declines sharply in the western provinces; for example, there are only 106 and 105 in Guizhou and Gansu. Qinghai and Tibet, each similar in size to the US state of Texas, have only five registered architects (http://www.cin.gov.cn). The statistics of registered structural engineers show a similar distributive picture in China. The Chinese government called for developing the western part of the country at the beginning of the twenty-first century. Considering the huge disparity between east and west, coastal and interior cities, there should be great potential for building professionals in developing the west.

The 12,000 architects are still a small number compared with the 1.3 billion population. The registered architects are highly sought after, and the profession of architect is a "golden collar" career (even more valuable than the conventional "white collar"). This could be seen from the various recruitment advertisements in magazines and newspapers. The registration system has gradually eliminated the restrictions on individual professionals that were imposed by "design institutes," and no doubt marks an important step towards private practice.

THE EMERGENCE OF PRIVATE PRACTICE

Private practice in interior design and construction has existed since the mid-1980s. However, private practice was still rare in the field of architectural design even in 1997.

In 1985, a joint-venture design firm, "Great Earth," was incorporated in Beijing, led mainly by Alfred Pei-Gen Peng, a Tsinghua University professor returning from Canada. This firm is the first of its kind in China, and some directors are retired government officials who have extensive connections in China. The founders bravely "jumped into the icy river," as repeatedly described by

Alfred Peng.[4] However, the river was not so chilly; the firm enjoyed navigating in the vast sea of the market. "Great Earth" has completed numerous urban designs, master plans, and institutional and residential buildings.

The Zuo Xiaosi Architectural Firm, approved as Class A, was set up in Shenzhen in 1994 and attracted much attention. In 1995, the Ministry of Construction issued a notice that each coastal or provincial capital city could have from one to three private firms of architectural design as an experiment. In March 1996, the Ministry of Construction approved the Wang Xiao-xiong Architectural Firm in Taiyuan, Shanxi Province, as Class A. It soon became the standard for private firms in central China.

In 2000, the central government hoped to reform thoroughly service industries such as law, accounting, and design. All law firms were incorporated, completely separating them from government organizations. The design trade followed. In the beginning of 2000, the General Office of the State Council issued *The system reform of engineering, survey and design institute of Ministry of Construction* ([1999] No. 101). The percentage of state-owned design and surveying institutes dropped from 82.4 in 1999 to 71.2 in 2001. Up to February 2003, the Ministry of Construction had approved seventy-four incorporated design firms, among which forty-nine are in Shanghai, including four Class A design firms and eight structural design firms (Li 2003).

In fact, almost all design firms (design institutes) have run on a self-financing basis since the late 1980s. They have to pay tax and are responsible for the salaries and welfare of their staff, as well as all costs for production. In fact, architects in China nowadays work in various forms of private practice in the market economy. Generally, there are several types of competitors in China's design market today, as analyzed below.

First, there are the main design institutes. These large, old design institutes, for example, Northwest Design Institute, Southwest Design Institute, Beijing Design Institute of Architecture, usually have a staff of over 1000. These institutes are adopted from the Soviet Union model in the 1950s. In the 1990s, the wave of reform swallowed the whole country, and these old state-owned companies were gradually further divided. The smaller units became "cost centers," having self-reliance and self-responsibility in finance and bidding commitments. For example, the Shenzhen Design Institute and Shanghai Design Institute divide their organizations into "Section 1," "Section 2," "Section 3," etc. Each section has the right to bid on design commissions and sign contracts.

The design institutes undertake large commissions, eased by the relationship with their local construction committee and their strong technical competence and resources. No doubt, they are the foundations of China's design market today. In some important design competitions, like the opera house, airport, and convention center, the owner (the government) will invite a local or Chinese firm to submit schemes. Even if they fail in the design competition, they will be assigned the work of construction drawing for the winning international firms. In this way, their income is ensured, and they can gain experience from this international cooperation.

Architectural design is labor intensive but highly individual. In the US, UK, and Hong Kong, a firm of over fifty people is considered large. How can a firm of 1000 survive and operate? The crisis of a "collapse" has not often happened in the large Chinese design firms since the mid-1990s. They are the desired workplace for talented young people. High-caliber band-A graduate students compete to enter such large companies; the application to vacancy ratio is more than 10:1 in the past ten years. The pressures and challenges are offset by the job satisfaction of young men and women, who can usually lead a project of 100,000 sq m or even larger after several years' training.

The burdens for such large, old, state-owned companies are the huge staff, both current and retired. The firms cannot easily lay people off. For example, in some old design institutes, people have been working in the reference library and other non-productive positions for decades. These companies have to bid on design projects with very low prices. At the end of the 1990s, for example, the design fee for residential buildings was around 10–20 yuan (US$1.20–2.50) per sq m, but this could be two yuan in some provinces. The book *Great Leap Forward* by Rem Koolhaas and his students has this comment: "The Chinese architects design the largest volume, in the shortest time, for the lowest fee. There is one-tenth the number of architects in China as in the United States, designing five times the project volume in one-fifth the time, earning one-tenth the design fee. This implies an efficiency of 2500 times that of an American architect" (2001, 161). Given the low income and the high staff costs, many big companies are almost bankrupt and have to rely on loans from banks to survive.

The second group is the overseas companies. Chapter Three discusses some operations of the overseas companies. Currently, the major international companies have done jobs in China or opened branches in China; for example, John Portman, KPF, SOM, HOK from the US;

Terry Farrell from the UK; Jean-Marie Charpentier et Associés from France; Peddel and Thorp from Australia; and a group of Hong Kong consultancy companies such as P & T, Leigh & Orange, and Taoho. Overseas companies are only interested in large government projects (for example, "city beautification" mentioned in Chapter Five), joint venture projects, or those funded by investment from overseas, to offset the huge cost.

For example, when Paul Andreu of Paris was designing the Grand National Theater of Beijing in the early 2000s, he had to fly to the capital city almost every month (Phoenix TV News, Nov. 2001). Another French architect, Jean-Marie Charpentier, was so popular in Shanghai that he was commissioned to design the Shanghai Grand Theater, the pedestrian Nanjing Road, and other important designs. Half of his working time is in Shanghai, and he is also proud to be in Shanghai. Many Hong Kong and Taiwan architects relocated to Shanghai and Beijing. As these international architects are involved mainly in large projects, they are not a threat in the market for medium- or small-scale buildings. The overseas companies usually excel in the design of those large-scale, comprehensive, and technically sophisticated buildings. Their experience in compiling specifications, managing the job, and doing the construction are what China needs today.

The third group is the private companies. They may give the impression of being "state-owned" or being run by a state-owned company, but they are essentially privately owned. These companies are usually managed by overseas Chinese who are familiar with both China's situation and global trends. They are the strong competitors of the state-owned and foreign companies.

Entering the twenty-first century, more young people have elected to run their own firms or work as freelance. Compared with the old state-owned companies, private companies are more flexible and efficient in personnel and resources. They lose the stable and safe umbrella of the state-owned companies, but they realize their own value and dreams. In these young firms, each person is capable of handling many duties.

The working efficiency and revenue created are usually double or triple that of the state-owned companies. The maximum design fee revenue in the old state-owned design institutes was around 300,000 yuan (around US$36,144) per staff per year in 2000. The figures in some private firms in Shenzhen, Guangzhou, Shanghai, Beijing, and other cities are higher. However, the annual revenue per staff member in China is about one-seventh to one-tenth that of their Hong Kong, US, and UK counterparts.[5] The average construction cost in mainland China is only about one-fifth of that at the international level. These factors contribute to the low income of Chinese architects.

It is clear that private practice is more appealing to young people. In 2002, many architectural graduates of South China University of Technology opted for freelance work as designers, model makers, and illustrators, based on their training in their five years of architecture school.[6]

In Chapter Seven, we mention several Fellows of the China Academy of Engineering and China Academy of Science. The government gave the green light to these people to run a practice under their own names. For example, Fellow Mo Bozhi, eighty-nine years old in 2003, runs his design firm with thirty staff members, located in the five-star White Swan Hotel he designed in the early 1980s. He is among the most successful first generation of private practitioners.

Further analyzing this group of Fellows, we find that the youngest was around fifty-eight in 2002; the others ranged in age from sixty to ninety. Except one or two Fellows who were running their own private firms, the majority work in studios at big design institutes or universities; for example, Professor Dai Fudong's office in Tongji University and Professor Qi Kang's research institute in Southeast University, Nanjing. These studios are filled mostly by "hopeful" young people under or around thirty years old, and usually on a temporary basis. When the young people are older, they may not be satisfied in assistant postions. When they leave, new graduates soon fill the vacancies. This partly impedes the implementation of imagination and pencil plans of those masters.

Shi Wei investigated eighteen non-state-owned design firms in Shanghai from January to April 2003. These companies are partnerships, privately owned, or joint ventures. Some company owners are from overseas or are university teachers. The companies are commercially registered overseas or in China, therefore sometimes appearing to be "international." They usually have a staff of more than thirty. Ninety percent of the companies charge a design fee higher than the national standard. In the prevailing design competition or tendering, most design schemes cannot be built. But in this investigation, sixteen companies could have 50 percent of their work constructed, eight companies could have 85 to 100 percent, and three companies have never participated in any design competition (Shi 2003).

Several private companies made their debut after years of quiet but hard work. For example, New East of

Shenyang in north China, Standard Architecture of Beijing, Huahui Design Ltd. of Tianjin. From 25 Architects, Studio, Pan-Pacific Design, Tianhua and MADA s.p.a.m. (see Chapter Eight) of Shanghai, Urban Practice and X-Urban in Shenzhen (Figures 9.1–9.3). Their design and office

(a)

(b)

(c)

(d)

(e)

(f)

Figure 9.1 Works of From 25 Architects Studio, (a, b) Seine Villa, Beijing, 2002, (c) Sanxin Garden, Shanghai, 2002, (d) Waigaoqiao Administration building, Shanghai, (e) Zhang Jiajing (f) Office of From 25

(a)

(b)

Figure 9.2 Fei Xiaohua and X-Urban, the public washroom of Lotus Mountain, Shenzhen, 2002

(a)

(b)

(c)

Figure 9.3 Pan-Pacific Design & Develoment Group Ltd., office and design work, (a) Building of automobile industry, (b) Delong Building, (c) The office accommodates seventy staff members

management are obviously different from the traditional state-owned design institutes. Their work is imbued with the exploratory trends discussed in Chapter Eight, and they gradually built up their own portfolios. Their designs include comprehensive developments of over 100,000 sq m, urban designs, museums, residential estates, and public washrooms. Private firms, especially those led by the foreign-educated Chinese architects, soon emerged as strong competitors of state-owned and foreign companies (Larsen 2004).

The portfolio of the Original Design Studio of Shanghai includes an academic building of a technical institute in Guangxi Province, the TV station of Jiashan City, Zhejiang Province, landscape architecture of Xihu in Hangzhou, campus planning, a pedestrian street in Hunan Province, Financial Museum of Hangzhou, a residential subdivision in Shanghai, and a commercial building in the heart of Shanghai. Most of their designs mentioned above were completed after 2000 (*Time and Architecture, No. 3, 2003*).

Last but not least, there are university teachers or staff from the major design institutes. Working in their spare time, they are strong in schematic design and are usually active in the market for small building projects or interior design. As mentioned in Appendix II, teachers and students from universities form a very active force in design, especially in schematic design in China. They understand Chinese and local culture well.

In the increasingly keen market competition, developers hope to offer unique products, and they are prepared to hire capable workers, no matter where they come from. When the scheme is procured, the design can actually be sent to any design firm for approval and further development.

In Chifeng Road of Shanghai, a street adjacent to Tongji University, there are more than 500 firms related to architecture. Of the design, production, modeling, rendering, printing, and architectural bookstores in this street of less than 300 m, more than 80 percent are run by the students, graduates, teachers, and retired staff members of Tongji University. The annual revenue in 2002 was more than 1 billion yuan. The office rent rose 10 percent in the second half of 2002 (Yuan and Xu, February 9, 2003). People jokingly call this street the "Hollywood of architecture," as in Hollywood where there are many large and small companies related to the movie industry (Figure 9.4).

When all construction tasks were planned by the government, the state-owned design institutes shouldered the design work. When the tide of privatization and the market economy is high, most clients are privately owned

(a)

(b)

Figure 9.4 Business related to architectural design is everywhere on Chifeng Road, Shanghai (a) The street adjacent to Tongji is filled with companies related to design, (b) A graphics and printing company

sole proprietorships, partnerships, or corporations. It is natural that private practice provides design service; indeed, this trend is irreversible. The market competition and struggle for recognition make very thrilling scenes of China's building revolution.

NOTES

1. The name "design institute" is a result of learning from the Soviet Union in the 1950s. As employees usually numbered several hundred to a thousand, the "institute" is obviously different from the privately owned design "firm" or "company."
2. The standards of Class A, B and C design companies are set by the Ministry of Construction and are available in its website. The author introduced the system, with more details, in another book, *Building Practice in China* (Pace Publishing Ltd., Hong Kong, 1999).
3. In the 1980s and 1990s, some cities launched an election of "ten celebrities" or "fifty celebrities," important buildings of their cities for the past forty, fifty, or a hundred years, mainly chosen by citizens. Those events attracted the notice of the public and the media. In Beijing's event of 1999, Beijing Library, People's Congress, and most of the "ten grand buildings" of 1959 (see Chapter Two) were selected. Shanghai celebrated the fiftieth anniversary of the People's Republic of China and selected its favorite buildings in 1999. After several rounds of voting by Shanghai residents and experts from Shanghai and other provinces, thirty buildings were awarded gold, silver, and

bronze awards. Five top celebrity buildings were designed by overseas architects; the others were designed by local architectural design institutes. Most of the buildings that form the skyline of Shanghai are included; for example, Jin Mao Building, Shanghai Grand Theater, Pearl TV Tower, Pudong International Airport, Shanghai Museum, Shanghai Exhibition Center, Shanghai Stadium, Shanghai Library; and New Jinjiang Hotel. See Charlie Xue, "Ten Celebrity Buildings in Shanghai and Hong Kong," *World Architecture*, No. 9, 2000.
4. Professor Alfred Peng was interviewed by newspapers and TV in the 1980s. "Jumping into the icy river" was a frequent topic to describe his determination. This saying also appears in the introductory article of his company profile materials.
5. The data of design fees are from *World Architecture*, London, 2000–03. Take the per capita figure of 2002 as example. KPF was US$297,000; Sasaki Associates of the US was US$634,000. Some Hong Kong companies performed as follows: Rocco Design, US$530,000; Dennis Lau & Ng Chun Man, US$428,000; P & T Group, US$263,000.
6. Discussion with Professor Zhao Honghong of South China University of Technology in June 2002.

Economists, politicians, and ordinary people are concerned about where China will go, so that they can make their own choices. The building professionals in China have no other choice but to show their advantages, overcome weaknesses, and surf the wave of opportunities and threats. Architects and developers should find a new balance and position in the framework of contemporary China and the world. China should, and will, provide more pleasure to its people through a better built environment, and vigorously contribute to the wealth of world architecture in the new millennium.

CHAPTER TEN

CHINESE ARCHITECTURE
IN THE TWENTY-FIRST CENTURY: AN EPILOGUE

WHERE WILL CHINA GO FROM HERE?

The previous nine chapters talk about architecture, a very visible profession that speaks for a nation. However, where and how will this nation go, in turn, determines its future shape of architecture. This chapter first analyzes the directions and scenarios of China's development in the twenty-first century. It then presents the strengths, weaknesses, opportunities, and challenges in architecture, planning, and built form.

China is the fastest growing economy in the world, its per capita income increasing fivefold since 1980. In the past quarter century, it has achieved what took other countries centuries to do. Swift growth and structural change, although resolving many problems, has created new challenges; for example, employment insecurity, growing inequality, persistent poverty, inefficient bureaucracy, inconsistent policies, widespread corruption, lack of infrastructure, and mounting environmental pressures (World Bank 1997; World Economic Forum 2003). The World Bank, in its research report, argues that China can meet the challenges and sustain rapid growth. Although the difficulties ahead should not be underestimated, neither should China's strengths: relative stability, a remarkably high saving rate, a strong record of pragmatic reforms, a disciplined and literate labor force, a supportive Chinese diaspora, and a growing administrative capacity (World Bank 1997).

"The transformation of an economy as large as China's, from low- to middle-income status, from rural to urban, from agricultural to industrial (and services), will inevitably cause ripples in the world economy." "The past two decades have seen sustained, rapid modernization unlike in any other period in China's long history. The next two decades promise more of the same. The huge risks that China faces could yet take the shine off this potential. But with resolute leadership at home and statesmanlike policies from the world's industrial powers, China can overcome these challenges. One-fifth of humanity would then have within its grasp the power to break free of the shackles of poverty and under-development and accomplish what could become the most remarkable economic transformation the world has ever seen" (World Bank 1997).

Many world experts on economics acknowledge China's phenomenal growth on a macro scale, but fail to recognize the problems associated with the pace of the development. From the top leaders to the workers in China, everyone sees the imperative of economic prosperity. Money and development are the only goals and measures to gauge success. Even when SARS (severe acute respiratory syndrome) affected China in 2003, the country recorded an increase in GDP of 9.1 percent.[1] The physical construction of modernization continuously exhibits proud achievements. Without this speed, tens of thousands of people will lose jobs, triggering social upheaval. To maintain a booming economy seems to be the sole objective of the government at various levels.

How to showcase the rapid development and make a profit from the process are two questions that need answering. The "image projects" are the best means. Scattered throughout the countries, these bridges, highways, central business districts, and impressive theaters are lucrative business for the officials in charge, and the manifestation of the achievements of local governments and officials. Countless grand scenes parade in the mass media, and people's lust for materials has reached a climax. Woman can sell their bodies, officials sell their power, intellectuals sell their souls, a nation sells its land, and people sell their dignity — all for money! Corruption is rampant in various administrative levels and academic institutions. The social, moral, and honest conscience has gradually disappeared in this 5000-year-old civilization. The traditional religions and the spiritual pillars collapsed during the communist rule, and the new common belief and world values have not yet been established.

Nine hundred million peasants and rural inhabitants account for more than 60 percent of the population in China. The structural poverty of rural areas, and a series of irrational policies, will enlarge the already huge gap between the countryside and cities, rural people and city-dwellers. The voices of disadvantaged and vulnerable groups, both in the countryside and cities, are rarely heard. The fruits of growth cannot be fairly shared by all people, and that will create more instability in society (also see Preface and notes).[2]

Social problems directly or indirectly lead to environmental disasters. China's growth has brought both dramatic improvements in living standards and serious damage to the environment. China's air and water, particularly in urban areas, are among the most polluted in the world. Ambient concentrations of most pollutants exceed international standards several times over, burdening China with vast human and economic costs, estimated at 3 to 8 percent of the GDP a year (World Bank 1997; also see Preface and Chapter One). An alarming scientific report, "Climate change," indicated "the planet is carrying a higher population than it can sustain. By 2020 'catastrophic' shortages of water and energy supply will become increasingly harder to overcome, plunging the planet into war. 8,200 years ago climatic conditions brought widespread crop failure, famine, disease and mass migration of populations that could soon be repeated" (The Observer, Feb 22, 2004). Accounting for almost one-quarter of the residents on Earth, China is no exception, as "China's huge population and food demand make it particularly vulnerable." When "major European cities will be sunk beneath rising sea" (The Observer, Feb 22, 2004), Shanghai and other Chinese coastal cities have no escape.

In an authoritative global ranking conducted by the World Economic Forum and Swiss International Institute of Management Development, China's growth competitiveness dropped from number twenty-six in 1996 and twenty-four in 1997 to forty-four in 2003, and around forty to forty-four since 2000 (World Economic Forum 1995–2003). Apparently the social, environmental and other problems are affecting the country's competitiveness.

All of those barriers can be attributed to the reluctance to reform China's political system and the strict censorship of the media. According to many analyses, modernization will only be assured by liberal democracy (Fukuyama 1992; www.cnd.org). The Chinese government "must begin serving markets by building the legal, social, physical, and institutional infrastructure needed for their rapid growth" (World Bank 1997). Only by taking this direction can China sustain further growth and steadily enter the strongest rank in the twenty-first century.

STRENGTH, WEAKNESS, OPPORTUNITIES, AND CHALLENGES IN ARCHITECTURE

While the macro condition in China is one of rapid growth with potential instability, China's architecture is also in a state of flux. To predict how Chinese architecture will perform in the twenty-first century, four aspects will be discussed: strengths, weaknesses, opportunities, and challenges.

Strengths

The healthy development of Chinese architecture has benefited from the ambitions of various levels of governments to improve their cities. As revealed in the previous chapters, China not only embraces the international norms but aspires to lead the world trends. This is reflected in the rapidly expanding building quantities, gradually enhanced qualities, and more frequently held international activities. If the economy keeps a healthy momentum, it will be financially viable to build a series of more impressive urban and building projects.

After twenty and more years of exchange with and immersion in international architecture, Chinese architects have accumulated valuable experience in design and management, which in turn contributes to their building works in the twenty-first century. Trained in the top Chinese and overseas architectural schools, the architects mentioned in Chapter Eight entered the golden age of their career in this new millennium and will soon reach the frontier of China's construction of modernization. They know China's past shortcomings and aim to be world class in design and services. Their activities and work will be part of the international scene of pioneering architecture.

In spite of the shortcomings mentioned in the previous sections, the general education level and people's qualities have been enhanced. "Educating clients" has been mentioned by the professional world for a long time, as it "is a slow job and often lags as much as a quarter century behind the education of architects which is not always a

Figure 10.3 Jianwai SOHO, Beijing

Figure 10.1 New town in Shunde, Pearl River Delta

fast moving process" (Lang *et al.* 1997). In twenty-first-century China, it is hoped that the clients have a better vision and higher mission in doing building, which directly demands more forward-looking, durable, sustainable, and ingenious design. The authentic and serious designs and buildings will be based on China's economic, and available technical and material situations, instead of merely showing off wealth and mimicking foreign counterparts.

Weaknesses

Although the large number of design tasks gives designers more practice opportunities, it takes away the time required for careful thinking. It is a common problem of Chinese architecture that a building has an impressive visual effect when viewed from afar, but it cannot be read closely. The details and maintenance have the typically embarrassing problems that can often be seen in developing nations.

Figure 10.2 Seminar in a small design firm, Zhuhai, Guangdong Province

As the funding is volatile and decisions are usually made in haste, most buildings are designed and constructed in a very short period (see Chapters Four and Five). For example, the construction of the Zhuhai campus of Dr Sun Yat-sen University, a site of around 200 ha, the academic buildings, canteens, and students halls of around 200,000 sq m. GFA, was completed in less than a year in 2000. So was a neighboring campus, Beijing Teachers' University in Zhuhai. The Dongguan Convention Center of 190,000 sq m was also delivered to clients after eight months of intensive construction in 2001. Foundations were laid when other drawings had not yet been issued. The hard-working clients, designers, and construction companies deserve applause. But those buildings fail to present appropriate details here and there, not to mention the lack durable of qualities required for fifty or even a hundred years.

In this regard, Chinese architects and their clients are generally not mature. More exposure to international architecture, or examination of Hong Kong architecture, will help Chinese architects to establish the concept and techniques of carrying out projects from design through procurement.

Opportunities

The ample opportunities of practice, both in quality and quantity, give architects (especially younger ones) the best environment to learn and accumulate experience. From 2000 to 2010, the urbanization level will increase from 36 percent to around 50 percent, which means another 130 million people will move to the towns and cities. Some social scientists estimate this migration figure as 200 million (Jakes 2004). Suppose each person needs 15 sq m. That means 1.95 billion sq m in floor area for residential buildings alone. Assume the current 12,000 architects continue to work in these ten years. Each architect will design 160,000 sq m of residential buildings, not including the 2008 Olympic Games in Beijing, 2010 World Expo in Shanghai, and numerous urban beautification projects in various towns. The chances of real building are so immense: a young architect under thirty years old may act as design or project architect for a building of 100,000 sq m. Good works, it is hoped, are increasing proportionally to the vast quantity. The boom in the 1990s and early 2000s gave opportunities mainly to international masters. The rising young Chinese architects cannot compete in building quantities and scale. When this generation matures and has ample chance to practice,

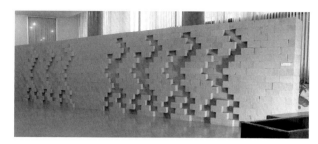

Figure 10.4 Students' design, arts exhibition, Shanghai, 2002

Chinese architects will rise in prominence. A similar phenomenon happened in Japan in the second half of the twentieth century, which also saw a large quantity of construction and trained Japanese and overseas architects.

"Fifty years ago, the architectural scene was not about a unique individual, the genius, but about the group, the movement. There was no scene … Architecture was not about the largest possible difference, but about the subtleties that could be developed within a narrow range of similarities within the generic … This kind of architecture saw itself as ideological. Its politics stretched all the way from socialism to communism and all the points in between … Our client is no longer the state or its derivation, but the private individuals often embarked on daring ambitions and expensive trajectories, which we architects support whole heartedly." "The system is final. The market economy. We work in a post-ideological era and for lack of support we have abandoned the city or any more general issues… At best our work brilliantly explores and exploits a series of unique conditions" (Koolhaas 2000, www.pritzkerprize.com). Koolhaas's words succinctly describe the transitions of both world and Chinese architecture, as evidenced by the narrative in this book. The market economy and ambitious private developers are encouraging individual design and unique qualities in planning and buildings.

As the lower-stream computer industry moves to China and India, the twentieth century saw a tendency for Hong Kong's design firms to outsource the rendering and technical documentation to the Mainland. The relatively inexpensive technical labor in architectural rendering, animation, printing, and binding may also attract employers from overseas. This may be an opportunity for China to export its building services.

In addition to the market, technological advancement provides opportunities for better design and quality of urban architecture. One development is in the continuously improved building materials and creative structural and mechanical engineering, which generate high-intensity, low weight and brand-new-looking structures. Another development is in the design process itself, which benefits from the current information technology, including digital architecture, a larger database, design intelligence, virtual realities, and faster and more extensive communications. In this regard, China shares the global efforts in expediting the advancement of building science and technology.

The changes in ideas, culture, and technical means will inevitably influence the future curriculum of architectural education. The youth in the twenty-first century live and grow in an environment obviously different from that of their parents. In the 1980s, students had limited material resources and reference materials; therefore, at that time they could take only one or two directions. In the 2000s, students have too many choices in a more lively cultural background, and they may be bewildered about what and how to choose. They have their own cultural values, aesthetic goals, and technical dimension. Teaching them needs a completely new way of thinking and pedagogic methodology.

The building boom creates an urgent need for new blood — the expansion of architectural education has been and will be continuously ongoing. There are currently around 120 architectural programs, either in an architectural program attached to an engineering department or in an architectural school under the university system. Architectural education will be particularly in demand in two areas. One is the undergraduates, who will directly join the army of drafting and designing. The other is the higher graduate and research degree holders, who will satisfy the teaching forces of continuous expansion in old and new schools. The latter is seen in top schools like Tsinghua, Tongji, and Southeast Universities. The opportunities of practice and education are for both the domestic Chinese and the overseas international professionals. China will become a new employment center for building professionals and scholars.

Threats

The strengths and opportunities are always encouraging; however, challenges and threats exist. The environmental and social crises, often mentioned in this book, saliently present several possible constraints for the future of architecture.

Figure 10.5 Old lane house in Shanghai

Figure 10.6 Residential tower in Pudong, Shanghai

First, the land supply is limited, as indicated in Chapters One and Four. The fast expansion and drive of cities and Special Economic Zones ruthlessly erode the agricultural lands; building development and "food demand" compete for pitifully limited land resources. The existing city centers are suffering from increasingly crowded use: more people, more buildings, more roads, and vehicles. The Chinese government's encouragement of the car industry has sharpened the contradiction. The land shortage will force people to dig for space underground. According to a study, the underground space of Beijing has a potential of providing 6.4 billion sq m of floor area, outnumbering the total of Beijing's buildings now (Qian 1998). In this case, the challenges may also be transformed to opportunities.

The shortage of electricity and clean water already constrain most Chinese cities in the beginning of the twenty-first century. The new development stretches the already tight supply, and it will have to slow down to adapt to the situation. The "opportunities" of abundant practice mentioned above can easily be lost at any time. What is the appropriate development speed? What is the suitable density for the urban areas, which can save the buildable land and cater for livable environment? These will be big challenges both for China and the world. This also explains why we believe that the environmental aspect should become the new criterion in evaluating (Chinese) architecture, as discussed in Chapter One. The environmental crisis may also stimulate more research and practice in sustainable, green, and intelligent buildings and relevant technologies.

Second, in the conflict of commercialism and preservation, traditional neighborhoods and relics are threatened and largely being razed. The pace of preservation and meager funds cannot save the valuable heritage from the bulldozers and short-sighted decision-makers. As discussed in the preceding chapters, the continuation of Chinese culture was broken on several occasions in modern times; the people's belief in their own tradition is amazingly weak or even nonexistent. The Chinese or local identity and tastes are almost swamped in the high tide of globalization. Imported buildings, architects, and styles are embraced, and they dominate the urban streets regardless of the local conditions. Most Chinese cities, if not all, soon fall into the rank of "generic city," a term coined by Rem Koolhaas (1995). It is good or bad, as repeatedly discussed in Chapters Two and Three, but it is definitely detrimental to China as a nation.

In our analysis in Chapters Two and Three, the mere and singular "Western" or "Chinese" will only exist in illusion. Chinese architects and developers should find new balance and position in the framework of contemporary China and the world. China should, and will, provide more pleasure to its people through a better built environment, and vigorously contribute to the wealth of world architecture in the new millennium.

NOTES

1. The World Bank, through its thorough study, suggests that an alternative (or perhaps real) picture may be 1.2 percentage points lower than is indicated by China's official statistics. See World Bank, *China 2020: Development Challenges in the New Century* (The World Bank, Washington DC, 1997, p 3).

2. Following the discussion in the Preface of this book, the problems of the countryside and peasants gradually draw the attention of the Chinese government and people in the cities. In the beginning of 2004, an investigation, *Report of Chinese Peasants*, by two writers in Anhui Province, shocked the country with its profound revealing of the poor conditions in rural areas and a series of scandals about the local leadership. The report was first published by People's Literature Press of Beijing, and then by numerous newspapers and websites.

Seen from the old president's office, Nanjing

CHRONICLE OF CHINESE ARCHITECTURE SINCE 1980

1980

Shenzhen, Zhuhai, Shantou and Xiamen are set up as Special Economic Zones.

Criminal trial and conviction of the "Gang of Four," the former conservative forces, including Mao Zedong's widow, Jiang Qing.

The central government says that the current design trade should be reformed.

The Fifth Congress, Architectural Society of China Design institutes allowed to charge design fees and have contracts with clients, a policy different from that of the planned economy in the past decade.

Inaugural issue of the bi-monthly magazine *World Architecture*, Beijing, October.

Representative buildings:

Jianguo Holiday Inn Hotel in Beijing, the first joint-venture hotel in China, designed by overseas architects.

Hangzhou Theater, a large and prominent theater in this period, set an example for theater design.

National design competitions of rural housing and theater design. These competitions motivated the architects to design creatively and look carefully at these building types.

Terminal of Beijing airport, integration of interior design and murals.

Nanlou Guest House of Great Buddha, Leshan Mountain, Sichuan Province.

1981

The Chinese government begins permitting peasants, almost eighty percent of China's population, to grow and sell their own food. Agriculture is in effect de-collectivized.

State Council starts to encourage property sales to individual citizens.

The People's Congress decides to continue the policies of reforming, adjusting, and restructuring the administration in the next five years.

Chinese troops invade Vietnam to help the Cambodian regime.

After normalization of tertiary education, the state implements the system of bachelor's and master's degrees in higher education.

Conference of earth-sheltered building held in Yan'an, Communist capital in the 1940s.

Aga Kahn Architectural Award and international conference held in Beijing.

The first national students' design competition held.

Representative buildings:

A scheme designed by four lecturers of Tongji University participating in the international competitions run by Japanese architectural journal awarded honorable mention.

Nanguan Mosque, Ningxia, No. 4, Huajiashan Hotel, Hangzhou, Tulufan Hotel, Xinjiang. These buildings explore indigenous identities.

Pagoda Park, Songjiang, Shanghai, planned by Tongji University, exploring modern Chinese style.

1982

The sixth five-year plan of the national economy and social development approved.

People's Republic of China Law of Heritage Preservation enacted and promulgated.

Ministry of City and Rural Construction and Environmental Protection (short name: Ministry of Construction) founded.

Pilot scheme of selling residential properties in the cities begins.

Conferences on library, sport, and medical building design held.

Conference on the planning of residential neighborhoods held in Hefei, Anhui Province.

Twenty-four historic cities announced by the State Council.

Representative buildings:

Fragrant Hill Hotel, Beijing, designed by I. M. Pei, indicating a way-out of "national form."

Longbai Hotel in Shanghai, on a site with old British colonist buildings, explores the local identities of Shanghai.

Qinglong Temple, Xi'an, commemorating a Japanese monk coming to China in the Tang Dynasty (618–907), designed by Zhang Jinqiu.

Yuanling Residential Area, Shenzhen, in the early 1980s.

Jiangsu Academy of Fine Arts, Nanjing.

1983

Zhou Yang, China's top art theorist and official, proposes reviewing the humanity, personality, and other discourses of Marxism, the theoretical basis for China's socialism.

Deng Xiaoping, chairman of Communist Party of China, discusses the problem of "spiritual pollution of the bourgeois" in culture and arts.

Ministry of Construction issues a notice on strengthening the planning of historic cities.

Symposium of building materials and policies held in Beijing.

Construction companies use contracts to do projects.

State-run design institutes no longer government-funded. The design fee will be their income.

Founding of the quarterly magazine *New Architecture*, Wuhan.

Death of Yang Tingbao and Tung Jun (both 1900–83), two influential architects of the first generation. Both were graduates of the University of Pennsylvania.

Representative buildings:

Great Wall Hotel, the first curtain wall building in China.

Jinling Hotel in the city center of Nanjing, designed by Parmer & Turner of Hong Kong.

Wuyi Mountain Village, Fujian, designed by Qi Kang and his colleagues, with strong indigenous style.

White Swan Hotel, in colonial Shamian, Guangzhou, designed by She Junnan and Mo Bozhi.

Shanghai Hotel in the city center of Shanghai.

Open housing system, Wuxi, application of open-building theory in China, designed by the faculty of Southeast University.

Round city park, Hefei, making the city famous for its city greenery.

1984

Deng Xiaoping, China's patriarch, expresses his opinions on housing and the building industry.

China and the United Kingdom sign the joint declaration, stating that the sovereignty of Hong Kong will be handed over to China on July 1, 1997.

Fourteen coastal cities opened for international trade.

US President Ronald Regan visits China.

Government officials and mass media appeal for the reform of design system.

Thirty-seven building designs given award of excellence by the Ministry of Construction.

National trends of building technology established, especially CAAD, and its application in design.

Founding of quarterly magazine *Time + Architecture*, Shanghai

The first Ph.D. degree in urban planning awarded, to Zhao Dazhuang.

Representative buildings:

Scheme of renovating the old city of Xi'an designed by thirteen students won students' design competition in the Fifteenth UIA Congress.

Taihu Lake sanitarium for oil workers, Wuxi, designed by Lu Jiwei and Gu Ruzhen. Building complex comfortably integrated with the hilly topography.

Qingchuan Hotel, Wuhan, the classiest hotel in the city.

1985

The conference of computer application in architecture held in Beijing, at which four foreign experts give speeches.

National competitions of primary and middle school buildings. The scheme guided design practice in later years.

Launch of investigation of modern Chinese architecture since 1840, led by Professor Wang Tan and Terunobu Fujimori, sponsored by Japanese consortium.

China Year Book of Building Industry (1949–1964) published.

Seminar of architecture and creation held in Guangzhou.

The first joint-venture design firm "Great Earth," led by Alfred P. G. Peng, a professor returning from North America, founded in Beijing. Several small design firms led by young architects are approved.

The first Ph.D. degree in architecture awarded, to Xiang Bingrun.

Representative buildings:

Queli Hotel in Qufu, Shandong Province, designed by Dai Nianchi, located in the sensitive historic area next to the Confucian family home.

Public buildings of people's congress, science museum, overseas Chinese buildings, hotels, Islamic college, children's palace, banks, bus and train stations completed in Xinjiang to celebrate the thirtieth anniversary of the autonomous region.

Street of Song Dynasty built in Kaifeng, Henan Province, "fake-antiquity" design.

Dragon Hotel, Hangzhou, designed by Cheng Taining, in the scenic West Lake district of Hangzhou.

Hangzhou Hotel, Hangzhou, uses traditional language.

Cultural street of Liulichang, Beijing, imitation of ancient buildings.

Lhasa Hotel, Lhasa, indigenous Tibetan style.

"Sunset on ancient cornice (*gu die xie yang*)," cultural building in the West Lake, Fuzhou.

Shenzhen Gymnasium, Shenzhen, a sports building.

International Exhibition Center, Beijing, uses a bold modern style.

International Trade Building, Shenzhen, 160 m high, tallest in China at that time.

Dunhuang Airport, Dunhuang, Gansu, with characteristics of the desert.

1986

Liberal intellectuals ask for democracy and freedom of speech.

Student demonstrations for democracy and freedom in Beijing, Hefei, and Shanghai.

China implements the "863" high-technology plan.

Ministry of Construction and State Bureau of Statistics issues census data of buildings in China's cities.

Huayi Deisgn Ltd., a state-run company, registers in Hong Kong and Tokyo.

The government states that foreign architects (including those from Taiwan, Hong Kong, and Macau) could design in China only with the cooperation of a local Chinese design institute.

Exhibition of Hong Kong architecture held in Beijing and Shanghai.

Representative buildings:

Buildings and street imitating the Qing Dynasty (1644–1911) style completed in Shijiazhuan city. This begins the trend of imitating ancient buildings.

South China Sea Hotel, Shenzhen.

"Huang He Lou," an imitation of a historic "crane" pagoda, standing at the bank of Yangtze River, Wuhan, "fake-antiquity" design.

Memorial Hall of the Japanese Massacre, Nanjing, designed by Qi Kang, in memory of 300,000 Chinese people killed by Japanese invaders in 1938.

Quyang Residential Area, Shanghai, a model for residential planning in the 1980s, markets, and schools all within a 200-m radius.

Old temple market street, Fuzhi Temple, Nanjing, renovation of a traditional market.

Ice sports center, Changchun, the new face of structures integrated with sport functions.

Taihu Lake Hotel, Wuxi, building well integrated with the hills.

Dinosaur Museum, Zigong, Sichuan.

1987

Hu Yaobang, the open-minded representative in the central government, steps down. The top liberal intellectuals are criticized or stripped of their administrative duties.

The Thirteenth Congress of the Communist Party of China is held.

Chinese architects participate in the Sixteenth UIA Congress; Professor Wu Liangyong elected vice chairman.

Conference on architectural education held.

Activities of the International Year of Housing and commemoration of the 100th birthday of Le Corbusier.

The Society of Construction Industry decides to issue Lu Ban award to quality construction work every year. Lu Ban is a legendary carpenter.

Exhibition of architectural drawings held.

Sixtieth anniversary of architectural department at Southeast University, Nanjing.

Representative buildings:

Yuhuatai Revolutionary Martyrs' Memorial Hall in Nanjing, designed by the faculty of Southeast University.

Beijing Library, the largest in Asia, started in the 1970s, is completed in the national style.

Shanghai Train Station terminals are above the tracks. International Hotel, Beijing.

Nationality Museum, Dali, Yunnan Province.

National competition of cultural amenities building.

Stepped modular housing, Tsinghua University staff quarters, Beijing.

Tianhe Sports Center, Guangzhou, for the Fifth National Sports and Games.

Yungu Mountain Village, in the tourist resort Yellow Mountain (*Huang Shan*), Anhui Province.

No. 4 Middle School, Beijing, uses a new shape for classrooms.

Science Building, Shenzhen, uses geometry as a design element.

1988

China starts to reform its housing supply system in cities, thus alleviating the government from the burden of providing housing.

The central government asks to limit the construction of entertainment and memorial buildings, to avoid wasting money.

The central government researches prices and salaries.

Liberal intellectuals are more active in speech and in the media.

National economy is heated and inflated.

Closed in 1949, share stock market reopens in China. Two stock exchange markets are established, in Shanghai and Shenzhen.

Two hundred thousand people vote for the "ten celebrated buildings" in Beijing.

"Service fee for urban planning" is issued.

School of Architecture founded, based on the original department in Tsinghua University.

The government strictly controls the construction of entertainment buildings, to save land and governmental investment.

The first architects and scholars meeting from the two sides of Taiwan Strait held in Hong Kong.

Start of investigation and listing of historic buildings from 1840 to 1949.

Up to 1988, more than 110 Chinese architects and students receive awards in various international design competitions.

Representative buildings:

Tang Dynasty style hotel and restaurant, Xi'an.

"Dream of the sea" resort, designed by Qi Kang, in Changle beach, Fujian.

"He Lou Xian Pavilion," a bamboo structured teahouse at Pagoda Park, Songjiang, Shanghai, designed by Feng Jizhong.

Jiuzhai Valley Hotel, in the primeval forest of Sichuan.

Capital Hotel, Beijing.

College of Architecture building, Tongji University, Shanghai, designed by Dai Fudong and Huang Ren.

Nandaihe Training Center, Nandaihe, Hebei.

Research Institute of Ancient Vertebrates and Sample Hall, China Academy of Science.

Performance and meeting center, Shenzhen University, a semi-open assembly plaza.

Crystal Hotel, Tianjin, a high-class hotel invested and designed by American.

1989

Tens of thousands of students and citizens in Beijing and other cities call for an end to corruption and for the establishment of democracy. The army cracks down on the demonstration in June.

Fall of the Berlin Wall and the reunification of East and West Germany.

Conservative power prevails; Jiang Zeming assumes power under Deng Xiaoping. Zhao Ziyang steps down as secretary general of the Communist Party.

Top democratic representatives, intellectuals, and students are arrested and prosecuted.

Deng Xiaoping reiterates that the open-door policy will not change. (The political climate did not influence architecture.)

Labor surplus in construction industry.

To curb inflation, 14,400 projects in development or construction are stopped.

The first volume of *Contemporary Chinese Architects* published.

Second conference on modern history of Chinese architecture takes place.

Activities relating to choosing ten celebrities of world architecture and ten Chinese buildings in the 1980s.

International symposium of "Asian cities and architecture in transition," sponsored by the Asian and Australian region of UIA, held in Beijing.

Representative buildings:

Shanghai Center, designed by John Portman, completed; a high-density complex in historic West Nanjing Road.

The second China Antarctic station completed.

Jigong's (a legendary monk) court, Tiantai Mountain, Zhejiang, an interesting tourist building, designed by Qi Kang.

Changfu Palace Hotel, Beijing, invested in and jointly designed with Japanese.

Yanzhishan Residential Area, Jinan, model residential area.

Sichuan Provincial Gymnasium, Chengdu.

China International Trade Center, Beijing.

1990

The central government decides to develop Pudong, the east bank of Huangpu River in Shanghai.

The Eleventh Asian Games held in Beijing.

Debate on the Sino-Japan Youth Friendship Center, jointly designed by Kisho Kurokawa and Beijing's design institute, on the credits and responsibilities of architects.

Representative buildings:

A gymnasium, sports facilities, and athletes' villages are completed for the Asian Games.

Hongqiao Economic Development District, office building, exhibition hall, and comprehensive development, Shanghai.

Ju'er Hutong, courtyard housing, Beijing, three-story courtyard housing, Beijing, awarded internationally for its "organic restoration."

Guo Village of West Lake, Hangzhou, a tourist resort.

Humanities Building, in the historic campus of Wuhan University, Wuhan.

School of Architecture building, Tianjin University.

Media center, Beijing.

Memorial Hall of former premier (1949–76) Zhou Enlai, Huai'an, Jiangshu.

Headquarters, China People's Bank, Beijing.

1991

War in the Persian Gulf.

Shanghai starts to reform its housing system. Citizens should contribute money to their own housing. The plan is adopted by other provinces in China.

"Looking at the future" seminar to celebrate World Day of Architecture.

Asian forum of architecture held at Fragrant Hill Hotel, Beijing.

Dai Nianchi, design master and former deputy minister of construction, dies (1920–91).

Representative buildings:

Experimental housing, Kangle Neighborhood, Shanghai, innovative design of housing.

Shaanxi Provincial Historic Museum, designed by Zhang Jinqiu, traditional form and layout.

North Dipper Village (*bei dou shan zhuang*), Shandong, uses seaweed as roofing material and clay wall, designed by Dai Fudong.

China folk culture village, theme park, Shenzhen, an early theme park in China.

Yanhuang Arts Gallery, Beijing, Chinese characteristics with some traditional symbols.

New addition to the library of Tsinghua University, Beijing.

Department of Oriental Arts, Nankai University, Tianjin, the plan features a traditional *taiji* pattern.

1992

Deng Xiaoping inspects southern China and repeats his policy of prioritizing national economy over politics: "speedy development is the only truth."

Up to 799 cities and counties open to foreigners.

The Fourteenth Congress of the Communist Party of China.

"Hope" project launched to help poor rural children complete primary and secondary school.

Four universities accredited for bachelor of architecture degrees. China previously only awarded bachelor of engineering for students of architecture.

The Eighth Congress of Architectural Society of China (ASC).

Activities relating to sustainable housing on the World Day of Housing.

Shenzhen given an award by the United Nations Habitat Center.

Representative buildings:

Renovation and broadening of the historic Bund, Shanghai.

Lujiazui, Pudong of Shanghai, international master plan competition; Richard Rogers wins first prize.

Enjili Residential Area, Beijing and Hongmei Residential Area, Changzhou, are models of residential planning in China.

Laishan Airport, Yantai, designed by Bu Zhengwei, high quality and low cost.

Run Run Shaw Science Building, South China University of Technology.

Library and Run Run Shaw Academic Center, Chongqing University.

Research institute of an airplane manufacturer, Chengdu.

Memorial Gallery of Lingnan Painting School, Guangzhou, reminiscent of Art Nouveau, by Mo Bozhi and He Jingtang.

The Lufthansa Center, Beijing, invested in by German company.

1993

Inflation, chaotic finance, and economic overexpansion in China. The central government adjusts and regulates the finance and banking sector.

Founding of construction committee of the Three Gorges Dam.

System of civil servants introduced from central to local government.

The government starts projects to help poor counties and areas.

The State Council eliminates some ministries, to scale back the government.

Universities should raise funding in addition to government allocation. Tuition fee starts being charged.

Commemoration of the 100th birthday of Liu Shiying, an architect and educationist of the first generation, by Hunan University.

International symposium of "The future of the Architect's Profession" held in Beijing, attended by ASC, RIBA, AIA, and HKIA.

Symposium on architecture and literature held in Nanchang.

In the Eighteenth UIA Congress held in Chicago, Beijing chosen as venue for the twentieth congress.

Association of Architectural History founded under the ASC.

China Society of Urban Planning founded.

ASC celebrates its fortieth anniversary.

Ministry of Construction announces 312 Class A construction contracting companies and 59 Class A construction supervision companies.

Representative buildings:

Shanghai Museum, designed by Xing Tonghe, in the heart of the city.

Nanyue King Tomb Museum, Guangzhou, designed by Mo Bozhi and He Jingtang.

Hualu Electronic Ltd., Dalian.

People's Square, Shanghai, where Shanghai Museum, Grand Theater, and municipal government are located.

Taierzhuang Campaign (1938) Memorial Hall, Shandong, designed by Charlie Q. L. Xue, for patriotic education.

Lantern Museum, Zigong, Sichuan.

1994

Reform of state-owned companies. Looser controls on the price of food. More state-owned factories and companies incorporated.

White Paper on the development of the twenty-first century.

System of forty-four working hours per week introduced, replacing the old system of forty-eight hours.

Chinese government issues bonds of US$1 billion.

Inflation at 25%.

Publication of *Selected Works of Deng Xiaoping*.

The Chinese currency, Renminbi (RMB), drops from US$1 = 3.8¥ to US$1 = 8.3¥, and pegged to US dollar.

A pilot examination of registered architects held in Shenyang, observed by AIA, RIBA, and HKIA.

Outstanding works designed by young architects awarded by the journal *Architect*.

Xi'an gazetted as world cultural heritage by UNESCO.

One hundred twenty elderly people awarded degree of design and surveying masters.

China Architectural Education Committee and American Collegiate Committee of Architecture sign agreement of cooperation.

Design institutes incorporated.

Zuo Xiaosi Architect Design Ltd., the first private practice, founded in Shenzhen.

Canadian architect Arthur Erickson's works exhibited.

Representative buildings:

Window of the World, theme park, Shenzhen; wonders of the world in miniature.

Oriental Pearl, Shanghai TV tower, new landmark in the city.

Run Run Shaw Building, Tongji University, Shanghai, designed by Wu Lusheng.

Fengzeyuan Restaurant, Beijing, by Cui Kai, Chinese characteristics with some traditional symbols.

Grottoes arts and heritage gallery, Dunhuang, Gansu.

Potala Palace in Lhasa renovated. The palace is a symbol of Tibetan Buddhist religion.

1995

Minimum wage for workers enacted in various provinces.

Science convention in China.

Commemoration of the fiftieth anniversary of victory in the anti-Japanese war.

Ten new buildings of the 1990s selected in Shanghai.

Ten design works awarded for outstanding environmental arts.

Ordinance of registered architects in People's Republic of China promulgated.

The first examination of registered architects, observed by professional bodies from the US, UK, Japan, Korea, Singapore, and Hong Kong, and attended by 9100 people.

Property appraisers examined and registered.

Ten universities accredited to award architectural degree.

Mutual recognition of architects' qualifications between China and the US signed; valid from 1998.

Representative buildings:

Sino-Japan Naval War (1894) Memorial, Weihai, designed by Peng Yigang, integrating sculpture and building in the seashore.

Speed skating rink, Harbin.

Zhuhai Airport, Zhuhai.

China Political Consultancy Council, headquarters, Beijing.

School of Architecture, Tsinghua University, academic building.

Hall of Macau, Great Hall of People, Beijing, interior design of an old room.

Gourmet City, Yantai, Shandong, designed by Bu Zhengwei.

1996

Gross National Product (GNP) increasing at an annual rate of 11.6 from 1992 to 1996.

Eighty-eight cities implement projects to settle low-income citizens.

China's foreign currency reserve over US$100 billion.

Examination of construction supervision engineers held.

Government puts more effort into residential neighborhoods.

Four thousand people attend the examination of registered structural engineers.

The Ninth Congress of the Architectural Society of China.

The architectural education accreditation conference held in Xi'an, specifying the requirements of undergraduate education. National students' design competition held.

Scientific habitat symposium held in Guangzhou.

Asian association of computer-aided architectural design founded.

Promotion center of intelligent building established in the Ministry of Construction.

Beijing architectural and planning works exhibited.

Conference on hospital buildings and facilities held.

Points on housing technology and modernization issued.

Professor Wu Liangyong wins architectural education award at the Nineteenth UIA Congress.

Representative buildings:

Beijing West Train Station opens, a huge traditional kiosk to symbolize the city gate.

International housing design competition and symposium held in Shanghai.

Shanghai Library completed, after design and construction of over ten years.

Coastal Defense Memorial Hall, Ningbo, Zhejiang.

Post office headquarters, Nanjing, designed by Qi Kang.

Shun Hing Building, Shenzhen, claimed "land king" in the city.

Gaoqi International Airport, Xiamen, using traditional form.

Nationality Museum, Kunming, Yunnan.

Shanghai Stock Exchange Plaza, Pudong, Shanghai.

World Plaza, Pudong, Shanghai.

Drum and Bell Tower Plaza, Xi'an, traditional open space in the city center, designed by Zhang Jinqiu.

1997

Handover of Hong Kong sovereignty to China.

Death of Deng Xiaoping.

Asian financial crisis. China keeps the damage to a minimum.

The Fifteenth Congress of the Communist Party of China upholds the banner of Deng Xiaoping's theory, "constructing a socialist country with Chinese characteristics" and progressing to the twenty-first century.

Economy soft landing, inflation dropping to 1.8%.

Social security and pension system implemented.

Celebration of the seventieth anniversary of the People's Liberation Army.

Practice notes on sustainable design in civil buildings.

ASC meetings to regulate various chapters and branches in different disciplines.

China-Japan architectural symposium held in Beijing.

Conference of joint design by China and overseas architects held in Shanghai.

Israeli architecture exhibited in Beijing.

Congress of building science held in Xuzhou.

International exposition of building and interiors held in Shanghai.

Conference of nationality buildings, sponsored by the relevant parties of China and Japan.

International conference on hilly buildings held in Chongqing, a mountainous city in the southwest.

Symposium on industry building held in Shenzhen. Association of educational buildings founded and conference on this building type held in Zhuhai.

Zoning of Beijing exhibited.

Conference on landscape and gardening held.

"Future cities," sponsored by the British Council, held in Shanghai.

Representative buildings:

Stadium for 80,000 people, Shanghai.

Memorial hall of Hong Xian Nu, a famous actress of Cantonese opera, Guangzhou.

Pit Gui Yuan, large residential development, near Guangzhou.

Gubei New District of Housing, Shanghai.

The gate of Tianjin tax-protection district, tensile structure.

San Xing Dui Museum, Chengdu, Sichuan, a unique design to accommodate the splendid ancient culture and heritage.

Tong Fang Gang (lane) residential area, vernacular-style housing, Suzhou.

Library, Beijing University, to harmonize with the old campus environment.

Dong'an Market, multistory shopping mall on commercial Wangfujing Street, Beijing.

Building of architectural engineering college, Shanghai Jiaotong University, designed by Charlie Q. L. Xue, an example of low-cost building.

1998

Severe flooding in the southern provinces along the Yangtze River.

The reserve of government foreign currency over US$140 billion.

China becomes the second largest country in absorbing foreign investment, after the US. US$45.5 billion taken in.

Real estate price index first announces in thirty-five cities.

Commemoration of the 100th birthday of Zhou Enlai, China's premier from 1949 to 1976.

French government provides fifty scholarships for Chinese architects studying in France in a program "50 architects in France."

Intelligent building symposium held in Guangzhou.

Forty companies compete in the scheme of Grand National Theater in Beijing.

Agreement of mutual recognition between China and Britain signed on structural engineering degree.

Symposium on history of Chinese architecture held.

"Soul of the city," jointly run by ASC and Culture and Education section of the British Embassy.

International building, machinery, and facility exposition held in Beijing.

"Housing salon" forum.

Representative buildings:

China Center of Architectural Culture, Beijing.

Shanghai Science and Technology City, designed by RTKL; ribbon cut by US President Clinton and mayor of Shanghai.

Young architects' design competition "Research center of the ancient Ba-su (Sichuan) culture."

Singapore Industrial Park, Suzhou, invested in by the Singapore government.

Motorola electronic plant, Tianjin.

Provincial Museum, Jinan, Shandong.

Jin Mao Building, designed by SOM, Shanghai, the tallest building in the city.

CITIC Plaza, Guangzhou, the tallest building in the city, designed by Dennis Lau & Partners in Hong Kong.

Zunhua Hotel, Hebei, designed by Dai Fudong.

1999

Handover of Macau sovereignty to China.

Universities and colleges expand admission quotas from 1.4 million to 2.2 million each year, to help the economy.

Practioners of "Falun Gong" (a kind of meditation) encircle the central government area, Zhongnanhai. The government cracks down on the Falun Gong movement.

Seminar on population and resources attended by top officials.

Sandstorm hits Beijing.

The Twentieth World Congress of Architects, UIA, held in Beijing, with 6000 attendees; *Charter of Beijing* released.

"Architectural arts of China," "Experimental architecture of China" displayed in Beijing, as part of UIA Congress events.

Symposium on "Information society and architecture of the twenty-first century."

International building trade exposition held in Shanghai.

Exhibition of architectural rendering. One hundred drawings selected from 700 entries.

Two big design institutes, East China and Shanghai Civil, merge in Shanghai.

Research institute of architecture established in Beijing University, led by Yung Ho Chang, graduate program only.

Death of Zhang Bo (1911–99), design master and representative of "national form" of Beijing.

Representative buildings:

Shanghai Grand Theater, designed by Jean-Marie Charpentier et Associés.

Master plan of Shenzhen, a milestone in the development of the border city next to Hong Kong.

Swimming pool, Tsinghua University, Beijing, designed by Zhuang Weimin.

Train Station, Hangzhou, designed by Cheng Taining, an exploration of the "gate" of the delicate southern city.

Confucius Research Institute, Qufu, Shandong, designed by Wu Liangyong and Tsinghua University staff.

Municipal buildings and central plaza, Dongyin, Shandong, designed by Bu Zhengwei.

Jiushi Mansion, designed by Norman Foster & Partners, Shanghai.

World expo of gardening, Kunming, Yunnan.

Terminal, International Airport of Beijing.

"September 18" Memorial Hall, Shenyang, by Qi Kang. On this date in 1931, Japanese troops invaded the northeast provinces of China.

Grand National Theater, Beijing. ADP of France won the design, fueling fierce debate on national form, image, and technology.

2000

China admitted into the World Trade Organization (WTO).

Universities merge in various cities and provinces.

Gao Xingjian, an exiled Chinese writer, awarded Nobel Prize for Literature. Chinese government keeps low profile in reporting the event.

US troops bomb the Chinese Embassy in Yugoslavia, leading to demonstrations in Beijing, Shanghai, Guangzhou, and other cities.

University student intake jumps to three million.

Building Law promulgated.

Debate on the Grand National Theater. Fellows of Chinese Academy of Science, Academy of Engineering, architects, and engineers write letters to the central government, asking that construction of the theater stop.

International Symposium of Chinese Architectural Education held in Hong Kong.

Research institute of architecture established in Nanjing University, graduate program only.

Representative buildings:

Shanghai Planning Exhibition Building in the city center.
Lu Xun (a great writer) Memorial Hall, Shanghai.
Xintiandi, a renovated old *lilong* housing community and tourist attraction in Shanghai, a successful commercial venture, invested in by Hong Kong capital.
Arts Gallery, Guangzhou, designed by Mo Bozhi & Associates.
Meteorology and Radar Center, Guangzhou.
National College of Accounting, Beijing, contemporary form.
Building of Foreign Language Teaching Press, Beijing, designed by Cui Kai.

2001

Attacks on 9/11 in New York.
China strengthens the elimination of and cooperation in anti-terrorist programs.
Chinese and American fighter jets crash above the South China Sea. Chinese pilot killed and American jet forced to land on Hainan Island.
Round-Pacific summit held in Shanghai.
Beijing successfully bids for the 2008 Olympic Games, stimulating the city's construction of infrastructure.
World Congress of Urban Planning Schools and Institutes held in Tongji University.
International Conference on Architecture and Local Culture, attended by 650 delegates from ten countries, held in Beijing.
TUMU, *Young Architects in China*, exhibition in Berlin.

Representative buildings:

Electric power building, Chang'an Street, Beijing.
New sports building, designed by ADP of France, in Guangzhou.
Bank of China Headquarters, designed by Pei Architects, Beijing.
Convention Center in Dongguan, designed by Tongji University.
Pudong International Airport, Shanghai, designed by ADP of France.

Yu Garden shopping mall, Shanghai.
Commercial center, Ningbo, designed by Madus.

2002

At the Sixteenth Congress of the Communist Party of China, Hu Jintao replaces Jiang Zeming as secretary general of the Communist Party; Wen Jiabao replaces Zhu Rongji as premier of State Council.
Shanghai successfully bids for the 2010 World Exposition.
The Biannual Arts Exposition, *Urban Construction*, Shanghai.
Tongji University celebrates the fiftieth anniversary of its department of architecture.

Representative buildings:

Convention and Exhibition Center, Guangzhou, 400,000 sq m, designed by AXS Satow Inc, Japan.
New campus, Zhejiang University, Hangzhou, designed by He Jingtang and design institute of South China University of Technology.
Commune by the Great Wall, housing designed by twelve Asian architects.
China Central Television (CCTV) Headquarters design competition announced; Rem Koolhaas wins the project.
Provincial Museum, Fuzhou, Fujian, designed by Qi Kang.
Boao Canal Village, Hainan Island, designed by Rocco Design Ltd., Hong Kong and Seung H-Sang from South Korea, featuring modern lifestyle in a tranquil canal environment.
Sino-German College building, Tongji University, Shanghai; an interpretation of limited site and constraints in available building industry.

2003

US and allied forces invade Iraq.
Severe acute respiratory syndrome (SARS) breaks out in China; thousands of people affected; tourism, exchange activities paralyzed from March to June.
Successful crewed space mission.
Corruption spread throughout various levels of communist leadership in the past decade. This year, more than 5000 corrupt officials flee overseas with a huge amount of money.

The Three Gorges Dam supplies power to central and east China.

The US, Europe, and Japan force the value of China's money, RMB, to rise.

The expanded student cohort recruited in 1999 graduate this year; only seventy percent of the graduates find jobs.

Despite SARS, China's GDP keeps an annual increase of 9.1%.

The second awarding of Liang Si-cheng Prize in architecture, a high award for architects in China.

The Architect, a national journal founded in 1979, publishes in a new format.

New editorial board of *Architectural Journal*, the official journal of the Architectural Society of China (ASC).

Alors, La Chine, including contemporary Chinese architecture, exhibited in Paris.

Twenty-five world architects and artists gather in Nanjing, to design a new architectural exhibition.

Architecture and Urbanism of Tokyo and *Architectural Record* of New York publish special issue on Chinese architecture.

Representative buildings:

Guangzhou airport in Baiyun Shan, the fifth large international airport in the Pearl River Delta; the other four are in Hong Kong, Macau, Shenzhen, and Zhuhai.

Jianwai SOHO, Beijing, developed by SOHO China and designed by Riken Yamamoto. Commercial, retail stores and upscale apartments with a floor area of 700,000 sq m.

Design competitions for 2008 Olympic Games announced: swimming pool, "water cube" won by PTW of Australia and Arup, and "bird's nest" national stadium, won by Herzog & De Meron.

Grand Bazaar, Urumqi, Xinjiang, designed by Wang Xiaodong and Xinjiang Architectural Design Institute, exploring Islamic culture and Xinjiang environment.

2004

"Bird flu" threatens China; however, no human infection is found.

Global Construction Summit, convened by McGraw-Hill Construction, held in Beijing in April.

Young Architects Forum, held in Shenzhen in June, discusses constructivism of Soviet Union in the 1920s and the contemporary Chinese architecture.

International Architectural Biannual Exhibition, Beijing, September–October.

Representative buildings:

International Hotel of Jiuzhaigou, Sichuan, a tourist attraction of forests and lakes, designed by Tsinghua University.

Academic building, Tianjin Medical University, designed by Huahui Design Ltd.

2005

It is announced that Beijing will build its new airport in the south, to be designed by Norman Foster & Partners.

The government issues measurements to curb the escalating housing price in the big cities.

"Mega buildings in Asian and Pacific Areas" — International Symposium of Asian and Pacific Architecture, sponsored by the University of Hawaii and Tongji University, held in Shanghai in June.

"City, open doors" — biannual urban and architectural exhibition held in Shenzhen in December.

Disneyland opens in Hong Kong in September, and a new theme park of 160 hectares conceived by The Walt Disney Company starts building in Shanghai.

Representative buildings:

The Jinhua Architecture Park, a riverside stripe of 2200 meters long, Jinhua, Zhejiang Province. The 17 structures are designed by 17 groups of architect/artist from seven countries.

Sanya Tongji Science Park, designed by Charlie Xue and Li Lin, Sanya, Hainan Province. It creates a new prototype of recreation and research.

ARCHITECTURAL EDUCATION AND PUBLICATION

Gong Weimin, School of Architecture building, Shenzhen University, 2003

FROM EIGHT TO ONE HUNDRED TWENTY: PROLIFERATING ARCHITECTURAL EDUCATION

Architecture is a profession. Architectural education should closely follow this profession. Before 1949, the architectural schools in China were run by the first generation of architects in China; for example, the Department of Architecture at Northeast University in Shenyang in the 1930s and the Department of Architecture at Tsinghua University were founded by Professor Liang Sicheng and his wife, Lin Huiyin. The Department of Architecture at Central University (the best architectural school before 1949, now called Southeast University), the Department of Civil Engineering at Shanghai's Jiaotong, and Tongji University are others founded by the first generation of architects.

In 1952, China reorganized the system of higher education. Eight formal architectural schools provided graduates for the whole country: Tsinghua University, Tongji University, Nanjing Institute of Technology (now Southeast University), Tianjin University, Harbin Institute of Building Engineering (now Harbin University of Building), South China Institute of Technology (now South China University of Technology), Xi'an Institute of Metallurgical Building Engineering (now Xi'an University of Building Science), and Chongqing Institute of Building Engineering (now Chongqing University of Building).

These eight architectural schools supplied graduates for all of China during the period 1952–77. Of these schools, the first four are considered superior to the latter four (Xue 1999). Tsinghua and Tongji Universities are without a doubt ranked the top "suppliers" of architects. Before 1966, when all other institutions offered only four or five years of study, architecture students underwent six years of training at Tsinghua and Tongji Universities. Remarkably, Tongji University set up the first program in urban planning in 1956 and the first college of architecture and urban planning in China only in 1986.

The situation of the eight schools changed after 1978, as the eight could not satisfy the huge demands for building professionals when China entered an era of economic and building boom. There were forty-six universities and colleges with architectural studies in 1986. The number rose to nearly eighty in 2001. There exist, of course, informal divisions of "first-tier," "second-tier," and "third-tier" institutes.

Starting in 1981, China implemented the degree system. Graduates from architecture programs were awarded a Bachelor of Science degree or Master of Science degree at that time. In 1993, the State Council approved the Bachelor of Architecture degree for four universities: Tsinghua, Tongji, Tianjin, and Southeast. The architectural degrees awarded by these four institutions are also recognized by overseas professional bodies. There were eighty programs or architectural schools in 2001. This number jumped to 120 in 2004, among which fewer than thirty schools had been accredited and are allowed to award

Auditorium of Tsinghua University, built in 1916

Bachelor of Architecture degrees. The eight old schools are assessed every six years. The remaining schools receive assessment every two or four years (www.mochr.coom/renshi/gaodeng/, Jan., 2004).

The more than 120 architectural schools and programs are unfolded against the educational background of more than 1000 higher learning institutions in the thirty-one provinces, autonomous districts, and centrally administered cities. Around 1.5 million students graduated from these institutions each year before 2001. In 1998, the then Chinese premier, Zhu Rongji, suggested that more college students could increase the value of the GDP. The university intake increased sharply to 2.3 million in 1999, and gradually to 3.5 million in 2001. The drastic surplus of students poured into and stretched the already intense labor market in 2003 (www.cnd.org, February 2003).

Suppose there are fifty graduates per institute each year. There should be around 6000 graduate architects entering the job market. Compared with the population of 1.3 billion, the number is insignificant. The US has a population of about 240 million, but the schools (or programs) of architecture number 115, and they produce over 3000 graduates with a Bachelor of Architecture and close to 2000 graduates with a Master of Architecture each year. Assuming a fifty percent attrition rate, about 2,500 new architects enter the field each year. In the US, the historical concern has been that this may be too large a number for the American architectural profession, which is around 150,000 licensed architects for a total population of 240 million, or a ratio of roughly one architect for every 1500 people (Yeh 2000).

In 1992, China set up a national guidance committee of architectural education under the Ministry of Construction and the State Education Commission. The committee is responsible for the supervision of architectural education and accreditation of schools. It

meets every year and gives direction to old and new schools, functioning like the American Collegiate Society of Architecture (ACSA). The annual meeting gradually evolved to a conference of architectural education, sponsored by schools in various cities and attended by hundreds of delegates from all over China and even Hong Kong, Taiwan, and other regions.

Architectural education in China in the past emphasized rendering and (schematic) design. There were professional fine arts teachers, and painting classes for at least two years. Design studio teaching introduced spatial forms, tailored from simple to complicated. There were few classes in professional practice, management, and regulations. Site design, required for the registration examination, was not even taught in the old curricula. After the registration system was established, schools put more effort into relating their studies to professional demands. In the following sections, the curriculum is discussed through case studies of several architectural schools.

In addition to the program of architecture are some similar programs in those institutes with long traditions, e.g., urban planning, landscape architecture, interior design, and environmental design. The programs of structural and civil engineering, industrial and civil building, and building economics also teach some architectural courses.

DESIGN INSTITUTES IN UNIVERSITIES

A remarkable design force comes from universities. Those colleges and universities that have an architecture department or building-related department usually run an architectural design institute. They are commercial arms of the institutions. They might be a design group within a department or an institute within the university. In Tongji University (Shanghai), for example, a design group within the Department of Architecture started to undertake the design work inside and outside the university in 1958. The Design Institute separated from the Department of Architecture in 1980, and grew to around 200 full-time staff with purpose-built headquarters of 5000 sq m and several branches in other cities in 2002. In Southeast University of Nanjing, three departments can meet the requirements of architectural design: the Department of Architecture, the Design Institute of Architecture, and the Research Institute of Architecture, of which the Design Institute is a real commercial company, and the other two have teaching and research duties.

Design Institute, Shenzhen University, building designed by Gong Weimin, 2003

The original intention of running a design institute in universities was to link town and gown: both students and teachers benefit from a location for practice. In the early years (the 1980s) of design institutes, the main designers took teaching duties in the department and supervised graduate students. They had the titles of professor, associate professor, and lecturer. Some years later, these design institutes became self-funded and ceased to receive government grants for higher education. They are located within campuses and give a percentage of their income to the universities. They shoulder the salary, bonus, medicare, pension, operation, and tax. They are licensed by the Ministry of Construction or a local construction committee. Therefore, they are the only legal representatives of design in the name of that university. For example, the teaching staff of the Department of Architecture or Department of Civil Engineering of Tongji University hope to do designs with the name "Tongji," but they have to found the Design Institute first. Their design documents should bear the chop of the Design Institute.

Because of the keen competition in the market, the design institutes of universities gradually discarded the old academic style, as clients were sometimes skeptical of the design service from education institutions. Summer and winter vacations have been shortened. Teaching duties are reduced to the minimum. These design "professors" could not afford to teach again. A smaller niche practice is set for the institutes, and first-class services are rendered. To take the example of Design Institute of Tongji University again, the institute, despite a staff of hundreds, has been ranked as one of the top three design practices in Shanghai. The other two are East China Design Institute and Shanghai Institute of Architectural Design, institutes with more than 1000 staff members.

In those campuses with design institutes, for example, Tongji University of Shanghai, Tsinghua University of Beijing, Southeast University of Nanjing, all building designs are from the drafting board of the university staff — a unique phenomenon in China. Teachers' design works in the campus are the best living text for students.

"Design institute" is a large umbrella for all profit-making activities in some institutions. Bridge design is a special technology. In Tongji University, there is a Bridge Design Section of the Design Institute within the Department of Bridge Engineering. Because of the relatively loose control, interior design practice is found everywhere. The College of Architecture and Urban Planning of Tongji University also has an interior design and decoration company. A consultancy company, "T Y Lin and Li Guo Hau," was set up in Tongji in 1996. An investigation showed that, in 1998, nineteen companies were doing building design with the name of "Tongji University." Some universities run hundreds of affiliated companies. They have become a large sector of non-government funding within the higher education. The stocks of those university companies (Fudan and Jiaotong Universities of Shanghai and Tsinghua University of Beijing, for example) perform quite well in the market. This close combination of education and business reflects the kind of culture prevailing in China's higher education today.

NOTEWORTHY SCHOOLS

Of all the schools mentioned, several are worth noting; for example, Tsinghua, Tongji, Southeast and Shenzhen.

Tsinghua University was converted from a preparatory school for studying in the United States in the late Qing Dynasty (1644–1911). It has always been ranked as a top university in mainland China, especially in engineering. The School of Architecture at Tsinghua University was founded by Professor Liang Si-cheng in 1946.

In 1952, the central government adjusted the location of university specialties. The Department of Architectural Engineering of Beijing University merged with Tsinghua. It mainly took the model of the then Soviet Union and carried on a six-year system of undergraduate study.

In 1988, the Department of Architecture was renamed the School of Architecture in Tsinghua, with two departments of architecture and urban planning. In 2000, a department of architectural science, mainly air-conditioning and thermal energy, joined the school. In 2002, the Department of Architecture had forty-four teaching staff, including three fellows of the Chinese Academy of Engineering, the highest title an architect can achieve in China; fifteen professors; fifteen associate professors; and eleven lecturers. Eleven people have doctorates.

The 1920s buildings at the campus of Tsinghua University

Based on the five-year system of the professional bachelor's degree, the School of Architecture at Tsinghua has tried to implement a six-year Bachelor of Arts-Master of Architecture mode of study since 2000. Students study three years to develop basic skills. In the fourth year are more comprehensive design projects and architect's practice. The fifth and sixty years are the period of study for the master's degree. Students take taught courses in the first half-year of Year Five, and propose their thesis topics. The remaining eighteen months are devoted to writing the thesis and taking the oral examination. Design projects, in some cases, can replace the conventional thesis. After six years of such study, students can receive a B.A and a professional master's degree (M. Arch.)

There is a degree office under the State Council of the central government. The office administers the accreditation process of those national "key" universities. The discipline of architectural design and theory of Tsinghua was selected as a "key" discipline by the State Council in 1988. Tsinghua has continuously explored the smooth integration of teaching, learning, research, and design. Professors, associate professors, young teachers, graduate students, and senior undergraduate students are organized into working studios along the following directions: architecture-ecology-technology, architecture-space-environment, architecture-culture-regionalism, architecture-revitalization-urbanism, and architecture-philosophy-methodology (Li 2001).

The relationship of Tsinghua and Tongji is similar to that of Beijing and Shanghai. Tongji University was founded as a medical school by Germans in 1907. The Department of Civil Engineering has been part of the university since the 1930s. In 1952, some architectural and civil engineering departments from other colleges were merged into Tongji, including the architectural department from St. John's University and two architectural schools from Zhejiang Province. Administered by the then Ministry of Building Engineering of the central government, Tongji soon became the starting point of future architects and civil engineers.

In the 1950s, the teachers of Tongji were trained from various countries — the US, UK, Austria, Japan — and the spirit of Bauhaus was deeply rooted in Tongji's tradition. The late Professor Huang Zuoxin was a graduate of Walter Gropius at Harvard University in the early 1940s. He acted as chair of architecture at St. John's University (ceased in 1952) and later at Tongji University. Professor Feng Jizhong, who graduated from a university in Austria, designed several buildings such as a sanitarium, hospital,

New building of Tongji University school of architecture and planning, 2004

Wenyuan Building, venue of architectural school of Tongji University for 30 years since 1954

and academic buildings in the 1950s, all following functionalist principles. The Wenyuan Building, designed by Tongji teachers in 1952, is a Chinese version of a Bauhaus school building. Professor Feng was one of the first in China who upheld the principles of spatial design in architectural education. Tongji introduced the teaching methodology of the Bauhaus type workshop in the late 1970s, and two- and three-dimensional composition replacing the original watercolor wash. Currently, the porcelain arts, Batik, and installation are the major themes of the Year One preliminary design studio. Because of the prevalence of the classical revival, mainly advocated by Professor Liang Sicheng in the north (also see Chapter Two), the design and practice of Tongji showed a subtle counterbalance in south China.

In 1986, a college of architecture and urban planning was set up in Tongji, which included architecture, urban planning, interior design, industrial design, and landscape architecture. It was the first college of its kind in China at that time, with more than 2000 students and 200 teachers. In 2003, a bachelor's degree program of historic building preservation, a cross-discipline of architecture, planning, heritage preservation and technology, was founded to echo the increasing demands of conservation in Chinese cities.

Tongji has obviously benefited from its location in Shanghai, which provides plenty of opportunity in architectural design, site and building visits, and national

and international activities and exchanges. The international joint design studio at the senior undergraduate and graduate levels covers such schools as Princeton University, the University of Illinois at Urbana-Champaign and Hong Kong University. Students are exposed to the very colorful building industry and cultural environment of Shanghai. Teaching staff at Tongji contribute extensively to the busy construction in Shanghai and other provinces in China. As mentioned, students from Year Four have already participated in real projects with their teachers. Graduate students focus on design, which generates part of their income.

Southeast University was originally Central University, when the central government was in Nanjing from the 1920s to 1949. The university was once moved to Sichuan Province during the Anti-Japanese War of 1938–45. After the Communists took over in 1949, it was renamed Nanjing Institute of Technology. The old Central University ran its architectural program early in 1926, one of the only architectural schools at that time. The teachers

Design Studio, Southeast University

were trained from such countries as the US, UK, Japan and Germany. Several excellent 1920s-graduates from the University of Pennsylvania led the team. Their knowledge in classical building shaped the generation of 1940s–50s.

Professor Yang Ting-bao (1900–83), chair of the school from the 1950s to the 1970s, was a student and later assistant of Paul Cret at the University of Pennsylvania from 1920–24. His design works formed the major part of "national identity" in the 1930s and 1950s (see Chapter Two). Professor Tong Jun, also a student of Paul Cret, graduated from the University of Pennsylvania in 1927 and was a firm supporter of the modern movement. He designed a series of functional but beautiful public buildings in Nanjing and Shanghai before 1949. After teaching at Nanjing, he indulged in researching theory and history, and brought the rich Western and traditional Chinese concepts of architecture to his writings. His articles and books published from 1979 to 1983 shed light on the path of exploration in the early years of the open-door policy. The historian Liu Dunzhen was a leader in traditional Chinese architecture and a colleague of Liang Sicheng in investigating ancient buildings in the 1930s. He compiled several volumes of classical history books in the 1960s, recognized as the most authoritative source books in the field. Professor Qi Kang, a graduate of Central University in 1952, inherited his teachers' insights in design and theory, creating numerous valuable design works, especially monumental buildings on the land of China. Professor Qi was also an important theorist in the 1980s (see Chapter Seven). The discipline of architectural design and theory was selected as a national "key" discipline, and the computer-aided architectural design (CAAD) lab was selected as a laboratory at the national level. The school can confer degrees up to Ph.D. and train post-doctoral research fellows. It can also confer a master of fine arts degree (MFA). The library is famous for its abundant resources of old and new books. Southeast University is determined to shine again.

Shenzhen, a city next to Hong Kong, has grown as a result of the open-door policy, from a village to a modern city of 4 million. Shenzhen University was founded in 1984, mostly by professors from Tsinghua University. The campus and the city were under intense construction at the end of the twentieth century. Shenzhen University may be the only example of an "educational" design institute. The Design Institute of Shenzhen University has more than 100 full-time staff. Teachers at the College of Architecture have the opportunity to practice, too. This ensures a close relation between teaching and practice — an ideal way of running a design practice in the university. One person sits in the position of Dean of the Architectural College and Director of the Architectural Design Institute. The Department of Architecture and the Design Institute were, in fact, in the same building. Students learn architecture in a more "practical" physical environment.

Gong Weimin, School of Architecture building, Shenzhen University

Charlie Xue, Shanghai Jiaotong University college of architectural engineering, built at very low cost, 1992

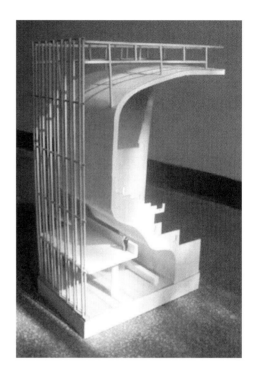

Design studio at Shanghai Jiaotong University

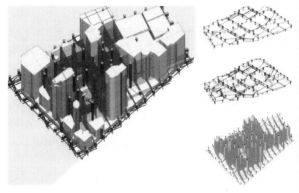

From 1991, the *Architect* journal of Beijing often held design competitions for university students. The topics include architects' homes, youth centers, cultural heritage etc. Essay competitions were also held. The editorial board members usually acted as the jury. These activities greatly motivated student learning in the schools scattered in various corners of China. Winning students come from many cities, and those from "third-tier" schools have a chance to reveal their talents. The national accreditation body of architectural education also held its annual meeting to exchange ideas and examine the state of education. Both the competition and the annual meeting provide a forum for students and schools.

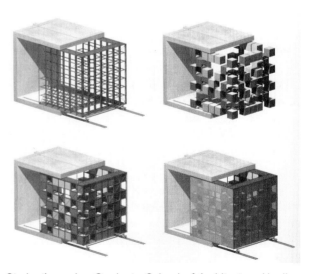

Student's works, Graduate School of Architecture Nanjing University, 2002

Various magazines and journals in China

PUBLICATIONS: A REFLECTION OF THEORETICAL CONTEMPLATION

Most architectural and building technology books were published by China Architecture and Building Press (translated as China Building Industry Press before 1999) in Beijing. Early in 1985, the press published one book a day, on average. The number tripled in the 2000s. China has such a vast land and a large population that the circulation a book was usually over 100,000 in the early 1980s.

In each province and city, there are usually publishing houses of science and technology, of culture etc. The presses gradually joined the lucrative career of printing architectural books, especially with big pictures and less text. These are easy to produce and cost little, making them particularly suitable for the busy designers who are eager to find inspiration from the color images. The Tianjin Press of Science and Technology, among others, is an outstanding house. It set up an ambitious goal of publishing up to 300 types of architectural book, a goal achieved in the early 1990s.

Some newly established private (or semi-private) publication houses also joined the market. There is an abundance of books on building regulations, international architecture, building types, gardens, traditional buildings, interior design, graphics and rendering skills, design masters (stars), construction drawings, etc. The quantity of building-related books in Shanghai, Beijing, Guangzhou, and Shenzhen's bookstores seems higher than what the author has seen in the bookstores in the UK and the US. However, compared to Japan, China's publication industry still has a lot of room for improvement.

Purpose-built "building (or architecture) bookstores" can be found in many cities. In Beijing, the architectural bookstore is a five-storey building on the east-west thoroughfare of Chang'an Street. In Shanghai, the building bookstore is near Tongji University. Guangzhou and Shenzhen have these kinds of building and architectural store, too.

Domus, an Italian design magazine, issued its Chinese version early in 1990. Books on Peter Eisenman, Tadao Ando, Frank Gehry, Gothic architecture, Baroque, classical revival, etc. were authorized for publication in Chinese with the same format as the original ones. The Chinese editions of magazines appear on bookshelves at about the same time as the originals from overseas. After these books appeared, KPF and SOM's design approaches and their treatment of crowns in high-rise buildings were soon seen on the streets of China. These books, journals, and magazines provide up to-date information to architects.

The *Architectural Journal* was chosen as the official journal of the Architectural Society of China (ASC) in 1954. It is an organ of the government, usually disseminating new official views. It was the only architectural journal in China before 1980 and collected by libraries all over the world.

The Architect of Beijing was first issued in 1981 by the China Architecture and Building Press. It is an influential journal of architectural history, theory, and design. In February 2003, Issue No. 101 was released. It is widely distributed among design institutes and colleges, and well received by graduate students. Quite a number of good articles were adapted from master's degree or doctoral dissertations. It is the only architectural journal in China that can entertain articles longer than 10,000 words.

World Architecture was published by Tsinghua University in 1980. It appeared at the time China had just opened its doors and people were eager to breathe in the fresh air of outside world. American architecture, modern architecture, post-modernism, deconstruction, Kisho Kurukawa, Rem Koolhaas, etc. sere covered in these magazines, thus bridging China with the frontier of global architecture. It is an easy and handy tool for practitioners and students when they face the drawing board or computer monitor. Professor Zeng Zhaofeng, editor from 1983 to 1996, led the readers with his good taste, acute sensitivity, and profound understanding of architecture.

In 1984, Tongji University launched a magazine, *Time + Architecture*, which contains abundant information on Shanghai, a very busy construction site in China and the world. The magazine includes book reviews, information, and important websites, in addition to formal articles. As mentioned in Chapter Eight, the magazine is a fortress of experimental architecture, because of the style of the editor, Professor Zhi Wenjun, and a group of devoted young people around him. *New Architecture*, run by the Technical University of Central China (Wuhan) in 1983, is also well received by students and young people. *Architecture of Southern China*, based in Guangzhou, and *Architecture of Central China* in Wuhan mainly report on architecture and trends in the south, as southern China is obviously different from the north physically, geographically, and politically.

Trade journals, like *Architectural Review, World Architecture* of the UK, *Architectural Record* of the US, *A + U* of Japan, are well received by professionals and students. Refereed journals are not so popular in the architectural world. They include *Journal of Architectural Education, Journal of Architectural and Planning Research, Urban Design International, Environment and Planning*, among others. *The Architect* of Beijing is close to this kind of journal. More time is needed for the academics of China to become aware of the importance of refereed journals, and for the prevailing citations and indices of the world to open their doors to the journals in Chinese.

The busy design and construction activities appeal to high culture and theory. A few theorists are silently working in this direction. The late Professor Wang Tan, of Tsinghua University, systematically introduced Western theories to China's architectural field. He disseminated the theories of modern and late modern architecture through his lectures at Tsinghua, Tongji, and other universities. Tsinghua professor Chen Zhihua is an expert in the ancient history of world architecture. His books on ancient Western history (before the mid-nineteenth century) have been extensively used in all universities in China from 1980 to the present. His comments on contemporary Chinese architecture and social drawbacks, mainly published in *The Architect* and *Architectural Journal*, won applause. From 1990 to now, Chen Zhihua's works have concentrated on the vernacular buildings in Zhejiang Province. His archeology-like works were published in Taiwan and mainland China.

Zeng Zhaofeng, editor of *World Architecture* from 1983 to 1996, audaciously published a series of articles on Chinese architecture since the 1950s, pointing out the relationships of national form and modernism. Xue Qiuli's (Charlie Xue) essays and articles helped Chinese readers to understand theory and Western trends in the 1980s and 1990s. From the late 1990s, his research shifted to the topics of contemporary China and Hong Kong architecture, and his publications appeared in international conferences and overseas journals and books. After Wang Tan, Shen Kening, now in the United States, introduced much American architectural concepts starting in 1993, his articles were mainly published in *The Architect* of Beijing.

Compared with the busy building construction, the cultural construction of architecture is generally ignored in China. Most of the writings and publications only provide information and images for front-line professionals. Contemplation and theoretical conclusions are rarely seen. This book, together with other efforts, is intended to partially improve the situation.

BIBLIOGRAPHY

Abel, Chris. *Architecture and Identities: Responses to Cultural and Technological Change*. Oxford: Architectural Press, 1997.

Abel, Chris. Architecture in the Pacific Century. In Miao, Pu (ed.) *Public Places in Asia Pacific Cities, Current Issues and Strategies*. Dordrecht, The Netherlands: Kluwer Academic Publishers, 2001, pp. 215–36.

Ando, Tadao. *Tadao Ando on Architecture*. Beijing: China Architecture & Building Press, 2002.

Albert Speer & Partner. Urban Design of the Central Axis in Beijing. *Architecture and Urbanism*, No. 399, December 2003, pp. 18–23.

Andreu, Paul. Defiant Design. South China Morning Post, July 10, 2000.

Balfour, Alan and Zheng Shiling. Shanghai. World Cities Series. Chichester, West Sussex: Wiley-Academy, 2002.

Birchall, Johnston (ed.) *Housing Policy in the 1990s*. London: Routledge, 1992.

Bognar, Botand. *Contemporary Japanese Architecture, Its Development and Challenge*. New York: Van Nostrand Reinhold Company, 1985.

Broadbent, Geoffrey, Richard Bunt, and Charles Jencks (eds.) *Signs, Symbols and Architecture*. Chichester, West Sussex: John Wiley and Sons, Ltd., 1980.

Broadbent, Geoffrey, Richard Bunt, and Tomas Liorens. *Meaning and Behaviour in The Built Environment*. Chichester, West Sussex: John Wiley and Sons, Ltd., 1980.

Brown, Lester Russell. *Who Will Feed China: Wake-up Call for a Small Planet*. London and New York: Earthscan Publications Ltd, 1995.

Carmona, Matthew. *Housing Design Quality Through Policy, Guidance and Review*. London: Spon Press, 2001.

Chan Kam Wing and Ying Hu. Urbanization in China in the 1990s: New Definition, Different Series, and Revised Trends. *The China Review*. Hong Kong: Chinese University Press. Vol. 3, No. 2, pp. 49–71.

Chang Qing. *Jiangwan Forest: A Proposed Plan*. Unpublished report submitted to the Yangpu District government, Shanghai, 2003. 常青，《江灣森林建議計畫》

Chang Yong He. The Third Attitude. *The Architect*, No. 108, 2004, pp. 24–6. 張永和，《第三種態度》，《建築師》叢刊

Chang Yong He. Three Questions in Architectural Education. *Time + Architecture*. Shanghai. Special Issue on Architectural Education, 2001, pp. 40–2. 張永和，《對建築教育三個問題的思考》，《時代建築》，2001年增刊"中國當代建築教育"

Chen Baoshen. *Chinese Architecture in the Forty Years (1949–1989)*. Tongji University Press. Hong Kong: Urban Architecture Press, 1992. 陳保勝，《中國建築四十年》，同濟大學出版社，香港建築城市出版社

Chen Chong-zhou, Zhang Ming, *et al. Modern History of Shanghai Architecture*. Shanghai Science and Technology Press, 1986. 陳從周，章明，《上海近代建築史稿》，上海科學技術出版社

Chesneaux, Jean. *China: The People's Republic, 1949–1976*. New York: Pantheon, 1979.

Chen Qi and Zhao Jingzhao. *Fifty Years of Residential Design — Selected Works of Beijing Institute of Architectural Design & Research*. China Architecture & Building Press, 1999, pp. 2–30. 陳奇，趙景昭，《50年的住宅設計 — 北京建築設計研究院作品選》，中國建築工業出版社

Chow, Paula K. and Gregory C. Chow (eds.) *Asia in the Twenty-first Century: Economics, Socio-political and Diplomatic Issues*. Singapore and River Edge, NJ: World Scientific Press, 1997.

Chung, Judi Chuihua, Jeffrey Raba, Rem Koolhaas, and Sze Tsung Leong (eds.) *Great Leap Forward*. Project on the City 1, Harvard Design School. Köln: Taschen, 2001.

Cody, Jeffrey W. *Building in China: Henry K Murphy's "Adaptive Architecture,"* 1914–1935. Hong Kong: The Chinese University Press, and Seattle, WA: University of Washington Press, 2001.

Cody, Jeffery W. *Exporting American Architecture, 1870–2000*. London and New York: Routledge, 2003.

China Building Industry Yearbook, 1994–2000. China Building Industry Press, 1995–2001. 《中國建築年鑒》，中國建築工業出版社

Compilation of Building Regulations, China Building Industry Press, 1994. 《建築規範選編》，中國建築工業出版社

Contemporary Chinese Architect — Cheng Taining. China Building Industry Press, 1997. 《中國當代建築師 — 程泰寧》，中國建築工業出版社

Cruickshank, Dan (ed.) *Sir Banister Fletcher's A History of Architecture*. Oxford: Architectural Press, 1996.

Cui Yong. Interview with Zhao Bing. *The Architect*, No. 104, August 2003, pp. 12–6. 崔勇，《風生水起 — 趙冰訪談》《建築師》

Dai Nianci. On Architectural Styles, Forms, Contents and Beyond. *Architectural Journal*, 1986/2, pp. 3–12. 戴念慈，《論建築的風格，形式，內容及其他》，《建築學報》

Design Bureau, Ministry of Construction (ed.) *Collection of Excellent Housing Designs*. China Press of Construction Material Industry, 1999. 建設部設計局，《優秀住宅設計選編》，中國建材出版社

Dietsch, Deborah K. Carpetbagging in Asia. *Architecture*, September 1994, p. 15.

Editorial Committee. *China's Housing Design in the Eighth Five-year Plan*. Beijing: China Building & Architecture Press, 1992. 《八五計畫時期中國住宅》，中國建築工業出版社

Eisenman, Peter. Blurred Zones: Investigations of the Interesitial, Eisenman Architects 1988–1998. New York: Monaceli Press, 2003.

Environment and Development Study Center of China Social Sciences Institution. *China Environment and Development Review*, volume 1. Social Sciences Documentation Publishing House, 2001. 中國社會科學院環境與發展研究中心，《中國環境與發展評論》，第一卷，社會科學文獻出版社

Fang Ke. *Contemporary Redevelopment in the Inner City of Beijing: Survey, Analysis and Investigation*. Beijing: China Architecture & Building Press, 2000. 方可，《北京舊城改造》，中國建築工業出版社

Feng Yuan and Yang Xiaoyan. The Ostentatious Pearl River Delta. *Building Review*, No. 326, July 2004, pp. 49–56. 馮原，楊小彥，《金色的土改》，《建築學導報》

Frampton, Kenneth. *Modern Architecture — A Critical History*. London: Thames and Hudson Ltd., 1992.

Frampton, Kenneth. Opening Address, Symposium on "Structure, Fabric and Topography," Nanjing, China, 2004.

———. Seven Points for the Millennium: An Untimely Manifesto. Keynote speech at the Twentieth UIA Congress, Beijing. *Architectural Review*, November 1999, pp. 76–80.

———. Study in Tectonic Culture: *The Poetics of Construction in Nineteenth and Twentieth Century Architecture*. Edited by John Cava. Cambridge, MA: The MIT Press, 1995.

Fu Chao-qing. *Neo-classicism of Modern Chinese Architecture*. Taiwan: South Heaven Publisher, 1992. 傅朝卿，《中國官式現代建築》，南天書局

Fukuyama, Francis. *The End of History and the Last Man*. New York: Free Press, 1992.

Gandelsonas, Mario (ed.) *Shanghai Reflections: Architecture, Urbanism, and the Search for an Alternative Modernity*. New York: Princeton Architectural Press, 2002.

Giedion, Sigfried. Space, *Time and Architecture, the Growth of a New Tradition*, Fifth Edition (First Edition, 1941). Cambridge, MA: Harvard University Press, 1982.

The Global Competitiveness Report. World Economic Forum. Geneva, 1994–2003.

Gong Deshun, Zou Denong, and Dou Yide. *An Outline of Modern Chinese Architectural History (1949–1985)*. Tianjin Press of Science and Technology, 1989. 龔德順，鄒德儂，竇以德，《中國現代建築大綱》，天津科技出版社

Harvey, David. *The Condition of Postmodernity: An Enquiry into the Origins of Cultural Change*. Cambridge, MA: Blackwell, 1990.

He Qinglian. *The Primary Capital Accumulation in Contemporary China*. Hong Kong: Mirror Books, 1997.

Ho, Samuel P.S. and Y.Y.Kueh, *Sustainable Economic Development in South China*. New York: St. Martin's Press, 2000.

Hou Youbin. The "Soft" Tradition and "Soft" Inheritance in Architecture, *The Architects*, No. 39, June 1990, pp.1-13. 侯幼斌，《建築的"軟"傳統和"軟"繼承》，《建築師》

Huang Guangui and Zeng Weijie. The Challenge of Sustainable Development China Faces in the Twenty-first Century — Research on the Environmental Management. In Zhang Mujin and Joseph Cheng (eds.) *The Strategies of China's Sustainable Development in the 21st Century*. Beijing: Tsinghua University Press, 2001, pp. 85–96. 黃關貴，甄偉傑，《中國21世紀可持續發展的挑戰—環境管理制度的探討》，張慕津，鄭宇碩主編，《面向21世紀中國可持續發展戰略研究》，清華大學出版社

Ioan, Augustin. A Postmodern Critic's Kit for Interpreting Socialist Realism. In Neil Leach (ed.) *Architecture and Revolution, Contemporary Perspectives on Central and Eastern Europe*. London: Routledge, 1999, pp. 62–8.

Jakes, Susan. Soaring Ambitions: The World's Most Visionary Architects are Rebuilding China. *Time*. May 3, 2004, pp. 32–37.

Jia Dongdong (eds). *Joint Venture Design in China*. China Architecture & Building Press, 1998. 賈東東編，《海內外建築師合作設計作品選》，中國建築工業出版社

Jencks, Charles. *Heteropolis, Los Angeles. The Riots and the Strange Beauty of Hetero Architecture*. London: Academy Editions, 1993.

Koolhaas, Rem. Address at the award ceremony of the Prizker Architectural Prize, 2000. Available at: www.pritzkerprize.com

Koolhaas, Rem (ed.) *Content*. New York: Taschen, 2003.

Koolhaas, Rem and Bruce Mau. S, M, L, XL. New York: The Monacelli Press, 1995.

Kostof, Spiro. *A History of Architecture: Settings and Rituals*. New York: Oxford University Press, 1985.

Lang, Jon T. *Urban Design, the American Experience*. New York: Van Nostrand Reinhold, 1994.

Lang, Joh T., Madhavi Desai, and Miki Desai. *Architecture and Independence, The Search of Identity: India, 1880– 1980*. Delhi: Oxford University Press, 1997.

Larsen, Tom. Practice Matters. *Architectural Record*, March 2004, pp. 51–4.

Leach, Neil (ed.) *Architecture and Revolution: Contemporary Perspectives on Central and Eastern Europe*. London: Routledge, 1999.

Li Fang. Such Urbanization! *Urban and Rural Development*, No. 7, 2002, p. 57. 李芳，《如此城市化》，《城鄉規劃》

Li Dexiang. Characteristics of Education at Department of Architecture of Tsinghua University. *Time + Architecture*. Special Issue on Architectural Education, 2001, pp. 10– 2. 栗德祥，《清華大學建築系的教學特色》，《時代建築》，2001年增刊"中國當代建築教育"

Li Wuying. Potential Space for the Design Firms. *Building Time*, March 17, 2003. 李武英，《設計事務所的發展空間》，《建築時報》

Li Xiangning. *The Real and Imagined: An Analysis of Value Perspectives in Contemporary Urban Studies*. Unpublished Ph.D. Dissertation, Tongji University, Shanghai, 李翔寧，2003a.《想像與真實 — 城市研究中價值視角的分析》，同濟大學博士論文

Li Xiangning, *New 798, Art Area, Architecture and Urbanism*, No. 12, 2003b, p. 145.

Li Yaopei. *New Housing Design Regulations, Living Conditions, and Good Housing Design in China,* Southeast University Press, 1999. 李耀培，《中國住宅的新規範、居住條件和設計》

Liang Sicheng (Liang Ssu-ch'eng) edited by Wilma Fairbank. *A Pictorial History of Chinese Architecture*. Cambridge, MA: MIT Press, 1984.

Liang Sicheng. *Complete Works of Liang Sicheng*, Volume 5. China Architecture & Building Press, 2001 梁思成，《梁思成全集》，中國建築工業出版社

Lin Yu Sheng. *The Creative Transformation of China's Tradition*. Beijing: Joint Publication, 1988. 林毓生，《中國傳統的創造性轉變》，三聯書店

Lim, William S. W. *Alternative (Post) Modernity: An Asian Perspective*. Singapore: Select Publishing Pte. Ltd., 2003.

Liu Jiakun. *Here and Now*. Beijing: China Architecture and Building Press, 2002. 劉家琨，《此時此地》，中國建築工業出版社

Lopez, José and Garry Potter (eds.) After Postmodernism: *An Introduction to Critical Realism*. London: Athlone, 2001.

Lu Junhua, Peter G. Rowe, and Zhang Jie. *Modern Urban Housing in China, 1840–2000*. Munich: Prestel Verlag, 2001.

Luo, Xiao-wei and Wu Jiang (eds.) *Index of Shanghai Architecture*. Shanghai Press of Science and Technology, 1996. 羅小未，伍江，《上海建築指南》，上海科技出版社

Mao Zedong. *Selected Works of Mao Zedong*. Beijing: People's Press, 1963. 毛澤東，《毛澤東選集》，人民出版社

Master Planning of Beijing. *The Architect*, No. 65, 1995. 北京總體規劃，《建築師》叢刊

Master Plan of Beijing, Beijing, City Planning Committee, 1996

Marsh, Alex and David Mullins (eds.) *Housing and Public Policy: Citizenship, Choice and Control*. Buckingham: Open University Press, 1998.

McBride, Stephen and John Wiseman (eds.) *Globalization and its Discontents*. London: MacMillan Press Ltd., 2000.

Miao Pu. In the Absence of Authenticity: An Interpretation of Contemporary Chinese Architecture. *Nordisk Arkitekturforskning*, No. 3, 1995, pp. 7–24.

Miao Pu. The Genius of Tradition: Thirteen Characteristics of Chinese Traditional Architecture. *The Architect*, No. 36, pp. 56–67 and No. 40, pp. 61–9, 1989. 繆朴，《傳統的本質 — 中國傳統建築的十三個特點》，《建築師》叢刊

Mingpao Monthly. Hong Kong, March 2003. Special Edition on China's Academic Corruption. 《明報月刊》，中國學術腐敗專輯

Moughtin, Cliff. *Urban Design, Method and Techniques*. Oxford and Boston: Architectural Press, 1999.

Municipal Government of Dongguan. *Welcome to Dongguan*, 2002

Musgrove, John (ed.) *Sir Banister Fletcher's A History of Architecture*, Nineteenth Edition. London: Butterworths, 1987.

Nie Meisheng. Hot Topics in the Housing Industry. *Architectural Journal*, No. 9, 2000, pp. 6–7. 聶梅生，《住宅工業的熱點》，《建築學報》

Norberg-Schulz, Christian. *Meaning in Western Architecture*. London: Praeger Publishers, Inc., 1975.

The Observer. London. Available at: http://observer.guardian.co.uk. February 22, 2004.

Organizing Committee of Design Competition. *Competition Entries of Cross-century Real Estate Property*. China Architecture & Building Press, 1999.

Organizing Committee of Shanghai International Communications on Residential Design '96. *Selected Projects and Dissertations of Shanghai International Residential Design*. Beijing: China Architecture and Building Press, 1997.

Pan Guxi. *Opinions on Revitalizing Creative Architecture Architectural Journal*, No. 3 1986, p. 15. 潘谷西，《繁榮建築創作的幾點意見》，《建築學報》

Pan Shiyi et al. (eds.) *Commune by the Great Wall*. Tianjin: The Tianjin Academy of Social Science Press, 2002.

Pearson, Clifford A. China: Moving Heaven and Earth, and Doing it Faster than you Thought Possible. *Architectural Record*, March 2004, pp. 71–2.

Pei Minxin. An Expression of Idealism, or Self-righteous Hypocrisy? *Foreign Policy Journal*. Washington DC. Reprinted in The South China Morning Post, April 17, 2003.

Peng Pei-Gen. Why do we Oppose the French Architect's Scheme of the Grand National Theater? *Architectural Journal*, No. 11, 2000, pp. 11–2.彭培根，《我們為什麼反對法國建築師的國家大劇院設計？》，《建築學報》

Peng Zaide. *Theory and Practice of Sustainable Development in Big Cities*. Ph.D. dissertation. Research Institute of Western Europe and North America. East China Normal University, 1997. 彭載德，《大城市可持續發展的理論和實踐》，華東師範大學博士論文

Peng Nu and Zhi Wenjun. A Mosaic of Contemporary Experimental Architecture in China: Theoretical Discourses and Practicing Strategies. *Time + Architecture*, No. 5, 2002, pp. 20–5. 彭怒，支文軍，《中國當代實驗建築拼圖》，《時代建築》

People's Republic of China Year Book 2002. Beijing: China Year Book Press, 2002. 《中華人民共和國年鑒》，中國年鑒出版社

Pevsner, Nikolaus. *A History of Building Types*. London: Thames and Hudson, 1976.

Proceedings of Continuity & Innovation, Chinese Conference on Architectural Education. Chinese University of Hong Kong, Hong Kong, 2000.

Proceedings of the Symposium on Modern Chinese Architectural History, Vol. 1, Vol. 2, Hua Zhong Architecture, 1987, 1989, Vol. 3, Vol. 4, China Building Industry Press, 1989, 1993.《中國近代建築史討論會文集》

Qian Qihu. Sustainable Urban Development and Underground Space. *Underground Space*, No. 2, 1998. 錢七虎，《可持續城市開發和地下空間》，《地下建築》

Qingdao Institute of Building Engineering, Department of Architecture. *Qingdao Architecture*. 1986. 青島建築工程學院，《青島建築》

Quantrill, Malcolm and Bruce Webb (eds.) *The Culture of Silence: Architecture's Fifth Dimension*. College Station, TX: Texas A & M University Press, 1998.

Rogers, Richard. London, *A Call for Action*. London: Penguin Books, 1992.

Rowe, Peter G. and Seng Kuan. *Architectural Encounters with Essence and Form in Modern China*. Cambridge, MA: MIT Press, 2002.

Raporport, Amos. *House Form and Culture*. Englewood Cliffs, NJ: Prentice-Hall, 1969.

Research Department of Development Strategy and Regional Economy. *An Analysis on the Features of District Economic Development in China*. Development Research Center of the State Council, People's Republic of China, 2000.

Said, Edward W. *Orientalism*. New York: Pantheon Books, 1978.

Scoffham, Ernie R. *The Shape of British Housing*. London: George Godwin, 1984.

Sha Yongjie. *A Comparative Research on Development of Architecture between China and Japan in Modern Times*. Shanghai: Shanghai Press of Science and Technology, 2001. 沙永傑，《"西化"的歷程 — 中日建築近代化過程比較研究》，上海科學技術出版社

Shi Wei. Shanghai Phenomenon: From Studio to Firm. *Time + Architecture*, No. 4, 2003, pp. 20–5. 史巍，《上海現象 — 從工作室到事務所》，《時代建築》

Simon, Sherry and Paul St-Pierre (eds.) *Changing the Terms: Translating in the Postcolonial Era*. Ottawa, ON: University of Ottawa Press, 2000.

Singtao Daily News. Hong Kong, August 6, 2004. 《星島日報》

Sit, Victor F. S. *Hong Kong Development Map*. Hong Kong: Joint Publication, 2001.

Smith, Anthony D. *Nations and Nationalism in a Global Era*. Cambridge: Polity Press, 1995.

Sommer, Robert. *Social Design*. Englewood Cliffs, NJ: Prentice Hall, 1983.

South China Morning Post. June 2, 2004.

Spence, Jonathan D. *The Search for Modern China*. New York: Norton, 1990.

State Council. *Government Report*. Beijing: State Council, 2000.

Tafuri, Manfredo and Francesco Dal Co. *Modern Architecture*. Trans. by Robert Erich Wolf. London: Faber and Faber, 1986.

Teeple, Gary. What is Globalization? In Stephen McBride and John Wiseman (eds.) *Globalization and its Discontents*. London: MacMillan Press Ltd., 2000, pp. 9–23.

The Architect, Vol. 46, 1992.

Tschumi, Bernard. *Architecture and Disjunction*. Cambridge, MA: MIT Press, 1996.

Tu Wei-ming. *Confucian Thought: Selfhood as Creative Transformation*. Albany, NY: State University of New York Press, 1989.

Tu Wei-ming (ed.) *Confucian Traditions in East Asian Modernity: Moral Education and Economic Culture in Japan and the Four Mini-dragons*. Cambridge, MA: Harvard University Press, 1996.

Twitchett, Denis and John King Fairbank (eds.) *The Cambridge History of China*. Cambridge University Press, 1978.

Venturi, Robert. *Complexity and Contradiction in Architecture*, Second Edition. London: Architectural Press, 1977.

Vitruvius, Pollio. *The Ten Books on Architecture*. Trans. by Ingrid D. Rowland. Cambridge University Press, 1999.

Wang Ban. *History and Memory in the Shadows of Globalization*. Hong Kong: Oxford University Press, 2004.

Wang Shaozhou. *Modern Architecture in Shanghai*. Zhejiang Press of Science and Technology, 1986. 王紹周，《上海近代建築史》，浙江科學技術出版社

Wang Shaozhou. *Terraced Lane Housing in Shanghai*. Shanghai Science and Technology Press, 1987. 王紹周，《上海里弄》，上海科學技術出版社

Wang Tan and Terunobu Fujimori (ed.) *The Architectural Heritage of Modern China: Shanghai, Xiamen, Beijing, Qindao, Chongqing, Shenyang, Harbin, Dalian, Nanjing, etc*. China Building Industry Press, 1993. 汪坦，藤森照信主編，《中國近代建築總覽》，中國建築工業出版社

Weston, Richard. *Modernism*. London: Phaidon Press Limited, 1996.

What are buyers' concerns? Spring Report on the Housing Market. *Shenzhen Commercial News*, May 8, 1999.《消費者關心什麼？— 房屋市場春季報告》，《深圳商報》

World Bank. *China 2020: Development Challenges in the New Century*, Washington, DC: The World Bank, 1997.

World Economic Forum. *Global Competitiveness Report*, Geneva: World Economic Forum, 1995-2003

World Bank. *World Development Report*, 1990–2003. New York: The World Bank and Oxford University Press, 1990–2003.

Wu Jiang. *One Hundred Years of the History of Architecture in Shanghai* (1840–1949). Tongji University Press, 1997. 伍江，《上海百年建築史》，同濟大學出版社

Wu Liangyong. *Revitalizing the Old Housing in Beijing*. Vancouver, BC: The University of British Columbia Press, 2000.

Wu Yaodong. *Modern Japanese Architecture*. Beijing: China Architecture & Building Press, 1997. 吳耀東，《日本現代建築》，中國建築工業出版社

Xue, Charlie Q. L. *Building Practice in China*. Hong Kong: Pace Publishing Ltd., 1999.

Xue, Charlie Q. L. Chronicle of Chinese Architecture: 1980–2003. *Architecture and Urbanism*. No. 399, December 2003, pp. 152–5.

———. *Contemplating on Architecture*. Hong Kong: Pace Publishing Ltd., 2001.

———. Evolution of House Form in China: An Outline. *International Journal of Housing Science and Its Application*, Vol. 23, No. 1, 1999, pp. 47–58.

———. Hong Kong Architecture: Identities and Prospects: A Discourse on Tradition and Creation. Division of Building Science and Technology, City University of Hong Kong (ed.) *Building Design and Development in Hong Kong*, Hong Kong: City University of Hong Kong Press, 2003, pp. 75–98.

———. Organic Renewal of Housing in Old City Areas: A Case Study of Hong Kong. *International Journal of Housing Science and Its Application*, Vol. 26, No. 1, 2002, pp. 27–38.

———. Ten Celebrities in Shanghai and Hong Kong. *Hong Kong Institute of Architects Journal*, No. 4, 2000, pp. 48–53.

———. Artistic Reflection in Contemporary Chinese Architecture. *TAASA, The Journal of Asian Arts Society of Australia*, Vol. 13, No. 4, 2004, pp. 14–5.

Xue, Charlie Q. L. and Chen Xiaoyang. Chinese Architects and Their Practice. *Journal of Architectural and Planning Research*. Vol. 20, No. 4, Winter 2003, pp. 291–306.

Xue, Charlie Q. L. and Kevin Manuel. Where Can We Find Lingnan Architecture? A Quest for the Integration of Greater Pearl River Delta. International Conference on Tropical Architecture (iNTA). National University of Singapore, February 2004.

Xue, Charlie Q. L., Kevin Manuel, and Rex Chung. Public Space in the Derelict Old City Area: A Case Study of Mongkok, Hong Kong. *Urban Design International*, No. 1, Vol. 6, 2001, pp. 15–31.

Xue, Charlie Q. L. and Ernie Scoffham. China's Housing in Transition: A Case Study of Shanghai. International *Journal for Housing Science and Its Applications*, Vol. 20, No. 4, 1996, pp. 231–44.

Xue, Charlie Q. L. and Shi Wei. Design Tendering in China. *Hong Kong Institute of Architects Journal*, No. 3, 2002, pp. 20–5.

Xue, Charlie Q. L. and Xin Ziyu. Housing Price and Affordability. *World Architecture*, No. 3, 1992, pp. 20–3. 薛求理，辛志宇，《住房價格和購屋能力》，《世界建築》

Yang Bing-de (ed.) *City and Architecture of Modern China*. China Building Industry Press, 1992. 楊秉德主編，《中國近代城市和建築》，中國建築工業出版社

Yang Wanzhong. The Industrial Layout in Shanghai Across the Centuries. *Urban Planning Forum*, Shanghai, No. 4, 2000. 楊萬鐘《跨世紀上海工業佈局》，《城市規劃論壇》

Yang Yongsheng and Gu Mengcao (eds.) *Chinese Architecture in the Twentieth Century*. Tianjin: Tianjin Press of Science and Technology, 1999. 楊永生，顧孟潮主編，《20世紀中國建築》，天津科技出版社

Yang Yongsheng (ed.) *A Hundred Opinions on Architecture*. China Building Architecture & Press, 2000. 楊永生主編，《建築百家評論集》，中國建築工業出版社

Ye Bu. Comment on the First Phase of the Great Wall Commune Project. *Time + Architecture*, No. 3, 2002, pp. 42–7. 野卜，《長城公社第一期評論》，《時代建築》

Ye Guixun, Xu Yisong et al. *Strategies of Shanghai Urban Development*. Beijing: China Building and Architecture Press, 2003. 葉貴勳，徐逸松，《上海城市發展策略》，中國建築工業出版社

Yeh, Raymond W. H. Model for a Professional Degree Program in Architecture at the University of Hawaii, Manoa. *Continuity and Innovation: Chinese Conference on Architectural Education*, Hong Kong, 2000

Yuan Xialiang and Xu Kenmei. The Knowledge Economy has Given Rise to a "Street of Architectural Design." *Wenhui Bao*. Shanghai, February 9, 2003. 袁夏良，許懇美，《知識經濟產出"建築設計一條街"》，《文匯報》

Zhang Bo. *My Path of Architecture*. China Building Industry Press, 1993. 張鎛，《我的建築道路》，中國建築工業出版社

Zevi, Bruno. *The Modern Language of Architecture*. Seattle: University of Washington Press, 1980.

Zhang Kaiji. Maintaining Features of Ancient Cities and Carrying Forward the Chinese Culture. *Architectural Journal*, No. 1987, p. 32. 張開濟，《維護古都風貌，發揚中華文化》，《建築學報》

Zhang Jinqiu. Architecture of Xi'an: A City of Historic Culture. *Architectural Journal*, No. 1, 1994, pp. 30–2. 張錦秋，《歷史文化名城西安的建築》，《建築學報》

Zhang Mujin and Joseph Cheng. *The Strategies of China's Sustainable Development in the Twenty-First Century*. Tsinghua University Press, 2001. 張慕津，鄭宇碩主編，《中國21世紀可持續發展策略》，清華大學出版社

Zhang Zhai-yuan and Stephen Lau. *Image of Central Hong Kong*. Beijing: China Planning Press and Hong Kong:

Pace Publishing Ltd., 1997. 張在元，劉少瑜，《香港中環城市形象》，中國計畫出版社，香港貝思出版公司

Zhao Guanqian and Kai Yan. The Hard Way and Plenty of Results: Fifty Years of Building Housing in China. *Architecture Journal*, No. 12, 1999, pp. 35–9. 趙冠謙，開彥，《中國住宅建築50年》，《建築學報》

Zheng Shiling. *Study of Architectural Criticism*. China Architecture & Building Press, 2001. 鄭時齡，《建築批評學》，中國建築工業出版社

Zheng Yi. *China's Ecological Winter*. Hong Kong: Mirror Books, 2001.

Zhu Jianfei. Beyond Revolution: Notes on Contemporary Chinese Architecture. *AA Files* 35, 1998, pp. 3–14.

Zhu Jianfei. Configuring a New Modernity: Architectural Agenda of a Cultural China in the Twenty-first Century. *Academic Treaties*, Vol. 2, UIA XXth Congress, Beijing, 1999.

———. Modernization: Yung Ho Chang in the Historic Matrix. *Architect*, No. 108, April 2004, pp. 14–7. 朱劍飛，《現代化：在歷史大關係中尋找張永和及其非常建築》，《建築師》

Zou Deci. Preface. In Wang Jianguo (ed.) *Urban Design*. Nanjing: Southeast University Press, 1999, pp. 1–2. 鄒德慈，《前言》，王建國：《城市設計》，東南大學出版社

Zou Denong. *A history of Modern Chinese Architecture*. Tianjin Press of Science and Technology, 2001. 鄒德儂，《中國現代建築史》，天津科技出版社

Zou Denong and Dou Yide. *Fifty Years of Chinese Architecture (1949–1999)*. China Building Materials Industry Press, 1999. 鄒德儂，竇以德，《中國建築五十年》，中國建材出版社

Zweig, David. China Joins the Global Economy. *Yale Global Online*. Available at: www.yaleglobal.yale.edu. September 15, 2003.

http://www.realestate.gov.cn/default.asp

http://www.far2000.com (Free report of building, based in Beijing)

http://www.abbs.com.cn (architectural forum based in Shanghai)

http://www.welcome-to-china.com

http://www.cin.gov.cn (Ministry of Construction, China)

http://www.housecenter.com/

http://pudong.shanghaichina.org (Pudong District, Shanghai)

http://search.sina.com.hk/

http://china-window.com/

http://www.sina.com.cn

http://wamp.abcd.com.cn (Tsinghua University)

http://www.china-up.com (city planning in China)

http://www.cnup.com/ (city planning in China)

http://urban.netsh.net (forum of city planning)

ILLUSTRATION CREDITS

Map of China, Changjiang River Delta and Pearl River Delta were drawn by Raymond Pit Hang Chan.

Color plates 1, 2, 5, 14, 26, shot by Raymond W. M. Wong.

Chapter 1 title picture, from *Forbidden City*, China Antiquities Press, 1997.

Figure 1.1, *Selected Architectural Works of Tongji University*, Heilonjiang Science and Technology Press, 1999.

Figures 1.6 (a), (b), 2.1 (b), (c), (d), (e), Figures 2.4 (a), (b), 2.6 (b), 2.7, 2.8, 2.9(a), 2.12, 2.13, 2.14, Figures 6.1, 6.3, 6.4(b), 6.8, 6.9, 1.6, *China Modern Fine Arts Selection — Architectural Arts,* Vol. 2, 3, 4, China Architecture and Building Press, 1998.

Figure 2.1 (f), Li Hui, *Liang Sicheng*, Joint Publication, Hong Kong, 2003.

Figure 2.10, 5.3, Chapter 2 title picture, color plates 6, 7, courtesy of Zhang Jinqiu.

Figures 2.15 (e), 4.11, 4.21 *Time + Architecture*, No. 3, 2002.

Figure 3.1, photo by Chen Xiaoyang.

Figures 3.3, 3.5, 3.6, 3.9, 3.13, Jia Dongdong (ed.), *Joint Venture Design in China*, China Architecture and Building Press, 1998; 3.8(a), photo by Shi Wei.

Figure 3.16(a), (c), (d), *World Architecture*, Feb. 2000.

Figure 3.17, courtesy of OMA; 3.18 (a), courtesy of Zhao Xiaojun, the others are from *Architectural Journal*, No.5, 2003.

Figure 3.22(c), 3.23(c), www.abbs.com.cn, Nov. 2003.

Figure 3.23 (b), website of Pei Architects, 2002.

Figure 4.1, 5.1 (b), Pan Guxi (ed.), *History of Chinese Architecture*, China Architecture and Building Press, 1997.

Figures 4.2, 4.3, adapted from Gao Yilan & Wang Menghui, Liang Si-cheng's proposal of protection of ancient city and planning, *Collection of Research on Liang Si-cheng 1946–1996*, Tsinghua University Press, 1996.

Figure 4.4, http://www.bjall.com/guide/bjmap.htm

Figures 4.5, 4.6: http://www.hua2.com/mapworld" http://www.hua2.com/mapworld.

Figure 4.12, Chen Chongzhou & Zhang Ming, *History of Modern Shanghai Architecture*, Joint Publication, Shanghai, 1988.

Figure 4.15, Shanghai Institute of Surveying, *The Pudong New District of Shanghai*, China Map Study & Press, 1996.

Figure 4.16(b) from the pamphlet of Pudong District government, Shanghai, 1996.

Figure 4.20 adapted from Zhang Shaoliang, Exploration of Optimizing Shanghai Urban Space, *Urban Planning Forum*, No. 2, 2001.

Figure 4.24 adapted from the planning pamphlet of Nansha Town government, 2003.

Figure 4.21, Dong Jianhong, *Ancient City Construction of China*, China Building Industry Press, 1988; Figures 5.4, 5.5, shot from the planning exhibition of Shenzhen.

Figure 5.7, *World Architectural Review*, 05:06, 1997.

Figure 5.10, *Time + Architecture*, No.2, 2003.

Figure 5.11 and color plates 14, 25, courtesy of Lu Jiwei.

Figure 5.13 and color plate 13, courtesy of Chang Qing.

Figure 6.13 (a), sales materials, Pit Gui Yuan, 2001.

Figure 6.15, sales materials, Horizon Cove.

Figure 6.16 (a), (d), sales materials, Le Parc.

Figures 6.17 (c), (d) and 9.2, color plate 47, courtesy of X-Urban.

Figure 6.19, courtesy of Xiang Bingren.

Figure 6.20, courtesy of Steven Holl Architects.

Figures 7.1 to Figure 7.4, color plates 19, 20, courtesy of Professor Qi Kang.

Figures 7.5 to 7.10, color plate 27, courtesy of Cheng Taining.

Figure 7.11, courtesy of Bu Zhengwei.

Figures 7.12, 7.13, courtesy of Professor Peng Yigang.

Figures 7.14 to 7.18, color plates 21, 22, courtesy of Professor Dai Fudong.

Figures 7.19, color plate 25, courtesy of Professor Lu Jiwei.

Figure 7.20 and color plate 24, courtesy of Xiang Bingren.

Figure 7.24(b) courtesy of Xing Tonghe.

Figures 7.32 to 7.35, content page picture and color plate 30, courtesy of Professor He Jingtang

Figure 7.36(b), (c), color plate 29, courtesy of Professor Guan Zhaoye.

Figure 8.2 and color plate 33, *Time + Architecture*, No.5, 2002.

Figures 8.4, 8.5, courtesy of Chang Yong He and Dong Yugan.

Figure 8.6, color plates 35, 42, courtesy of Zhang Lei.

Figure 8.7, color plate 44, courtesy of Ma Qingyun.

Figure 8.8, courtesy of Meng Jianmin.

Figure 8.9 and color plate 31, courtesy of Miao Pu.

Figure 8.10, color plates 37-39, courtesy of Zhao Bing.

Figure 8.11 and color plate 34, courtesy of Liu Jiakun.

Figure 8.12 (b), courtesy of Li Xiangning, (c), (d), color plate 41, courtesy of Wang Shu.

Figure 8.13 (a), (d), (e), courtesy of Wang Lifang.

Figure 8.17, color plates 40, 41, courtesy of Yin Jia.

Figures 8.15(a), (b), (c), 8.16, 8.18, 8.20, *Time + Architecture*, No.2, No.5, 2003.

Figure 8.15 (d), (e), color plate 45, courtesy of Li Linxue;

Figure 8.21, color plate 46, courtesy of Teng Kunyen.

Figure 8.22 (c), color plate 36, Pan Shiyi *et al.* (eds.), *Commune by the Great Wall*. Tianjin: The Tianjin Academy of Social Sciences Press, 2002.

Figure 9.1, courtesy of Zhang Jiajin.

Figure 9.3, 10.6, color plate 46, courtesy of Pan-Pacific Design & Development Ltd.

Figure 9.4 (b), shot by Wang Hongjun.

Chapter 10 title picture, *China*, No.10, 2002.

Appendix II, title picture, courtesy of Gong Weimin; Students' works of Nanjing University, Graduate School of Architecture, Nanjing University, No.2, 2002-2003 year book.

The other pictures were shot and produced by the author. If copyright can be established for any illustration not specifically or erroneously attributed above, please contact the publisher. Any omission are inadvertent and will be remedied in future reprints.

INDEX

Hebei Province, 75
Heilongjiang, 73
Herzog & De Meron, 36, 43
high tech, 10
Holl, Steven, 36, 97, 100, 153
HOK (Hellmuth, Obata + Kassabaum), 36, 74
Hong Kong, viii, xii, 32, 50, 55–6, 66, 68, 95–7, 102, 142, 149,
    163
Hu Shaoxue, 125, 128
Huahui Design Ltd., 164
Hunan (Province), 68, 164
Hungary, 157
hutong, 55–6

imperialism, 30–1
India, ix
Italy (Italian), 153, 155

Japan (Japanese), ix–x, 29, 41, 57, 61, 65, 73–4, 105–7, 114,
    127, 151, 185, 187, 189
Jencks, Charles, 19
Jiangsu, 58, 102
Jianguo Hotel, 32
Jiangxi, 68
Jilin, 73, 77
Journal of Architectural and Planning Research, 190

Kahn, Louis, 29
Kales, F. H., 26
Kanika R'kul, 151
Kalach, Alberto, 153
Klotz, Mathias, 153
Koolhaas, Rem (and OMA), xiii, 17, 43, 135–6, 154, 160, 168,
    189
    CCTV Headquarters, 43–44, 136
Kostof, Spiro, 7
KPF (Kohn Pedersen Fox Associates), 7, 37, 39, 45, 136, 160,
    163
    Global Financial Center, 39
    Plaza 66, 37
Kuma, Kengo, 151
Kurokawa, Kisho, 36, 78, 189
    Sino-Japan Youth Friendship Center, 35–6
Kwan, Wu & Yang, 157

Lao Tzu, 113
Legorreta, Ricardo, 142
Leigh & Orange, 160

Lerup, Lars, 135
Li, John M. Y. (and Michael Timchula), 74, 78
Li Lin, 97–8
Li Linxue, 146
Li Zongze , 36
Li Xinggang, 144
Liang Si-cheng (Liang Ssu Ch'eng), 13–4, 17, 29, 52–3, 68, 72,
    81, 185
Liaoning Province, 73, 158
lilong (lane house), 25, 83
Lin Huiyin, 29
Lin Keming, 14
Lingnan style (Lingnan architecture), 24, 123
Liu, Doreen Heng, 144, 153
Liu Dunzhen, 81
Liu Jiakun, 132, 142–3, 153–4
    Luyeyuan Museum of Stone Sculpture, 142–3
Liu Li, 25
    Yan Huang Art Gallery, 25
Liu Taige, 79
Llewelyn-Davis, 73, 76
London, 135, 163
Lu Jiwei, 118
Lu Yanzhi (Lu Yen-chih), 14, 16
Lufthansa Center, 34
Luke H. S., 105
Lynch, Kevin, 73, 118

Ma Qingyun, 132, 136, 138, 153
Macau, 50, 66, 68, 96
MADA s.p.a.m., 136, 161
Malaysia, x, xiv, 28
Mansilla, Luis M., 153
Mao Zedong, ix, 4
Marx, Karl (Marxism), ix, xiv, 105
Meier, Richard, 45
Meng Jianmin, 136, 138, 155
Mexico, 153
Miao, Pu, 14, 139–140
    Reception, Minhang Ecological Garden, 139
    Teahouse at Xiaolangdi Dam Park, 139
Ministry of Construction, 11, 73–5, 90, 92, 158–9, 184
Ministry of Education, 144
Ming Dynasty, 51–2
Mo Bozhi, 24, 119, 123
    White Swan Hotel, 123
modernization, ix, 32, 167
Murphy, Henry K., 26, 157